The Third World and South Africa

**Recent Titles in
Contributions in Political Science**

Armed Forces and Political Power in Eastern Europe: The Soviet/Communist Control System
Bradley R. Gitz

Youth's Battle for the Ballot: A History of Voting Age in America
Wendell W. Cultice

Using Theory to Improve Program and Policy Evaluations
Huey-tysh Chen and Peter H. Rossi, editors

East Central Europe after the Warsaw Pact: Security Dilemmas in the 1990s
Andrew A. Michta

Public Management in an Interconnected World: Essays in the Minnowbrook Tradition
Mary Timney Bailey and Richard T. Mayer, editors

United Germany: The Past, Politics, Prospects
H. G. Peter Wallach and Ronald A. Francisco

Watergate and Afterward: The Legacy of Richard M. Nixon
Leon Friedman and William F. Levantrosser, editors

Health Insurance and Public Policy: Risk, Allocation, and Equity
Miriam K. Mills and Robert H. Blank, editors

Public Authorities and Public Policy: The Business of Government
Jerry Mitchell, editor

Shepherd of Democracy: America and Germany in the Twentieth Century
Carl C. Hodge and Cathal J. Nolan, editors

Gerald R. Ford and the Politics of Post-Watergate America
Bernard J. Firestone and Alexej Ugrinsky, editors

The Democratic System in the Eastern Caribbean
Donald C. Peters

THE THIRD WORLD AND SOUTH AFRICA

Post-Apartheid Challenges

Richard J. Payne

CONTRIBUTIONS IN POLITICAL SCIENCE,
NUMBER 304

GREENWOOD PRESS
WESTPORT, CONNECTICUT • LONDON

D
888
S6
P39
1992

Library of Congress Cataloging-in-Publication Data

Payne, Richard J.
   The Third World and South Africa : post-apartheid challenges / Richard J. Payne.
       p.   cm. — (Contributions in political science, ISSN 0147–1066 ; no. 304)
   Includes bibliographical references and index.
   ISBN 0–313–28542–X (alk. paper)
   1. Developing countries—Foreign relations—South Africa.
   2. South Africa—Foreign relations—Developing countries.
   3. Economic sanctions—South Africa.   4. Apartheid—South Africa.
   I. Title.   II. Series.
   D888.S6P39   1992
   327.680172′4—dc20   92–8847

British Library Cataloguing in Publication Data is available.

Copyright © 1992 by Richard J. Payne

All rights reserved. No portion of this book may be reproduced, by any process or technique, without the express written consent of the publisher.

Library of Congress Catalog Card Number: 92–8847
ISBN: 0–313–28542–X
ISSN: 0147–1066

First published in 1992

Greenwood Press, 88 Post Road West, Westport, CT 06881
An imprint of Greenwood Publishing Group, Inc.

Printed in the United States of America

The paper used in this book complies with the Permanent Paper Standard issued by the National Information Standards Organization (Z39.48–1984).

10 9 8 7 6 5 4 3 2 1

For Elaine and Mildred

Contents

Acknowledgments	ix
Introduction	xi
1. The Third World and South Africa: Interests, Strategies, and Change	1
2. Sub-Saharan Africa: Nigeria and Zambia	19
3. Asia: India and Taiwan	63
4. Latin America: Brazil	97
5. The Middle East: The Arab States, Iran, and the PLO	125
6. Post-Apartheid Challenges	149
Notes	159
Selected Bibliography	181
Index	197

Acknowledgments

This book is a continuation of research on the major industrial countries' relations with South Africa. I am therefore indebted, once again, to many anti-apartheid groups, governments, colleagues, and students who contributed to the earlier book. In addition, I would like to thank Michele Steinbacher-Kemp, Amy Atchison, Troy Bollinger, and Nadja Sadeghian for their research assistance, and Carol Ruyle, Garold Cole, and Sharon Wetzel at Illinois State University for their skill in locating library materials.

I am especially grateful to Samuel Huntington, Myron Weiner, Lucian Pye, and other participants in the 1988–89 Harvard University–Massachusetts Institute of Technology Joint Seminar on Political Development for their insights on Third World problems. Jamal Nassar of Illinois State University, Roger Fisher of Harvard Law School, Dov Ronen and Jennifer Widner of Harvard University's Center for International Affairs, Andre du Pisani of the South African Institute of International Relations, Sotorios Mousouris of the UN Center Against Apartheid, and Erik Blumer of the South African Consulate-General in Chicago were extremely helpful.

Michele Steinbacher-Kemp and Amy Atchison are due special thanks for the care and efficiency with which they prepared the manuscript. I am also indebted to many friends, especially Cyndi Hamlin, Donna Richter, Howard Wiarda, Jo Sullivan, William Foltz, Jane Guyer, and Denis Thornton for their encouragement. Above all, I would like to thank my son Jason for his support and understanding.

Introduction

Apartheid, more than any other issue, persistently dominated the international agendas of many Third World countries from 1946, when India brought the treatment of Indians in South Africa to the United Nations (UN), until significant steps toward dismantling the legal underpinnings of racial domination in South Africa were taken in 1990. Given the racial component inherent in European colonialism in Asia, Africa, Latin America, and the Middle East, apartheid became a very emotive issue in many Third World countries, particularly those in Africa. Even in societies where racial discrimination was not a principal concern of policymakers, the common struggle against European control engendered a degree of solidarity among the newly emerging states, a development that often found expression in anti-apartheid resolutions in the UN and other international organizations.

Growing competition between the United States and the former Soviet Union, coupled with the decline of Britain and France—the two major colonial powers—facilitated the elevation of apartheid as a major international issue. Superpower rivalry enhanced the leverage of the developing countries vis-à-vis the West and South Africa. Revolutionary changes in Eastern Europe and the Soviet Union in 1989 and 1990 fundamentally affected Third World relations with South Africa. The end of the Cold War, symbolized by German unification in late 1990 and growing cooperation between the superpowers in southern Africa, the Persian Gulf, the Middle East, and elsewhere, allowed apartheid to be challenged without the encumbrance of the East-West rivalry. The Soviet threat, long used by

Pretoria to justify perpetuating apartheid, restricting opposition to white minority rule, and destabilizing neighboring states to keep them subservient, was now clearly irrelevant. Relations between South Africa and the Soviet Union improved, economic and political ties between Pretoria and Eastern Europe were strengthened, and Mikhail Gorbachev's "new thinking" focused Moscow's attention on seemingly insurmountable political and economic problems at home and on the negotiated settlement of conflicts abroad. Furthermore, significant developments within South Africa itself—influenced in part by unacceptably high costs of maintaining apartheid, domestic pressures for reforms, the effectiveness of international sanctions, military setbacks in Angola, and the collapse of East European dictatorships—altered fundamentally Third World approaches to Pretoria. Moreover, changes in the communist world had serious implications for many Third World countries themselves.

The Third World as an economic concept was challenged by radical transformations in the international economic system. The movement of Eastern Europe and the former Soviet Union toward market economies effectively blurred the distinction between, arguably, the First and Second Worlds, or, in some cases, between the Second and Third Worlds. And given the wide economic disparities among Third World countries, putting Taiwan and Zambia in the same category was undoubtedly questionable. The Third World as an ideological concept was rendered virtually meaningless by the end of the Cold War and growing cooperation between Washington and Moscow. Nonalignment, albeit debatable, had been the cornerstone of several Third World countries' foreign policies. However, in the new strategic international environment the Nonaligned Movement seemed increasingly anachronistic. But Eastern Europe's and the Soviet Union's transition to either democracy or market economies appeared more difficult than the earlier optimism had suggested. Consequently, the Third World as an analytical concept was nonetheless still useful. Most countries in this group, with the obvious exceptions of Taiwan, Brazil, and oil-exporting Middle Eastern states, were characterized by widespread and seemingly insurmountable poverty. All of them, to varying degrees, suffered from political turbulence, questionable legitimacy, ethnic fragmentation, endemic corruption, violence, and human rights abuses. African states in particular were confronted with both political and economic marginalization as international aid donors turned their attention toward Eastern Europe. Africa's persistent economic decline highlighted the widespread corruption and inefficiency that continued to impede that continent's economic and political development.

The decline of superpower rivalry and the subsequent disintegration of the Soviet Union underscored the fact that many Third World countries, despite their plethora of socioeconomic and political challenges, were emerging as regional powers. Akin to South Africa in southern Africa, states such as Brazil, India, Nigeria, and Egypt attempted to dominate their particular regions. Without the restraining influence of the Soviet-American rivalry, it was likely that regional hegemons would attempt to impose their own agenda on neighboring states. Simultaneously, however, post–Cold War power diffusion and increased cooperation between Washington and Moscow eliminated some of the problems faced by outcast or pariah states such as South Africa, Taiwan, and Korea. Communism's hasty retreat and the shift from military to economic power as the primary currency of transnational relations clearly enhanced Taiwan's and Korea's ability to function as normal states and to play a greater financial and technological role in South Africa as well as in the former Soviet Union and the People's Republic of China. Furthermore, major steps in 1990 and 1991 toward the abolition of apartheid diminished South Africa's relative international isolation, thereby decreasing Third World leverage vis-à-vis Pretoria. In fact, to some extent, Third World leaders became victims of their successful anti-apartheid campaigns.

Improved relations between the United States and the former Soviet Union, the functioning of the UN as originally intended after the Cold War ended, and positive European and American responses to developments in South Africa fundamentally altered Third World relations with Pretoria. Countries that had effectively utilized the UN to mobilize international opposition to apartheid and Western governments closely linked to South Africa were now themselves under closer international scrutiny for human rights violations. Progress toward abolishing apartheid, paradoxically, highlighted shortcomings within countries that vociferously opposed white minority rule in South Africa.

Third World countries' declaratory anti-apartheid policies were clearly undermined by domestic grassroots opposition to the personalization of power, official corruption, and widespread human rights violations. These problems were most pronounced in sub-Saharan Africa and India, leading critics of apartheid. Nigeria, Zambia, and Zimbabwe, influenced partly by the political and economic revolutions in Eastern Europe and bold initiatives of State President F. W. de Klerk in South Africa, struggled with internal pressures for political and economic reforms. Having castigated the minority regime in South Africa for racial oppression and the imposition of a draconian State of Emergency, Zimbabwe's Robert Mugabe found himself in the embarrassing situation of maintaining the State of

Emergency inherited from Ian Smith's regime after South Africa had abolished its own. Similarly, Zambia's Kenneth Kaunda, while advocating the virtues of democracy, belatedly lifted his seventeen-year ban on opposition parties and quietly terminated the State of Emergency that undergirded his control of the country for twenty-seven years. Ironically, Kaunda's reforms led to his resounding electoral defeat by Frederick Chiluba in late 1991. In India, the caste system, imbedded in culture and religion for centuries, continued to create problems for the government as the lower castes' rejection of their position in their country's rigid system of social stratification resulted in widespread violence, which was instigated by high caste Hindus who adamantly opposed government efforts to mitigate the deleterious effects of the caste system. India, with its ongoing religious, ethnic, social, and political conflicts, remained an uncertain democracy. Southern Africa's continuing economic decline almost guaranteed that a post-apartheid South Africa would play an even more dominant economic and political role in the region. And the Southern African Development Coordination Conference, an organization designed primarily to reduce member-states' economic dependence on South Africa, would itself be transformed by South Africa's membership and rapprochement between Pretoria and the Frontline States.

This book analyzes foreign policy-making in the Third World, the common and divergent interests among countries opposed to apartheid, conflict as well as cooperation between the various countries and Pretoria, and the implications of international changes for Third World countries themselves. It brings into sharper focus contradictions between Third World states' declaratory policies against apartheid and their actual practices both in relation to South Africa and domestically. It also examines the almost insurmountable post-apartheid challenges for South Africans as well as possible changes in the Third World's policies toward Pretoria.

Chapter 1

The Third World and South Africa: Interests, Strategies, and Change

Although Third World countries consistently and ardently demonstrated their opposition to apartheid, their policies toward Pretoria were far more complex than a cursory analysis would suggest. These countries' policies were complicated by obvious contradictions between declaratory positions strongly condemning apartheid and advocating its abolition on one hand and an unwillingness or inability to sacrifice national interests and a general realization that external influences on change in South Africa may have been limited on the other. As is generally the case with foreign policy-making in most countries, it was often difficult to ascertain which audience a particular government was addressing.[1] For example, Nigeria's strong anti-apartheid stance could have been construed as an attempt to convince other African states as well as the West that Nigeria was indeed the continent's leading power. Brazil's opposition to Pretoria could have been viewed as being aimed primarily at its domestic multi-racial audience, with the objective of perpetuating the myth of racial equality at home. In India's case, an unequivocal anti-apartheid stance undoubtedly enhanced that country's claim to leadership in the Nonaligned Movement. Furthermore, such a position was consistent with India's hubristic tendencies toward moral superiority. For the Arab countries, anti-apartheid pronouncements seemed to be only tangentially concerned with racial discrimination in South Africa. Having few deeply rooted democratic traditions and little empathy with blacks in South Africa, the Middle East was more preoccupied with linking the Palestinian cause to the anti-apartheid movement in order to mobilize African and international opinion against Israel. Zambia's vociferous castigation of Pretoria, which emanated in part from its vulnerability to South Africa's aggression, was instrumental in gaining international support. But Zambia's rhetoric was also intended to obscure its significant commercial ties with South Africa.

Third World South African policies were further complicated by domestic economic and political considerations, the various leaders' personalities, the inherent weakness of developing countries, regional factors, and South Africa's efforts to counter Third World strategies designed to undermine apartheid. In Zambia, for example, divergent views between the government and the private sector concerning trade with South Africa clearly contributed to the complexity of Zambia's policies. Furthermore, President Kenneth Kaunda's commitment to his philosophy of humanism prompted him to make diplomatic overtures to Pretoria, actions that were often at odds with Nigeria's more uncompromising approach. Geographic distance and economic realities seemed to exert tremendous influence on sub-Saharan African countries' relations with South Africa. The further the distance from and the lesser a country's dependence on trade with Pretoria, the more belligerent and inflexible the country's policy tended to be vis-à-vis South Africa. Personal rivalries, such as that between Kaunda and Robert Mugabe, for regional dominance also affected both Zambia's and Zimbabwe's policies. This problem was complicated by competition between Zimbabwe and South Africa, the two most industrialized countries in southern Africa, for regional economic and political supremacy. South Africa's comparative economic might and the higher standard of living, in economic terms, for that country's black majority were frequently marshaled in defense of apartheid, realities which could not be ignored by its neighbors. Moreover, policymakers in Pretoria often alluded to double standards that were applied by the international community to South Africa. The fact that many Third World countries suffered from a degree of moral parochialism, encouraged by European states' paternalistic attitudes toward their erstwhile colonies, made their criticisms of apartheid appear disingenuous. However, their policies toward South Africa were largely effective because they could appeal to Western guilt for past racial wrongs, without being scrutinized for current human rights violations themselves. Finally, any analysis of Third World policies toward South Africa would have to take into consideration the fact that in order to achieve their objectives, countries such as India, Nigeria, Zambia, and Brazil depended on their ability to influence Western Europe, Canada, and the United States. Consequently, complex interaction among forces within the policy-making establishments of those countries ultimately had a bearing on the failure or success of Third World anti-apartheid policies.

The foreign policies of Third World countries are expressions of what governments, individuals, and groups determine to be national interests. National interests may be defined as a finite set of intrinsically important goals either essential or beneficial to a country's survival, its prosperity, the psychological well-being of its population, or any combination of these.² Efficient foreign policies are generally grounded in an objective analysis of a hierarchy of interests. Like industrially advanced countries, the foreign policies of Third World states are inevitably influenced by international factors.³ Compared to Western Europe, North America, and Japan, Third World states are much more preoccupied with domestic problems. Their principal concerns are inevitably centered around issues such as economic development, the building of political and social institutions, and, in too many cases, the survival of inefficient and corrupt political regimes. Most Third World governments are preoccupied with domestic rather than international threats to their security, largely because the state itself is still in the process of consolidation. Yet the issue of apartheid resonated throughout the vast majority of Third World countries, primarily because of their experiences with racial discrimination. In general, the various countries' foreign policies are strongly influenced by internal factors and the personalities and perceptions of those responsible for formulating and implementing them. Since most developing states are ruled by personalized authoritarian regimes, leaders have significant influence on the content of foreign policy.⁴ But this does not mean that they are unrestrained by domestic and international factors. Thus, the international relations of these states are shaped in part by domestic needs and political demands articulated or imposed from within the political system, by the processes through which policy is made, and by those who manage them.⁵

In addition to strong anti-apartheid sentiments, several specific factors affected Third World relations with Pretoria. These included economic interests; family and cultural ties; military considerations; intra-Third World politics and trade; a country's relative international isolation; developments within South Africa itself; and significant changes in the international system. Given the diversity among the countries covered in this book, their commitment to undermining apartheid varied significantly, depending on their particular national interests, proximity to South Africa, the importance of racial issues within their own societies, and so on. But in light of the reality of economic and political interdependence among nations, it was virtually impossible for any of the countries to escape the consequences of each other's actions as well as those of South Africa's major trading partners. Economic interests, or the lack of them, played a major role in influencing the various countries' relations with South Africa.

Despite their staunch support for the imposition of economic sanctions against Pretoria by the industrialized countries, particularly the United States and Western Europe, the Third World states included in this book, with the possible exception of Nigeria, traded overtly or covertly with South Africa. The Middle East and Gulf states, while condemning Israel for its economic, military, and cultural links with Pretoria, were the principal sources of South Africa's oil supplies. Similarly, India's considerable interests in gold and diamonds as well as its close ties to Mauritius—a major outlet for South Africa's trade—inevitably brought New Delhi into contact, directly or indirectly, with De Beers Central Selling Organization and other South Africa–affiliated firms. Zambia, caught in the web of the interdependence of southern Africa, was simultaneously a leading critic of apartheid and a reliable trading partner and peace broker.[6] Brazil's dire economic conditions and its development strategy—based in part on capturing export markets—reduced that country's ability to sever economic relations with South Africa. Since Brazil and South Africa competed for many of the same markets, and because the former attempted to improve trade with Angola, Nigeria, and Mozambique, commercial transactions between Brazil and South Africa remained modest but constant. By contrast, Taiwan, with approximately $80 billion in reserves in 1992, dramatically increased its trade with Pretoria, precisely when the international community had implemented sanctions against the apartheid regime. By 1987 Taiwan had become South Africa's seventh largest trading partner, just behind France. Whereas American imports from and exports to South Africa had declined sharply between 1983 and 1987, Taiwan's imports and exports increased by about 115 percent and 102 percent, respectively.[7] Taiwan's economic relations with South Africa were bolstered by strong political and military links between the two countries.

Unlike the other Third World states, Taiwan, South Africa, and, to a lesser extent Korea, shared the dubious distinction of being regarded as pariah or outcast states, a categorization that engendered military and political cooperation between them. Taiwan's technological capabilities were an obvious asset to Pretoria, especially in the area of electronics and computers. Furthermore, since both Israel and Taiwan had access to American technology and military weapons, collaboration among the pariahs essentially reduced the effectiveness of international sanctions against South Africa. Thus, Taiwan pursued objectives that conflicted directly with the declaratory policies of the other Third World countries.

In addition to economic and military ties, cultural and family links also influenced relations between the Third World and South Africa.

India's early opposition to apartheid emanated from its concern about the treatment of South Africans of Indian origin. As racial segregation became permanently enshrined in law, India found it more difficult to separate problems confronting the Asian community from those faced by black South Africans. But Taiwan, like Japan, due to significant economic ties with Pretoria, was able to secure the status of "honorary whites" for the small South African Chinese community, thereby further distancing itself from the problems of both Indians and blacks. In contrast to India, Taiwan expanded cultural relations with South Africa, scheduled regular flights between the two countries, and encouraged tourism and other exchanges. The various countries' interests and capabilities influenced their strategies toward apartheid.

Several constraints prevent policymakers from selecting certain courses of action. Constraints are both internal and external and may range from very weak to very strong. The strongest constraints prohibit a state from moving in a particular field of action, while others provide motives for avoiding particular steps. Policymakers tend to balance the cost or risk the constraint imposes against probable benefits of the measures under consideration.[8] Internal constraints include the level of economic and political development; the foreign policy-making process; leadership skills; administrative competence; the size of the country; and the personality and priorities of the dominant leader and his or her inner circle. External constraints include the nature of the international public opinion and the priorities of major countries.[9] Given the widespread poverty that characterized the Third World, India, Nigeria, and Zambia, for example, had to exert pressure on countries that were capable of influencing change in South Africa. Consequently, developing states relied primarily on their numerical superiority in international organizations to persuade Britain, the United States, and other Western countries to adopt effective anti-apartheid measures.

Organizations such as the United Nations, the Nonaligned Movement, the Afro-Asian group, the Commonwealth, and the Organization of African Unity (OAU) were essential to the achievement of Third World foreign policy objectives. The implementation of apartheid in 1948, so soon after World War II, in which over 6 million Jews were exterminated in the Holocaust largely because they were regarded by the Nazis as racially inferior, was bound to be of concern to the world community in general and the emerging states in Asia, Africa, and Latin America in particular. Moreover, racial issues became intertwined with the superpowers' rivalry in the Third World. Since anticolonial struggles were primarily against racial discrimination, the issues of decolonization, East-West confrontation, racial equality, and human rights became inseparable. Apart from the fact that militarily weak states tend to base their foreign policies on morality and on a general appreciation for international law, organizations such as the UN and the Commonwealth had articulated policies that were consistent with basic Third World aspirations. By vigorously opposing apartheid and advocating respect for human rights, developing countries were simultaneously reaffirming their belief in racial equality in general. Consequently, they focused their cooperative efforts on abolishing apartheid, and argued that apartheid was directly inconsistent with the purposes and principles of the UN Charter and the Universal Declaration of Human Rights.[10]

The Sharpeville Massacre in March 1960 and the independence of the vast majority of African countries between 1960 and 1964 dramatically increased attention to racial domination in South Africa. Britain, pressured in the Commonwealth as well as in the UN, concluded that apartheid could no longer be treated simply as an internal matter. Third World countries used their majorities in both the UN and the Commonwealth to pressure the West to impose sanctions against South Africa. They advocated a complete trade and cultural embargo against Pretoria as well as its expulsion from the Commonwealth.[11] Western sensitivity to the issue of racial discrimination, among other factors, enabled Third World countries to achieve many of their objectives. But developments in South Africa, induced in part by external pressures, the collapse of communism in Eastern Europe and the Soviet Union, major changes in the international economic system, and the fragmentation of the Third World itself necessitated adjustments in Third World relations with Pretoria.[12]

Foreign policy is responsive to both internal and external stimuli and, as such, is a dynamic process. Relations among states are subject to several levels of change. These may include: (1) adjustment changes or changes in the intensity of effort; (2) program changes, or alterations in the instruments used to address a particular problem; (3) goal changes; and (4) international orientation changes, which occurs when a country redirects its entire approach to world affairs.[13] Among the myriad of sources of fundamental and major foreign policy change are: (1) a particular leader's vision of his or her country's role in the world; (2) bureaucratic initiatives; (3) the advocacy of new directions in policy by a politically relevant segment of society whose support is essential to the government's survival; and (4) external shocks emanating from significant developments in the international economic and political environment. These external shocks usually cannot be ignored by policy-making elites.[14] Revolutionary changes in world politics in 1989 and 1990 undoubtedly influenced shifts in Third World policies toward South Africa. Developments within South Africa itself, induced by several complex factors, forced Pretoria to adjust to new realities, thereby further affecting Third World policies. Moreover, these developments effectively reduced Third World leverage vis-à-vis South Africa and, paradoxically, brought Third World problems under closer international scrutiny.

Despite endemic violence in South Africa, it was obvious that President F. W. de Klerk's bold and imaginative initiatives in 1990 and 1991 had facilitated negotiations among all South Africans for the creation of a nonracial society. Releasing Nelson Mandela and other prominent political prisoners; lifting the State of Emergency; unbanning the African National Congress (ANC) and South African Communist Party, and other opposition groups; integrating public facilities and selected schools; and working with black leaders demonstrated a major departure from previous policies. The ANC's suspension of its armed struggle against the minority regime in early August 1990 indicated its recognition that a negotiated settlement was also in its interest.[15] The combination of internal and external factors had clearly eroded support for apartheid.

Sanctions advocated by the Third World were eventually implemented. Together with growing black empowerment in South Africa and divisions within the white community concerning the utility and costs of apartheid, economic measures against Pretoria ultimately had an impact on the economy and, consequently, on politics.[16] Although several factors may have been responsible for South Africa's economic decline during much of the 1980s, international sanctions ultimately played a pivotal role in the economic downturn by making it more difficult and expensive for South Africa to trade with other nations. Between 1981 and 1986 the economy declined by approximately 3 percent a year. Three consecutive quarters of declines in aggregate real production from the fourth quarter in 1989 onward confirmed the recessionary nature of the economy. The South African Reserve Bank concluded that developments in the first two quarters of 1990 did not leave much hope that positive real growth could be attained in 1990 vis-à-vis 1989.[17] These circumstances prompted de Klerk to enlist American and European support, with the ultimate objective of getting sanctions lifted. But removing sanctions depended to a large extent on progress toward eliminating apartheid.

Developments in Eastern Europe and the end of the Cold War facilitated the implementation of far-reaching reforms in South Africa. Communism, regarded by Pretoria as a threat to its existence, was no longer a primary influence on that country's domestic and foreign policies. South Africa, under U.S. leadership, had negotiated Namibia's independence and the phased-withdrawal of Cuban troops from Angola. Mikhail Gorbachev's new thinking in foreign policy and his preoccupation with perestroika and the disintegration of the Soviet Union diminished Soviet involvement in Third World conflicts, including Angola's civil war. Cuba was now becoming a liability, and Fidel Castro's refusal to abandon his economic programs created strains in the Cuban-Soviet alliance.[18] Furthermore, Moscow indicated its preference for a negotiated settlement between the ANC and Pretoria, thereby reducing the latter's fears of a "total communist onslaught." Communism's decline and the demise of East European dictators also signaled to Pretoria the futility of attempting to maintain the status quo in a rapidly changing international environment. These external shocks influenced public policies in South Africa. But if communism's collapse whetted the ANC's appetite for political power, it also caused many of that organization's leaders to abandon their commitment to a one-party state and a Marxist economy.[19] Recognizing the inevitability of change and new opportunities springing from it, South Africa decided to end its political isolation and to normalize trade relations by improving ties with its former nemesis, the erstwhile communist bloc.

Diplomatic contacts between Pretoria and Moscow were initiated in early 1989 when Soviet Deputy Foreign Minister Anatoly L. Adamishin, met South African Foreign Minister Pik Botha in Mozambique, before going to South Africa.[20] This visit was followed by an expansion of academic exchanges between the two countries and visits by Soviet diplomats to discuss Namibia's transition to independence. In mid-1990 the Soviet Union openly agreed to market its uncut diamonds through the Central Selling Organization, controlled by De Beers of South Africa. Under the agreement, De Beers advanced $1 billion to the Soviet Union against future diamond deliveries. The overall value of the sales contract was estimated to be around $5 billion.[21] These diplomatic and economic developments were strengthened, despite the ANC's disapproval.

South African officials also established economic and political relations with Hungary, Poland, Czechoslovakia, and other Eastern European states. Many of the 13,000 South Africans of Polish descent and the 10,000 South Africans of Hungarian extraction tended to be staunch supporters of the minority government. Nevertheless, both Poland and Hungary had consistently opposed apartheid, despite possible clandestine trade between Hungary and South Africa. However, in early 1990 Pik Botha and Hungary's Foreign Minister Gyuna Horn met in Budapest and expressed their intention to gradually establish official relations.[22] As a member of the UN Special Committee Against Apartheid, Hungary's decision to establish contacts with South Africa was viewed by many Third World governments as a major departure from previous policy. Although Horn emphasized that Hungary's foreign policy was concerned with promoting human rights and eliminating racial discrimination, and that it condemned all manifestations of apartheid, Alfred Nzo, general secretary of the ANC, strongly condemned the visit, and argued that similar initiatives had to be crushed because they supported the survival of the Pretoria regime.[23] But South Africa's decision to release Nelson Mandela, its dismantling of apartheid, and the revolutionary political and economic changes in Eastern Europe had clearly influenced these policy shifts. Bulgaria, Yugoslavia, Czechoslovakia, and Poland generally viewed developments in South Africa positively and moved toward establishing diplomatic and commercial relations with Pretoria.[24]

Paradoxically, Eastern Europe's movement toward democracy and capitalism and South Africa's reforms, combined with the European Community's advancement toward the Single Market and German unification, highlighted sub-Saharan Africa's shortcomings in the areas of human rights, democratic reform, and economic development. Eastern Europe's demand for capital, much of which was siphoned off by the 1990–91 Persian Gulf crisis, decreased the Europeans' willingness to invest scarce resources in Africa and prompted them to link economic assistance to progress toward democracy and economic development. Africans, long the champions of human rights in South Africa, were now subject to some of the same criticisms and pressures they had imposed on South Africa since their independence three decades earlier. Although most Third World countries had experienced setbacks with experiments with democracy, the African states were by far those most seriously challenged by the relative lack of progress toward democracy and economic development. India, Brazil, Taiwan, and South Korea had either achieved a significant level of political development or had built the economic foundations essential for democratic reforms. But such distinctions among Third World countries, most of which were solidly united against apartheid, were strenuously overlooked as the poorer countries appreciated the importance of collective action in their struggle for what they regarded to be a more just world order. While unity may have been essential to counter the West's economic and military power, as Michael Manley astutely observed, "in some cases this was a disservice to the legitimate aspirations and expectations of citizens of countries whose governments repressed or hindered the exercise of universally recognized human rights and economic freedoms."[25]

Global trends toward democracy, intellectual freedom, and private enterprise undoubtedly propelled Africa away from despotic dictatorships. However, equally important were internal developments such as the loss of credibility of ideologies which were utilized to justify autocracy; dismal economic performance, widespread corruption, and political repression that undermined arguments for one-party systems; and the emergence of more effective human rights movements within several African countries.[26] Ironically, many African opposition groups alluded to steps toward the realization of greater freedoms for South Africa's majority in order to persuade their own governments to abandon authoritarian rule.

Protests against undemocratic regimes marked the inchoate stages of Africa's second independence. The expectations of the first independence having been indefinitely postponed, if not denied entirely, ordinary Africans were now demanding from their leaders precisely what had been central objectives of the struggle against European control. In other words, whereas the anticolonial movement had spearheaded a revolt against British, French, and Portuguese rule, for example, the targets in the late 1980s and the early 1990s were the post-independence African ruling classes and, particularly, the political systems they created and sought to perpetuate by force and arbitrary means.[27] Analogous to South Africa's black majority—whose lack of political rights and economic opportunity had been deplored and condemned by African leaders throughout the continent—peasants, workers, and intellectuals in sub-Saharan Africa were becoming politically empowered; they refused to tolerate being victims of despotic regimes, regardless of their racial composition.[28] Attempts at political and economic empowerment in the 1990s represented a continuation of the struggle against external control. Post-colonial authoritarian rule was not radically different from that of the former European colonizers.

Unlike India, which experienced centuries of British governance and where Western political institutions were relatively compatible with firmly established indigenous bureaucratic traditions and social stratification, Nigeria and Zambia, for example, experienced a comparatively brief period of European colonization. British rule was not long enough to alter radically Africa's traditions or to consolidate the institutional foundations of democracy. Differences between India and Africa seemed to buttress Samuel Huntington's assertion that "the duration of democratic institutions after independence is a function of the duration of British rule before independence."[29] Furthermore, the short period of formal colonial domination in Africa could not be characterized as a paragon of democracy. With the exception of Kenya, few countries were regarded as places for

European settlement—a fact that influenced the nature of governance. In contrast to African states with large European populations, where human rights were more widely observed, countries with a small number of European settlers experienced fewer social and political freedoms. As Claude Welch noted, constitutional recognition and protection of rights were belated, with the constitutions created at independence being in many cases the first significant expression of them.[30] The artificial nature and fragility of the African state clearly exacerbated these problems shortly after formal independence was achieved. With traditional political institutions discredited by the implementation of superficial Western practices, the way for the personalization of power and the rise of military dictatorships was largely unobstructed. Equally important, several preconditions for democracy were generally absent.

Having championed the cause of democracy and human dignity in their struggle for independence, African leaders initially embraced outward trappings of parliamentary democracy. Their rejection of European authoritarianism heightened expectations that the social, political, and economic freedoms that were basically reserved for Europeans during colonialism would be enjoyed by Africans, especially urban residents. But since the majority of Africans had lived in smaller communities that were more conducive to egalitarianism and respect for individuals as group members, Western ideas were of dubious benefit. They were principally concerned with freedom from unjust and incomprehensible laws and directives that were formulated by Europeans and imposed by traditional authorities; with freedom to return to their land; and with their right to be left alone, to live as they desired, and to seek their own goals.[31] Nevertheless, ordinary Africans eventually subscribed to expectations articulated by the political elite. However, as leaders confronted almost insurmountable problems following independence, European institutions and principles were increasingly perceived as inappropriate for Africa. Subsequently, many aspects of Europeanization were equated with post-independence challenges, and leaders who sought to protect their privileged positions abandoned European democracy, where it existed, and justified their actions by claiming that the system was an alien importation.[32] In contradistinction to India, where the elites had strenuously observed democratic rules, to the extent possible in such a large and diverse country, African leaders essentially rejected political and economic freedoms. Therefore, the values of the dominant African elites militated against the growth of the democratic process. This, in turn, hindered the realization of an essential precondition for democracy—namely, economic development.

Africa, the least economically developed continent, is also the least democratic. With the exception of the Middle East, where religion and culture continued to impede democratic movements, which were generated by economic prosperity, countries in Asia and Latin America that had achieved substantial economic growth had also experienced greater democratization. In other words, there seems to be a relatively strong correlation between economic development and democracy.[33] Or, as Meddi Mugyenyi put it, "democracy comes in small installments behind development. Democracy comes in to protect the accomplishments of development."[34] Whatever the sequence, it is generally agreed that a wealthy country is more likely than a poor one to be democratic. In addition to making literacy more widespread and exposure to mass media more pervasive, a wealthy economy is more conducive to democracy for the following reasons: (1) wealth tends to moderate political conflict; (2) the availability of resources generally facilitates accommodation and compromise; (3) greater economic opportunities enhance political tranquility by providing unsuccessful contenders for political office with alternative sources of power; (4) wealthy societies tend to be more complex, thus necessitating the dispersion of decision-making; and (5) even if wealth is not equally distributed in a prosperous society, and it rarely is, the emergence of a relatively satisfied middle class provides the stability essential to democracy.[35] The existence of a large middle class is also conducive to the proliferation of interest groups, labor unions, and various civic and social organizations. These groups contribute to the dispersion of power and act as checks on political elites.

Equally important for the growth of democracy is the presence of an autonomous, indigenous business class.[36] Private enterprise and the existence of sufficiently large internal markets are essential to the emergence and survival of this class. Developments in India, Brazil, and, to a lesser extent, Taiwan and Korea seemed to support the assumption that market forces and entrepreneurs assisted the decline of authoritarian rule. Obviously, cultural and religious factors play a broader and sometimes more subtle role, as was demonstrated by Nigeria's lurching toward democracy. But when the economy is dominated by state-controlled enterprises in developing societies that lack high literacy rates, extensive communications, and so on, the personalization of power was more probable, precisely because alternative sources of wealth and upward mobility were severely limited. This reality continued to be the pivotal challenge confronting African societies, many of which had strongly condemned apartheid.

South Africa's relative wealth fostered the rise of trade unions and other interest groups; encouraged the shift of power away from the state to the private sector; contributed to both the complexity of society and the decentralization of decision-making; made racial integration difficult to avoid; and ultimately undermined the ideological foundations of apartheid. Thus, despite the fact that the future is fraught with dangers, South Africa is likely to become more democratic than Zambia or Nigeria. Most African countries are unlikely to sustain the momentum of the initial movement in a democratic direction due to endemic poverty and accompanying violence.[37]

Competitive party politics, generally regarded as a cornerstone of democracy in the West, had been widely repudiated by African leaders, many of whom argued that these Western institutions were not only inappropriate for Africa but were also harmful to political stability and economic development. More specifically, multiparty politics and political pluralism were viewed as tantamount to encouraging national disintegration along ethnic lines. Ethnic groups, defined as "distinct groups in society self-consciously united around shared histories, traditions, beliefs, cultures, and values which mobilized their membership for common political, economic, and social purposes,"[38] were perceived as being incompatible with the realization of democracy. But since ethnic groups are an integral component of African political reality, prohibiting the formation of political parties ultimately enabled corrupt political elites to perpetuate their control over society. The absence of political parties has not ensured stability or economic development. In essence, ethnic divisions were consolidated as various groups competed for scarce resources. As Donald Rothchild observed, to the extent that overt, tangible interests—rather than an abstract sense of unique, fixed, and total identities—are involved, ethnic groups can be regarded as utility maximizers who are responsible to the political exchange process.[39] Therefore, political competition exists, but without the restraints and benefits of the rule of law. Instead of promoting economic development and national unity, one-party states became increasingly repressive, corrupt, and inefficient. Growing African empowerment and revolutionary changes in the international political system forced many governments to grapple with citizens' demands for multiparty politics and the observance of human rights. Ironically, African critics of human rights abuses and political oppression pointed to the paradox of their black governments demanding democracy in South Africa but resenting pressure to democratize themselves.[40]

Given Zambia's and Zimbabwe's strong condemnation of apartheid, it was not surprising that in these countries citizens demonstrated assiduously for the same things their governments had demanded of South Africa, namely, political participation, political freedoms, and government accountability. Despite his reluctance to abandon the one-party system, Kenneth Kaunda was eventually compelled by public opinion, widespread protest, and the logic of his own anti-apartheid position to recognize the legitimacy of opposition political parties and to peacefully transfer power to Frederick Chiluba. The impetus for change came principally from individuals in the private sector, many of whom represented "the post-socialist, post-authoritarian reaction to black Africa's economic troubles."[41] Similar developments occurred in Zimbabwe, where Robert Mugabe had attempted to eliminate political opposition. Domestic pressures for multiparty democracy, coupled with "external shocks," rekindled debate about the inconsistency between Mugabe's strong advocacy of political freedom in South Africa and his suppression of political dissent at home. Mugabe's decision to create a one-party state by absorbing the opposition party, led by Joshua Nkomo, into the governing party ultimately broadened debate within the latter.[42]

Elsewhere in southern Africa, especially in Zaire and Mozambique, governments were pressured to move toward multiparty politics. President Joaquim A. Chissano of Mozambique invited the Mozambique National Resistance (Renamo) to participate in the political system, despite the widespread destruction it inflicted on Mozambique. It was largely the government's failure to end the civil war through military means that prompted Chissano to institute democratic reforms. In Zaire President Mobutu Sese Seko, often referred to as "the Father and God of the Nation," responded to demands for political change by announcing that a twenty-year ban on opposition parties would be lifted and by calling for a direct dialogue with the people to better gauge their concerns. But when confronted with the extraordinary outpouring of sentiment against him and his autocratic rule, Mobutu refused to publish the findings of his first public opinion survey.[43] Thus, despite declaratory policies favoring competitive party politics, it was apparent that political reforms would not be voluntarily implemented at the expense of the various leaders' political survival.

Widely regarded as one of the few African states with a comparatively strong economy and democratic inclinations, Kenya faced serious challenges to its one-party system in 1990 and 1991. Demonstrations for multiparty democracy occurred with greater frequency, and many who protested government repression and institutionalized corruption were detained without being charged with specific crimes. Lawyers, human rights advocates, religious leaders, and students were among the government's most vociferous critics as well as its targets of oppression.[44] Although President Daniel arap Moi argued that competitive party politics would exacerbate problems associated with ethnic loyalties, Kenya's educated urban residents were sufficiently empowered to oppose efforts to perpetuate the personalization of power and concomitant human rights violations. Conflict seemed to be more prevalent in Kenya than elsewhere in Africa partly because President Moi's resistance to change was contrary to the reality engendered by Kenya's relative economic prosperity. In other words, conflict demonstrated that Kenya had achieved some of the prerequisites for a transition to democratic government. Influenced to a large extent by events in the communist world, Western Europe and the United States viewed Africa as decreasingly relevant to their economic and strategic interests and were reluctant to allocate substantial foreign assistance to the various African countries that had not made tangible progress toward significant political reforms. Ironically, Europeans contemplated restricting economic aid to black Africa in order to pressure governments to adopt political reforms precisely when economic sanctions against South Africa were lifted, due to President de Klerk's abolition of apartheid legislation.

Cold War geostrategic calculations had facilitated the various African leaders' ability to relegate economic reforms to a much lower priority than their own enrichment and survival. Instead of developing, the vast majority of African states experienced deteriorating infrastructures, unpayable external debts, high levels of unemployment, declining exports, a decreasing ability to attract foreign investments, uncontrollable population growth rates, mass starvation, and rampant corruption at all levels of society. Consequently, Africa, which showed so much promise and had such high expectations at independence, contained twenty-six out of the world's forty-four poorest countries by 1990. African leaders, their countries' own worst enemies, were both amazed and frustrated by how economic and political reforms in Eastern Europe had marginalized their continent in international economic and political affairs. Although many African countries had implemented structural economic reforms at the behest of the International Monetary Fund (IMF), the World Bank, and other international financial institutions, economic conditions worsened. But as Richard Joseph astutely observed, economic restructuring on the continent, except in a few isolated instances, was not accompanied by political reforms. Perestroika without glasnost characterized the policies that were implemented with the IMF's and the World Bank's approval.[45] Economic reforms could not be divorced from long overdue political transformation.

Iraq's occupation of Kuwait and the subsequent American-led Operation Desert Storm further exacerbated Africa's economic problems. While

Nigeria benefited from oil price increases, most African countries paid higher prices for petroleum imports. Already suffering from severe economic difficulties, economic recessions in the United States, Canada, and Britain reduced demand for Third World commodity exports, thereby compounding the effects of higher energy costs. African governments raised gasoline, diesel, and kerosene prices by as much as 65 percent, which, in turn, increased the cost of almost everything else.[46] More developed Third World countries such as Brazil, Taiwan, Korea, and India were also affected. India, for example, was not only confronted with the problems created by large numbers of its citizens returning from working in the Gulf, but also had to deal with shortages of both crude and refined oil created by the termination of exports from Kuwait. Perhaps equally important, the Gulf War diverted resources away from Eastern Europe and from countries such as Germany, Britain, France, Japan, Saudi Arabia, and the United States, thus rendering Third World economic problems even more intractable. With fewer financial resources available for allocation to Africa, the view that economic aid should be linked to ending political repression and to instituting democratic reforms was strengthened.

Many members of the U.S. Congress who had staunchly supported sanctions against South Africa, often in cooperation with African leaders, advocated the adoption of a U.S. African policy based on consistent support for human rights and democratic governance. The African-American community, which spearheaded the anti-apartheid movement but was reluctant to criticize sub-Saharan governments for gross violations of internationally recognized human rights, was urged to turn its attention to encouraging the observance of democratic freedoms in all of Africa.[47] The main component of America's new approach to Africa was to link the provision of military assistance to Kenya, Zaire, and other African countries to releasing political prisoners; ending the mistreatment of prisoners; restoring the judiciary's independence; and upholding freedom of expression.[48] Prominent human rights activists throughout Africa, but primarily in Kenya, supported this shift in U.S. policy. For example, Gibson Kamau Kuria, a Kenyan human rights lawyer and leading proponent of democratic reform, urged the United States to impose economic sanctions against Kenya similar to those implemented against South Africa. These included the suspension of all aid programs and a ban on tourism, Kenya's principal source of foreign exchange.[49] While the complete termination of U.S. assistance to Kenya was unlikely to occur, especially in light of the fact that Kenya's strategic importance was highlighted by Operation Desert Storm in early 1991, it was evident that in the post–Cold War era human rights would assume a more significant role in U.S. policy toward Africa.

Western European governments, the European Community, the IMF, the World Bank, and the Group of Seven regarded the promotion of democracy as a post–Cold War imperative. To achieve this objective, they decided to link aid to African countries to improved governance and respect for human rights. John Major, when he was chancellor of the Exchequer and after he became prime minister in late 1990, had admonished African leaders that donor countries would place conditions on economic assistance. Asserting that there were too many cases of questionable military purchases and white elephant public sector projects in the Third World, Major noted that "donors cannot but take notice if resources are being wasted at a time when many of the countries involved are pressing for additional external support."[50] At the 1991 Commonwealth meeting in Harare, Major called upon member states for their unequivocal commitment to the principles of "good government." These included free elections, freedom of the press, respect for the rule of law, and the observance of human rights. Like Britain and the United States, France warned that future aid programs would be tied to political reforms. During the Franco-African Summit in June 1990, President François Mitterrand indicated a willingness to address demands of his domestic critics for the French government to commit itself to campaigning forcefully for democracy and human rights in Africa when he emphasized that France would be "lukewarm to countries that show no progress toward change, and more enthusiastic toward those who do."[51]

Predictably, African leaders were generally reluctant to face the new realities of the strategically altered post–Cold War environment. Accustomed to hiding behind their respective superpower in the intense periods of East-West rivalry, they attempted to avoid implementing the promises and expectations of independence by claiming that democratic reforms were too much to demand from relatively new countries. Crude conditionality was viewed as counterproductive. Many African leaders also challenged the right of donors to impose particular forms of democratic government as condition of further aid, particularly in the absence of any parallel moves to democratize the international economic system.[52] But apart from their diminished leverage vis-à-vis the West in the post–Cold War era, African leaders had strengthened the case for international sanctions to induce domestic reforms by their own inexorable and highly effective campaign for sanctions against apartheid.

Chapter 2

Sub-Saharan Africa: Nigeria and Zambia

Sub-Saharan Africa's relations with South Africa have been, and will undoubtedly continue to be, influenced by domestic economic and political realities within the various states as well as international factors. Although committed to the eradication of apartheid and what they regarded as vestiges of European colonialism, African countries were unable to achieve this objective by themselves, due largely to their internal political instability and the alarming deterioration of their economic infrastructure. Increasingly dependent on infusions of foreign aid, these states were essentially constrained in the area of foreign policy. Their ability to influence South Africa also depended on the support of their major donors, many of which had significant economic interests in South Africa. Consequently, the gap between their rhetoric condemning apartheid and the effectiveness of their policies grew as their political and economic conditions worsened.

Having gained their independence from the colonial powers, African states were recognized as sovereign entities by the international community. However, their international legitimacy was not necessarily accompanied by internal legitimacy. Unlike many Latin American states which had achieved a significant degree of internal cohesion before becoming independent, African countries managed to obtain only a veneer of internal consolidation. As Robert Jackson and Carl Rosberg observed, seldom did African nationalism result in the creation of a new national identity as a basis for the internal legitimacy of the new state.[1] This is largely due to the process by which African countries achieved their independence.

Anticolonial movements, primarily preoccupied with eliminating external control, articulated philosophies designed to appeal to international audiences and fragile domestic coalitions. The majority of the population saw the ideological component of the struggle against European domination as basically peripheral to their interests. And those who were mobilized politically were soon disillusioned. Following the attainment of independence, "nationalist thought was transformed into a gloss for the manipulation of the institutions of the new nation-states on behalf of the interests of the ruling political parties in a recession of one-party states."[2] Coalitions disintegrated, political struggles ensued, and ethnic rivalries were on the ascendancy. Attempting to undergird their declining legitimacy, political leaders resorted to coercive measures to enforce compliance with what were frequently arbitrary regulations. Thus, central political authority was threatened at a crucial early stage of the African countries' political development.[3]

Despite the growing centralization of political power, newly independent African states experienced constant erosion of internal legitimacy, a factor that ultimately reduced the effectiveness of their foreign policies. While many states could formulate policies, their ability to implement them was seriously diminished. This problem has been regarded as a central characteristic of the "soft state," that is, a state which is "limited in its control over society and is therefore incapable of implementing its regulations effectively throughout its territory and of achieving its many-faceted goals."[4] In order to survive, leaders in the soft state must engage in a process of bargaining and compromises with the most powerful political groups. They must also eliminate serious opposition. This, in turn, is conducive to the development of authoritarianism, the personalization of power, and institutionalized corruption, all of which contribute to the further weakening of the state and the dimunition of the government's authority.

But governance in sub-Saharan Africa is not principally concerned with the demands and opinions of the populace. As was usually the case under colonial rule, those who hold the reins of power in the contemporary African state generally view the state as their private estate for the duration of their tenure. African leaders, most of whom practice authoritarian rule, are neither responsible nor responsive to those they purportedly govern. In what Thomas Callaghy called the patrimonial administrative state,[5] the major objective of those in positions of power is to consolidate and perpetuate that power for as long as they can. To accomplish this, they surround themselves with small groups of loyal supporters and develop personality cults in order to obtain a modicum of political legitimacy.

Power becomes personalized. Personal rule aims at monopolizing power—locking in power in the hands of a political dynasty.6 Given the lack of significant alternative sources of power, control of government offices is jealously guarded against competing groups that endeavor to share the spoils that accompany political positions. Under these circumstances the general welfare suffers, matters that are not vital to the regime's survival are regarded as peripheral, and public officials are generally not expected to perform their nominal duties. While they are instrumentally attached to the offices they occupy and derive great personal and political advantages from them, they are likely to be legally and morally detached from them and therefore from the public interest and from the state.7 The personalization of power in the patrimonial administrative state ultimately destroys the government's claims to legitimacy and, simultaneously, prevents the realization of meaningful economic development. These factors undoubtedly diminished the overall effectiveness of sub-Saharan African policies toward South Africa. Thus, Africa's preoccupation with the personalization of power and political longevity was at cross-purposes with the objective of ending apartheid.

Poor governance has been largely responsible for Africa's economic decline. Personal rule, widespread corruption, unnecessary interference with market forces, and incompetent administration of the public sector contributed directly to Africa's dire economic problems. After an initial period of growth following independence in the early 1960s, Africa has experienced steady economic deterioration. Overall, Africans were almost as poor in 1991 as they were in 1961. Economic growth, averaging 3.4 percent a year since 1961, was only a fraction above population growth.8 Whereas per capita incomes grew by approximately 1.4 percent in the 1960s, this rate decreased to around 0.2 percent in the 1970s and to a negative 2.4 percent in the 1980s. Consequently, the number of Africans enduring absolute poverty grew by two-thirds between 1980 and 1985.9 This dramatic economic downturn was demonstrated by the change in status from middle-income countries to low-income countries for Nigeria, Ghana, Guinea, Liberia, and Zambia, among others.

Declining commodity prices, especially in the cases of Nigeria and Zambia, clearly exacerbated economic problems. Government policies did little to encourage agricultural production, and many farmers migrated to urban areas in search of jobs, thereby further undermining the agricultural sector. Food production has been unable to keep up with the population, and urban dwellers' changing consumption patterns influenced governments to increase imports of wheat and other products. Whereas industry grew roughly three times as fast as agriculture in the 1960s due to large infusions of capital in the industrial sector at the expense of the agricultural sector, during the latter half of the 1980s many African countries challenged assumptions of development models by actually deindustrializing. As Africa's share in world markets fell, its foreign debt escalated from about $6 billion in 1970 to around $134 billion by 1988. Sub-Saharan Africa's debt in 1991 was approximately the same as its gross national product and almost four times as large as its export earnings.10

Although external factors contributed to Africa's economic problems, domestic conditions and government policies were primarily responsible for the dismal economic performance. Excessive governmental involvement in the private sector and the absence of adequate incentives to produce needed goods and services combined to discourage additional investments essential to generate economic growth. The very nature of the patrimonial administrative state, with its arbitrary decision-making processes, and bureaucratic obstruction, militated against the development of a favorable investment climate. Political pressures to Africanize foreign enterprises and Africans' fears that foreigners would dominate the private sector helped to make most African countries unattractive to foreign investors. Moreover, substantial capital flight from African countries undermined investors' confidence in the economy. As R. Stephen Brent put it, as long as Africans themselves do not consider their countries safe places to invest, neither will foreigners.11 Much of the investment in the public sector was plagued by inefficiency. Weak public sector management, emanating partly from the personalization of power and its associated modes of behavior, resulted in significant financial losses by public enterprises, poor investment choices, costly and unreliable infrastructure, overvalued exchange rates, and inefficient resource allocation.12 The net result has been a downward spiral in economic growth and development.

Confronted with what appears to be almost insurmountable problems, many African governments have been more amenable to reforms suggested, or sometimes imposed, by international financial institutions and donor countries. The World Bank concluded that in order to stabilize Africa's economic decline and to prevent the number of poor from increasing, a growth rate of about 5.5 percent a year—nearly 2 percent higher than the projected rate—was needed to raise per capita consumption by enough to meet this target.13 In addition to a supportive policy environment that includes improvements in income distribution and the provision of more social services, massive infusions of foreign assistance and investments will be required to achieve this objective, an unlikely occurrence in light of demands of dwindling sources of capital in Eastern Europe, the Persian Gulf, and elsewhere. To be effective, foreign aid and investment must be combined with radical domestic changes. Unlike Eastern Europe, where economic reforms were accompanied by revolutionary changes in the political structure as well as in personnel, Africa attempted to make major economic reforms without implementing radical political changes, especially at the top. The same leaders who were responsible for Africa's economic deterioration endeavored to push through incremental changes that did not threaten their control of society. In fact, most African governments that managed to reduce their budget deficits did so by curtailing investments, reducing social welfare expenditures, and sacrificing maintenance. However, those personnel programs that sustained patronage networks and allocations for the military remained largely untouched.14 Continuing economic problems and the inherent weaknesses of African states influenced strategies adopted by African leaders.

Determined to see apartheid's demise but unable to exert pressure on South Africa as individual states, African countries decided to achieve their foreign policy objectives through collective action in international organizations such as the Commonwealth, the OAU, the UN, and the Nonaligned Movement. Overlapping memberships in some of the most powerful international bodies strengthened Africa's position vis-à-vis Pretoria. Cooperating with Canada, Australia, India, and the English-speaking Caribbean, Anglophone-African countries were able to exert pressure on Britain to change its relations with South Africa. Although not entirely successful in convincing Britain to implement a total trade embargo against Pretoria, their efforts, combined with developments within South Africa and other international anti-apartheid activities, had a considerable impact on apartheid. South Africa's desire to be regarded as an African state, together with the emotive nature of racial discrimination both in Africa and in the West, enhanced Africa's anti-apartheid leadership role in the UN and in various Western capitals. Africans also relied on the OAU as an instrument of their policies toward South Africa.

Prior to the OAU's founding in 1963, African states collaborated with Asian countries, principally India, to oppose apartheid. However, the need for a separate African movement to represent the continent in global affairs was expressed at the Accra Conference of Independent African States in 1958. Ethiopia, Ghana, Liberia, Libya, Morocco, Sudan, Tunisia, and the United Arab Republic (Egypt) established a permanent African caucus, known as the Informal Permanent Machinery, in the UN.15 While these states were clearly concerned about apartheid, the prevailing view favored inclusion of South Africa as an African country in the continent's international efforts. Thus, South Africa, the only other independent African state in 1958, was invited to attend the Accra conference, but declined. Perhaps overly confident of their ability to influence Pretoria to reverse its process of legalizing racial discrimination and domination by the example of their relative multiracial harmonious societies, emerging African countries such as Ghana did not attempt to ostracize South Africa. On the contrary, Kwame Nkrumah stated publicly that Ghana would not interfere in South Africa's internal affairs, and actively promoted closer economic, diplomatic, and cultural links between the two countries. To underscore this emphasis on cooperation, South Africa was invited to, and was officially represented at, Ghana's independence celebrations.[16] However, in the aftermath of the Sharpeville massacre in 1960 relations between the majority of sub-Saharan African countries and South Africa were radically altered.

Occurring at the zenith of Africa's achievement of independence from European colonialization, the Sharpeville massacre reverberated throughout the continent and was a catalyst for South Africa's withdrawal from the Commonwealth in 1961. Ghana, Nigeria, and India played a pivotal role in events that culminated in South Africa's decision. By 1963, when the OAU was formed, most African countries had subscribed to the view that the existence of apartheid threatened the entire continent. The system of legalized racial discrimination and domination was regarded as militating against the achievement of the fundamental objectives of justice, human dignity, and peace, which were viewed as essential to the stability and development of Africa.[17] In other words, apartheid and all vestiges of colonialism had to be eradicated before the expectations of Africa's independence could be realized. The OAU consistently advocated democracy for South Africa even as member states refused to practice it at home. The OAU called for an independent, nonracial judiciary, freedom to form and join political parties, and the right of all South Africans to participate in the government and administration of their country on the basis of universal suffrage, exercised through the one-person, one-vote system.[18] Yet few African governments had extended these rights to their own citizens, and generally resented external pressure to do so. However, despite their own human rights problems, African governments agreed that apartheid had to be abolished in order to complete the first phase of Africa's independence.

At the 1963 Addis Ababa summit, during which the OAU was established, African states formulated a general strategy for undermining apartheid in particular and white minority rule in southern Africa in general. The OAU's strategy contained three interrelated components. The first element, which involved isolating South Africa on the continent, focused on terminating diplomatic contacts with Pretoria, implementing an economic boycott against South Africa, closing African ports to South African ships, and preventing South African planes from entering the member-countries' airspace or landing at their airports. Another part of the strategy called for mobilizing international support to isolate South Africa economically, politically, culturally, and militarily. Consequently, the OAU worked through various international forums as well as with individual countries to achieve this objective. The final component of the liberation strategy focused on assisting armed struggle against South Africa by providing material and moral support for the various liberation movements. Economic and military aid from independent African countries and foreign sources was channeled through the African Liberation Committee, which was based in Dar es Salaam, Tanzania. In addition to directly assisting the armed struggle, the Liberation Committee provided scholarships, educational facilities, and employment for South African refugees.[19] Despite these commitments to armed struggle, many African states were generally opposed to a violent solution to the problem of apartheid. Furthermore, few OAU members were able or willing to fully meet their financial obligations to the Liberation Committee. Consequently, other countries, primarily the former Soviet Union and its erstwhile allies in Eastern Europe, assumed greater responsibility for assisting the armed struggle.

Despite widespread African opposition to apartheid, there was disagreement on strategies for effectuating change in South Africa. Sharing South Africa's concerns about communist expansion on the continent and close links between the African National Congress and the Soviet Union, President Houphouet-Boigny of the Ivory Coast believed that dialogue with South Africa would be a more effective approach than confrontation. Moreover, the OAU's view that Western industrialized countries were directly and indirectly helping to perpetuate apartheid through their economic, military, and political ties with South Africa was clearly inconsistent with the Ivory Coast's pro-Western stance.[20] Malawi, Kenya, Ghana, and Gabon seemed to endorse the Ivory Coast's preference for dialogue. While President Kenneth Kaunda of Zambia initiated dialogue with South Africa on several occasions, he also permitted the ANC to establish its headquarters in Lusaka. Kaunda's position—for political, economic, geostrategic, and personal reasons—was far more complex than those of most African leaders. Strongly opposed to any diplomatic contacts with Pretoria were Nigeria and Tanzania, among others. Nevertheless, the OAU seemed relatively powerless to prevent several African states from circumventing restrictions on commercial relations with South Africa.[21] Yet at the international level, beyond Africa, the OAU was relatively successful in mobilizing opposition to apartheid.

Given their numerical, and thus voting, strength within the UN, African states concentrated their efforts on passing anti-apartheid resolutions and on ostracizing South Africa from the international community. Unrelenting diplomatic pressure by OAU members resulted in the passage of a UN Security Council resolution in 1963 that urged arms-exporting countries to terminate military sales to South Africa. From the OAU's perspective, Western countries were undermining Africa's security interests by supplying weapons to South Africa. As Agrippah Mugomba noted, by arming South Africa, Western countries had helped Pretoria to dominate neighboring states and to diminish the OAU's ability to challenge the apartheid regime.[22] Yet the OAU could not prevent South Africa from obtaining military weapons from countries that were prepared to openly disregard the embargo or to covertly supply arms. Nonetheless, the African states rendered South Africa's acquisition of weapons a costly endeavor that was fraught with uncertainty and political embarrassment.

In addition to persuading most of the world community to agree in principle to observe the arms embargo, the OAU succeeded in getting South Africa expelled from the International Olympic Games Committee, the UN Economic Commission for Africa, the World Health Organization, UNESCO, the International Labor Organization, and other UN specialized agencies. In 1966 the OAU played the leading role in establishing a UN Special Committee on Apartheid, an organization designed to monitor developments pertaining to enforcing of anti-apartheid UN resolutions and to disseminate information about apartheid. Finally, in 1974 the OAU attempted to remove South Africa from the UN, an initiative that was eventually blocked by U.S., British, and French opposition to it in the UN Security Council.[23] However, South Africa, having been excluded from so many international organizations, was not helped significantly by its UN membership. The OAU had managed to disabuse the apartheid regime of any claim to legitimacy in international organizations.

While the UN was perceived by the OAU as the most appropriate forum in which to mobilize opposition to apartheid, attempts were made to enlist the assistance of both the Organization of Petroleum Exporting Countries (OPEC) and the Nonaligned Movement. As early as 1964 the OAU's Council of Ministers adopted a resolution that called on OPEC to implement an oil embargo against South Africa. But the resolution was defeated by OAU member-states, partly because many of them had maintained their own economic links with South Africa.[24] Yet contradictions between various African countries' declaratory policies and their actual behavior did not prevent the OAU from pursuing a policy of asking others to do what many African governments had tried to circumvent. The Yom Kippur War in October 1973 facilitated the OAU's efforts to enlist OPEC's support for the anti-apartheid campaign, largely because the Arab states needed African assistance in their struggle with Israel. Moreover, Israel's growing economic and military ties with South Africa were exploited by both African and Arab states that sought to portray Israel and South Africa as partners in the oppression of Palestinians in the West Bank and Gaza and the black majority in South Africa.[25] Due in part to Israel's occupation of Egyptian territory, as well as in response to Arab pressure, most African states severed diplomatic relations with Israel. Similarly, African states persuaded the Arab League to institute a petroleum boycott against South Africa. The OAU also tried to obtain the UN Security Council's approval of an oil embargo against Pretoria and requested all petroleum exporting countries to impose collective and individual penalties against those companies that supplied oil to South Africa.[26] The fact that South Africa conducted what was largely a covert oil trade demonstrated the OAU's effectiveness in convincing most countries to adhere to the oil embargo.

In order to consolidate international opposition to apartheid, the OAU and several of its members encouraged the Nonaligned Movement to adopt resolutions that would weaken international support for South Africa. Generally agreeing with the African view of apartheid, nonaligned countries called on the international community to deny legitimacy to Pretoria and requested that the UN Security Council impose comprehensive and mandatory sanctions against South Africa to compel it to end apartheid. Furthermore, consistent with the OAU's objectives and strategies, the Nonaligned Movement attempted to persuade the international community to increase its material assistance to the anti-apartheid liberation movements.[27] Concerted OAU efforts augmented Third World opposition to apartheid, despite the fact that several developing countries, for a variety of reasons, ignored many of the anti-apartheid sanctions they strongly endorsed in international and regional forums.

Anglophone OAU members also concentrated their efforts on the Commonwealth to pressure South Africa. Nigeria, Zambia, Zimbabwe, and other former British colonies collaborated with India, Jamaica, Canada, and Australia, among others, to try to convince Britain, one of South Africa's major trading partners and the Western country with the closest historical, cultural, and family links to that country, to impose economic sanctions against Pretoria. When Britain decided in July 1970 to allow British arms manufacturers to resume sales to South Africa, the Canadian and Indian governments protested to British prime minister Edward Heath, and the leaders of Tanzania, Kenya, Uganda, and Zambia threatened to withdraw from the Commonwealth, an organization that was decreasing in importance to Britain as it moved into the European Common Market. The Afro-Asian group was also instrumental in securing passage of the Commonwealth's Gleneagles Declaration in 1977, which prohibited sporting contacts with South Africa.[28] Even though Britain strongly opposed apartheid, it believed that economic measures and isolating South Africa would not achieve the objectives outlined by the African countries; instead, they would be counterproductive. Britain's perspective was obviously influenced by national interests to a much greater extent than by concerns with principles of racial equality and morality. Relatively powerless in the face of Britain's refusal to impose comprehensive economic sanctions against Pretoria, the African countries, despite their serious disagreement with British policy, had to accept incremental steps that were designed to eliminate apartheid without jeopardizing Britain's economic and other interests in South Africa. Nevertheless, combined with OAU activities in the UN and elsewhere, modest sanctions implemented by Britain contributed to the external pressure which was instrumental in forcing Pretoria to abandon its commitment to apartheid. By continuing economic relations with South Africa, while distancing themselves politically from Pretoria, several OAU members not only inadvertently buttressed Britain's position on economic sanctions but also facilitated South Africa's efforts to eventually improve diplomatic ties with many of the neighboring states, thereby diminishing the effectiveness of the OAU's attempts to prevent Pretoria from gaining political legitimacy in Africa.

Whereas all African countries, with the exception of Malawi, eschewed formal diplomatic links with Pretoria, the overwhelming majority of them, albeit covertly, maintained commercial relations with South Africa, a fact emphasized by government officials in Pretoria. For example, even though Kenya demonstrated its solidarity with the ANC and other anti-apartheid movements by providing an office for the ANC in Nairobi in 1988 and by collecting funds for the South West African People's Organization (SWAPO), the government permitted foreign airlines flying to South Africa to land and refuel in Nairobi. Incomprehensibly, in 1984 Kenya banned outgoing telex messages to South Africa, but did not extend the ban to telephone calls either way.[29] Similar to Kenya, the Ivory Coast allowed foreign aircraft on flights to and from South Africa to use facilities at Abidjan's Port Bouet international airport. These privileges were extended to South African Airways in 1988. Unlike Kenya, the Ivory Coast emphasized dialogue with Pretoria and did not conceal its opposition to the ANC. The government's conciliatory stance toward Pretoria was underlined when the local media were instructed by Ivory Coast officials not to cover the July 1987 conference in Dakar between liberal white South Africans and ANC representatives.[30]

Zaire, one of the world's poorest countries, due largely to political and economic mismanagement and ubiquitous corruption, seemed to disregard OAU guidelines on trade as well as on diplomatic contacts. South African products are commonly found in Zaire's stores, and South African airlines flew between Zaire and South Africa. Trade missions were established between the two countries and after November 1989, under the terms of a bilateral agreement, South Africans and Zairians were not required to obtain visas to visit each other's countries for periods of two weeks or less. Estimated to be one of Zaire's relatively insignificant trading partners prior to 1987, by 1990 South Africa was believed to rank as Zaire's fourth largest trading partner, after Belgium, the United States, and Germany.[31]

Determined to reduce its isolation, the South African government utilized the country's extensive economic links with sub-Saharan Africa to launch a concerted effort to obtain diplomatic recognition on the continent. Having suffered serious military and political setbacks in Angola and being confronted with escalating international pressures to abolish apartheid and to relinquish control over Namibia, Pretoria decided to transform its liabilities into assets by playing a constructive role in the U.S.-brokered Angolan peace initiatives, which linked the phased withdrawal of Cuban troops from Angola to Namibia's independence from South Africa.[32] By agreeing to end its illegal occupation of Namibia, South Africa hoped to gain greater acceptance by African governments. Given President Houphouet-Boigny's reluctance to endorse the OAU's diplomatic boycott against Pretoria, South African officials, including President P. W. Botha and his successor, de Klerk, visited the Ivory Coast as a first step toward diminishing their country's isolation on the continent. President de Klerk's bold initiatives at home were matched by innovative diplomatic overtures to Mozambique, Zaire, Zambia, the United States, and Europe.[33] By early 1990 the OAU itself, partly in response to dramatic developments in South Africa, had agreed to begin direct contacts with Pretoria in an effort to find a negotiated solution to its racial problems. But the OAU's policy reversal was also prompted by political considerations. To some extent, the new OAU policy was aimed at coordinating sub-Saharan Africa's contacts with South Africa, thereby preventing direct diplomatic approaches by Pretoria to individual African countries.[34] Whatever the political reasoning was behind the OAU's new policy, it was evident that isolating South Africa was rendered extremely difficult by substantial changes within South Africa itself. The South African policies of Nigeria and Zambia illustrate the complexity of sub-Saharan Africa's relations with Pretoria.

NIGERIA'S POLICY TOWARD SOUTH AFRICA

Having achieved its independence from the British, many of whom perceived themselves as racially superior to Africans, Nigeria supported the termination of European domination of Africa. Furthermore, Nigeria's achievement of independence subsequent to a war that was fought partly because of Germany's racial philosophies and the Nazis' attempts to exterminate Jews and other groups deemed to be either racially inferior or morally undesirable, heightened its awareness of the dangers of racial ideologies. The development of international human rights regimes and the general acceptance on the part of nations as well as individuals that racial discrimination was wrong further consolidated Nigeria's belief that human beings were entitled to basic human rights, regardless of their racial characteristics. Nigerians' experiences with the color bar, imposed on Africans by British colonial administrators as well as by ordinary British residents, inevitably influenced them to be sensitive to racial domination in South Africa. Apartheid was a painful reminder of Europe's assumptions concerning the relationship between racial characteristics and socioeconomic stratification. As Busari Adebisi observed, the brutality with which apartheid was identified and the indignity suffered by Africans under the system made for perfect agreement among the main political parties on a militant and dynamic policy against South Africa.[35] Yet Nigeria's domestic economic, political, and social problems effectively limited its ability to challenge the apartheid regime without obtaining the assistance of South Africa's closest allies and trading partners in the West, many of whom were reluctant to sacrifice their economic interests for moral causes. Moreover, Nigeria's preoccupation with its own domestic problems and its unpredictable and chaotic transfer of power conspired against the development of a concerted, consistent, and well-executed policy toward Pretoria.

Nigeria's foreign policy, like those of other states, is shaped by diverse domestic and international factors, including the personalities, values, priorities, and skills of foreign policymakers. Nigeria's perception of its regional, continental, and international roles also undoubtedly contributes to its external behavior. Given its huge population and abundant natural resources, Nigeria seemed capable of being not only a regional power but also of projecting its influence throughout the continent, thereby challenging South Africa's position as southern Africa's superpower. Although many Nigerians entertained such aspirations during the period of high oil prices, widespread mismanagement of petroleum revenues undermined the attainment of those objectives. Thus, despite the availability of resources, political constraints hampered their efficient utilization in relation to the achievement of foreign policy goals. Because Nigeria's foreign policy agenda was formulated and implemented by a relatively small group of political, military, traditional, and economic elites, the country's external relations were closely linked to the behaviors of those elites. Hence, Nigeria's foreign policy was affected by the lack of cohesiveness that characterized the national elite.[36] However, while most foreign policy objectives engendered little consensus among diverse ethnic, regional, religious, and ideological groupings, the emotive issue of apartheid was sufficiently powerful to galvanize and coalesce different groups and to enable Nigeria to pursue a relatively consistent anti-apartheid policy. However, Nigeria's domestic problems prevented successive governments from implementing many declaratory policies.

Concerned about Nigeria's inability to influence international events which ultimately affected the country, Bolaji Akinyemi, minister of External Affairs, developed the concept of a Concert of Medium Powers. The group, composed of Algeria, Argentina, Austria, Brazil, Egypt, India, Indonesia, Malaysia, Mexico, Senegal, Sweden, Switzerland, Venezuela, Yugoslavia, Zimbabwe, and Nigeria, was designed to play a mediatory role in international negotiations, with the general objective of strengthening global cooperation and enhancing peace and security. Required to be free of any military alignment and to be influential in their own region, member-states attempted to straddle North-South and East-West divisions, and concentrated on resolving issues such as apartheid, the militarization of outer space, and the UN's financial problems.[37] The first meeting of the Concert of Medium Powers was held in Lagos in March 1989 at the invitation of the Nigerian Foreign Ministry. Thus, despite its economic and political difficulties, Nigeria continued to perceive itself as a major international actor. Nonetheless, domestic problems impeded the achievement of its major foreign policy aims.

Plagued with tensions between the Muslim-dominated north and the primarily Christian south as well as ethnic rivalries, Nigeria has vacillated between promise and despair since its independence in 1960. The optimism that marked the birth of the new state was soon replaced with diminished expectations as the democratically elected prime minister, Abubaker Tafawa Balewa, was overthrown and assassinated in 1966. His successor Major-General Johnson Ironsi suffered the same fate in a military coup led by General Yakubu Gowon in July 1966. The instability that became an integral component of Nigeria's political life was manifested prior to independence. During the late 1950s, political intolerance had become deeply ingrained as incumbent political leaders attempted to eliminate potential as well as actual rivals for public office. With the departure of the British, repression, fraud, obstruction, and other violations of democratic rules of behavior escalated sharply.[38] The tenuousness of democracy became more apparent as political factions competed for the concomitant rewards of public office, a reality reflected in the frequency of successful military coups between 1966 and 1985. And the uneasy coexistence of the Muslim north and Christian south, a constant concern even during periods of relative political stability, was exacerbated in 1986 when the government of General Ibrahim Babangida decided that Nigeria would become a full member of the Organization of Islamic Conference. This decision, made and implemented without prior public consultation, antagonized many Christians who were apprehensive about Nigeria's future as a secular state.[39] Although confronted with significant political problems, or because of them, Nigeria decided to advance toward a transition from military rule to democracy.

Cognizant of the dynamic connection between economic and political development, President Babangida pursued political reforms and economic restructuring simultaneously. Having been instrumental in the demise of civilian rule under President Alhaji Shehu Shagari as well as in the skillful replacement of Shagari's successor, General Muhammadu Buhari, in a bloodless coup, Babangida initiated a transition to civilian rule. Originally scheduled for 1990, the transfer of power from military leaders to a democratically elected government was postponed until 1992. Partly in an effort to justify the delay, President Babangida emphasized that the political transition program would take effect immediately, with local government elections in 1987, state government elections in 1990, a census count in 1991, and federal elections in 1992, with all the processes "properly supervised by the military administration."[40]

The organization principally responsible for developing guidelines for democracy's inauguration in 1992 was the seventeen-member Political Bureau, established in 1985. While principally concerned with the number and composition of political parties that would exist under the new scheme, the Political Bureau and President Babangida also articulated broader principles that were designed to ensure the proper functioning of the democratic machinery of government. For instance, the federal system of government was to be retained; a general ban was imposed on individuals who held public office from 1960 to 1988, including those in office during the transition period; and all legislators at the federal as well as the state level would work part-time only, and would be awarded allowances instead of salaries.[41]

The Political Bureau's primary, and perhaps most difficult and controversial, task was to determine how many political parties were legally entitled to compete in national and local elections. Based largely on the assumption that several political parties would enhance ethnic rivalries and undermine democratic governance and institutions, the Political Bureau recommended that the number of political parties be limited to two. Conditions and restrictions placed upon these political parties included: (1) acceptance of the national philosophy of the government; (2) open membership to all Nigerians irrespective of origin, sex, religion, or ethnic grouping; (3) those in leadership positions would be drawn from different regions of Nigeria in order for parties to reflect the country's federal character; and (4) disagreements would be limited to national priorities and strategies for implementing them.[42] Furthermore, both parties were to be funded substantially from federal revenues, thereby reducing the prevalence of corruption associated with previous regimes. The National Electoral Commission would be responsible for allocating the funding and for monitoring additional financial contributions to the two parties. Politicians and bureaucrats found guilty of corruption were to be banned from politics for life. In an effort to improve the government's legitimacy, Babangida established a Code of Conduct Bureau and a Code of Conduct Tribunal "with appropriate laws to enable them to function as institutions for ensuring accountability and integrity in public office."[43]

If the first local elections, held in December 1987, were an indication of how the system would function, prospects for a successful transition to meaningful democratic rule after 1992 were not encouraging. These local elections were characterized by disorganization and violence. Several voters, who were admonished by the government that voting was part of their civic duty, discovered deserted polling booths when they went to vote. The National Election Committee, which was principally responsible for organizing the election, was unable to provide ballot boxes and voting papers on time to the correct polling stations. Moreover, the deliberate lack of any real election campaign, partly to avoid a return to corrupt political practices, inadvertently contributed to voter confusion on both the issues and the candidates.[44] Such problems were likely to be magnified in national elections. Despite efforts to limit the number of political parties, it was doubtful that the largest ethnic groups—the Ibo, Yoruba, and Hausa-Fulani—would not form three separate political parties. The multiplicity of ethnic groups and languages, approximately 250, virtually guaranteed the emergence of several political parties. Furthermore, north-south divisions between Muslims and Christians threatened to complicate a process that was so carefully crafted by the Political Bureau and the Babangida regime.[45] Equally important was the threat posed to the political experiment by escalating unemployment among college graduates and a general absence of enthusiasm for proposed changes. On the other hand, Babangida's economic achievements, albeit insufficient to deal effectively with the severe economic problems, offered some hope that the political experiment, while not working as originally planned, would at least contribute to improved governance and significant progress toward democracy.

Democratization of the Nigerian polity has been impeded by economic constraints, the foundations of which are deeply ingrained in the fabric of Nigerian society. Despite Nigerians' predilection toward democracy and the existence of an entrepreneurial class, there are several countervailing economic forces that render the achievement and maintenance of democracy extremely difficult. The country's rapidly growing population, expected to reach approximately 100 million by the year 2000, negated meaningful economic growth and development. In less than a decade Nigeria's exports, primarily petroleum, dropped from $26 billion to $9.4 billion. Per capita income fell from around $1,090 in 1980 to under $250 in 1989, amid rising levels of unemployment, a decaying infrastructure, and deteriorating social services. Faced with declining revenues, the government borrowed excessively from external sources. Consequently, the country's foreign debt soared, from $452 million in 1970 to over $32 billion in 1990.[46] Servicing the debt, estimated $4.2 billion a year, will undoubtedly militate against rapid economic recovery.

Even more menacing to the democratic process were the values and practices of Nigeria's political and economic elite. Ordinarily a country with a fairly large group of middle class families is regarded as having met one of the major prerequisites for democracy. However, in Nigeria this is not the case. As Richard Joseph noted, the Nigerian "bourgeoisie has an economic orientation and a set of priorities that render it fundamentally incapable of ruling without squeezing dry the arteries of the state itself."[47] Instead of becoming an alternative to state power, this group's interests were so intricately intertwined with the country's affairs that the state's coercive power was enhanced while the prospects of democracy were reduced. Public sector dominance of the petroleum-based economy facilitated the continuation of corruption and the transformation of government offices into prebends.[48]

Determined to reverse Nigeria's economic decline and to eliminate, or at least diminish, corruption in government as well as in the private sector, the Babangida regime instituted a radical economic adjustment program in 1986. Key elements of the new economic policy included devaluation of the country's currency, the naira, from 180 U.S. cents to 12.5 cents; privatization of many state-owned companies; termination of the essentially corrupt import licensing system; enhancement of the role of the private sector in the country's economy; greater reliance on market mechanisms for setting prices; increased emphasis on agricultural production; abolishment of inefficient agricultural boards; and greater efforts to attract private investment to Nigeria.[49] While the International Monetary Fund and other international financial agencies applauded Nigeria's bold austerity program and its stronger embrace of a market economy, groups that were adversely affected by structural adjustments attempted to undermine Babangida's reform efforts. Furthermore, in mid-1989 students throughout Nigeria demonstrated against what they perceived to be hardships emanating from the government's economic program. Similar to Zambia, where citizens demonstrated against President Kenneth Kaunda's austerity measures, Nigeria responded by reversing the major decisions that had triggered riots in which about fifty people were killed. Almost 62 thousand workers were promised jobs by the government, salaries and benefits for public employees were increased, and vacancies for teachers in primary and secondary schools were filled.[50] Despite these developments, the government continued to implement important economic reforms and to encourage foreign investment and agricultural productivity.

Whereas South Africa's experience with foreign firms disinvesting resulted in part from external pressures against apartheid, many of which were initiated by Nigeria and other African countries, the trend toward disinvestment in Nigeria in the late 1980s and early 1990s emanated principally from internal problems. Among the main causes for the outflow of foreign investment were high investment costs and comparatively low returns on investments. An inadequate and unreliable infrastructure forced companies to purchase their own emergency generators, to secure water supplies, and to develop alternatives to the public telephone system and postal services.[51] On the other hand, following the enactment of the 1990 Nigerian Enterprises Promotion decree, which allowed foreign companies to own 100 percent of the equity in certain activities, some smaller-scale Indian firms as well as larger enterprises from the United States and Western Europe began to invest or to explore investment opportunities. The trend away from disinvestment in 1990 was influenced not only by rising oil prices due to the Persian Gulf crisis, but was also the result of an intensive international campaign by the former External Affairs Minister Major-General Ike Nwachukwu to attract foreign investments to Nigeria.[52] Despite these efforts, developments in Eastern Europe as well as the war in the Persian Gulf drained badly needed financial resources away from Nigeria in particular and Africa in general. However, the government's decision to focus on increasing agricultural productivity seemed to reduce the need for food imports, a major cause of Nigeria's fiscal problems.

While Nigeria's agricultural decline may be attributed to factors ranging from inadequate credit and the government's failure to encourage private price setting to poor infrastructure and insufficient services in the areas of machinery maintenance, the principal factor that undermined agriculture was the petroleum boom of the mid-1970s. High oil prices encouraged large numbers of farmers and other agricultural workers to migrate to urban centers, thereby causing a severe disruption of the agricultural economy. Between 1970 and 1982 annual production of Nigeria's major cash crops—cocoa, rubber, cotton, and groundnuts—fell dramatically, and food imports increased significantly.[53]

In order to reverse Nigeria's agricultural decline, President Babangida implemented a comprehensive agricultural plan that included: (1) the encouragement of the upward integration by large-scale industrial users of agricultural materials; (2) the promotion of more ecological methods in food and agricultural production; (3) an increase in credit flows to agriculture; (4) the enhancement of economic efficiency; (5) a package of incentives that included higher prices derived from market forces; and (6) modernization of agricultural production.[54] Even though these changes have stimulated greater agricultural output, Nigeria's economic situation remained precarious.

The inflow of foreign investment was insufficient to stabilize the economy. Allowing for about $700 million in direct investments per year and international aid flows of around $1 billion, Nigeria still needed a large current account surplus in order to service its huge debt. Under these circumstances, recovery of the country's debilitated economy appeared elusive.[55] Continuing economic difficulties threatened to arrest progress toward democratization.

Although Nigeria, unlike South Africa, did not officially sanction discrimination or systematically engage in gross violations of internationally recognized human rights, severe economic problems and endemic political instability in Nigeria contributed to both discrimination and human rights abuses. The commanding role of the government in the country's economic affairs and the prebendary nature of public offices vitiated government efforts to avoid discrimination. Despite the fact that Nigeria, conscious of tensions among diverse ethnic groups, attempted to strike a balance among different groups in decision-making and in appointments to major governmental positions, individuals lacking family connections in a particular part of the country generally experienced difficulty in gaining access to schools and employment, among other things.[56] Similarly, relatively low levels of political development—manifested by weak national institutions, chronic political instability, and the lack of legitimacy on the part of political leaders—engendered conditions that were conducive to human rights violations. Preoccupied with their own survival, Nigeria's leaders instituted the State Security (Detention of Persons) Decree in 1984. This law empowered the chief of General Staff, the inspector-general of Police, and the minister of Internal Affairs to detain indefinitely, and without charge, persons considered to be a threat to the economy or security of the state.[57] Journalists and trade union members were usually principal targets, and many were detained for periods lasting several months.

Similar to South Africa, Nigeria had an extremely high number of executions. However, whereas South Africa's imposition of the death penalty was often racially motivated or strongly influenced by the very nature of the apartheid system, Nigeria's was more closely related to state insecurity and poverty. On the other hand, the court system in South Africa exhibited more outward vestiges of procedural due process of law. In Nigeria, special courts operated outside the ordinary legal system and were responsible for as many as sixty convictions that carried the death penalty in 1989. Known as Robbery and Firearms Tribunals, these courts were presided over by a High Court judge, a senior military officer, and a senior police officer. Persons who were convicted did not have the right to appeal to a higher court, although a State Military Governor had to confirm or deny the imposition of death sentences.[58] The fact that human rights violations were not institutionalized and varied according to the ruling elites' security perceptions differentiated Nigeria from South Africa. Nonetheless, for those affected by arbitrary legal decisions, the distinction was largely meaningless. However, regardless of the limited similarities between Nigeria and South Africa, the former consistently opposed the deliberate implementation by the latter of a system of racial domination that had systematically dehumanized blacks in all aspects of life. But Nigeria's economic and political problems had effectively diminished its ability to influence change in South Africa.

Nigeria's foreign policy, like that of any country, is shaped to a large extent by the remembered experiences of those who formulate policy as well as by the historical and political factors that defined the country's basic character. The issue of apartheid became a cardinal principle and preoccupation of Nigerian foreign policy not only because racial discrimination was a painful component of Nigeria's history, but also because the immorality of apartheid facilitated Nigeria's ability to mobilize public support at home. If the fear of majority rule in South Africa was used by Pretoria to galvanize white support for the continuation of apartheid, Nigeria's anti-apartheid activities were instrumental in mobilizing domestic and international opposition to racial domination anywhere in Africa. Yet the various Nigerian regimes' concern with apartheid diverted attention away from serious internal problems, including the lack of legitimacy of those in power. Thus, the emotive nature of apartheid, the tendency of relatively weak states to emphasize morality in foreign policy, and the personal and political calculations of Nigeria's leaders combined to elevate the elimination of apartheid as one of Nigeria's primary foreign policy objectives.

Nigeria's interests in South Africa transcended racial identification with and concerns about the oppressed black majority or the political survival of Nigerian leaders. The continuation of white minority rule was perceived as a direct threat to Nigeria's security and as a challenge to its dominant position in sub-Saharan Africa. During the 1967–70 Nigerian civil war, Portugal, Rhodesia (Zimbabwe), and South Africa actively supported the Biafrans. These white supremacist regimes, determined to maintain control over black majorities in southern Africa, viewed Nigeria's disintegration as providing an opportunity for them to permanently weaken a potential rival. Portugal, which endeavored to perpetuate its control of Angola and Mozambique, allowed Biafrans to establish their European headquarters in Lisbon. Rhodesia under Ian Smith's minority regime allowed its pilots to assist the Biafrans by flying Delfin fighter planes that dropped bombs manufactured in Rhodesia on Lagos. South Africa also permitted its pilots to engage in bombing raids on Nigeria, and a significant number of South African mercenaries fought on behalf of the secessionists. Following the cessation of hostilities, Nigerian leaders were convinced that their own country's security as well as that of sub-Saharan Africa as a whole was tenuous at best as long as Portugal, Rhodesia, and South Africa remained obdurate in their opposition to the emergence of majority-ruled governments in southern Africa.[59] Nigeria's views were clearly consistent with those of the OAU. Most African states, to varying degrees, assumed that their own independence would be circumscribed until colonial rule and racial domination were eradicated from the entire continent. To accomplish these objectives, Nigeria adopted several strategies. These included mobilizing domestic as well as international public opinion against apartheid; applying diplomatic pressure; assisting the ANC and other liberation movements; threatening to use military force, if necessary; and imposing economic and cultural sanctions against South Africa.

Unlike many African states, where anti-apartheid activities by independent interest groups were generally regarded as potentially dangerous to national security and were therefore discouraged, Nigeria encouraged the formation and functioning of anti-apartheid groups. During the Lagos Apartheid Conference in November 1988, Nigeria's minister of External Affairs, Major General Ike Nwachukwu, urged African countries that did not have anti-apartheid movements to take immediate measures to promote such organizations as a means of mobilizing their citizens and providing support for the various governments' anti-apartheid actions.[60] However, given the political insecurity of many African regimes, they were clearly apprehensive about the direct and indirect consequences of encouraging widespread domestic political activity for their own survival. While Nigeria's internal problems threatened its leaders' political longevity, anti-apartheid activities were tolerated by successive governments. Most Nigerians were not only generally aware of South Africa's problems but also were largely supportive of their leaders' efforts to dismantle apartheid. Prominent Nigerian thinkers, leading politicians, and interest groups such as the National Committee Against Apartheid, the Nigerian Students Union, the Nigeria Labor Congress, and the Academic Staff Union of Universities were actively opposed to apartheid. There was little divergence between the government's position on apartheid and the public's views. Nigerian leaders had succeeded in mobilizing public opposition to apartheid and, consequently, support for an important component of Nigeria's foreign policy.

The Nigerian government established a National Committee on the Dissemination of Information on the Evils of Apartheid in the mid-1970s. Composed of government officials and media representatives, the committee was designed to inform Nigerians about racial discrimination in South Africa. The committee's activities were also instrumental in focusing public attention on the need to dismantle apartheid, thereby predisposing Nigerians to support the government's attempts to achieve its foreign policy objectives in southern Africa.[61] Further efforts were made to influence international public opinion. These included hosting the World Conference on Action Against Apartheid during August 1977 in Lagos. Organized by the UN, the OAU, and the Nigerian government, the conference was attended by several national liberation movements, intergovernmental organizations, and about two-thirds of the UN-member countries. Similarly, the National Committee Against Apartheid held a conference in Lagos in November 1988 to focus international attention on strategies for dismantling apartheid. These activities helped to mobilize world public opinion against South Africa and demonstrated Nigeria's determination to end apartheid. Nigeria's diplomatic activities buttressed its efforts to induce greater international and domestic anti-apartheid sentiment.

Because of its leadership position in sub-Saharan Africa, Nigeria assumed primary responsibility for initiating anti-apartheid policies in the OAU, the UN, and elsewhere. For example, General Olusegun Obasanjo, the former Nigerian president, emerged as a prominent anti-apartheid spokesperson within the OAU and the Commonwealth. Retired Major General Joseph Garba, Nigeria's permanent representative to the UN, was instrumental in getting the UN Anti-Apartheid Committee to pursue aggressively alleged violations of sanctions implemented against South Africa and to disseminate its findings to the international community.

Nigeria, like Ghana, had originally eschewed a policy of confrontation in relation to South Africa and had tried to encourage peaceful change through dialogue. Furthermore, Prime Minister Tafawa Balewa's ideological views predisposed him to cooperate with Britain and other Western countries to resolve the apartheid issue. Balewa had indicated Nigeria's willingness to exchange ambassadors with South Africa, but Pretoria refused to develop diplomatic ties with Nigeria.[62] Following the Sharpeville massacre in 1960 Nigeria's approach to South Africa shifted away from dialogue toward increased confrontation. By 1961, shortly after Nigeria became fully independent, South Africa's membership in the Commonwealth was challenged by Nigeria and other former British colonies. Nigeria's major departure from the policy of dialogue was prompted by South Africa's participation in the Biafran conflict. This trend was strengthened when South Africa invaded Angola in 1975 to overthrow the Soviet–Cuban-backed government in Luanda. South Africa's actions against the Angolan regime not only influenced Nigeria to recognize the Popular Movement for the Liberation of Angola (MPLA) as the legitimate government but also diminished the credibility of any Angolan group, principally the National Union for the Total Independence of Angola (UNITA), that was supported by Pretoria. South Africa's determination to destabilize its neighbors, especially the former Portuguese colonies that had provided Pretoria with a buffer against what it regarded as the "total onslaught" by communist-inspired African liberation groups, led Nigerians to conclude that only more assertive strategies toward South Africa could dismantle apartheid.

Due in part to its newly acquired power, derived mainly from escalating oil revenues that came in the aftermath of the Organization of Petroleum

Exporting Countries' success in determining oil prices, Nigeria adopted more aggressive policies toward South Africa. Both Murtala Muhammad and his successor, Olusegun Obasanjo, made a concerted effort to isolate Pretoria from the world community and to persuade other countries, particularly the United States and Western Europe, to do likewise. Similarly, Alhaji Shehu Shagari, who became Nigeria's first president following the 1978 transition from military to civilian rule, pursued policies that were largely consistent with those of his predecessors. Shagari, who was openly critical of the Reagan administration's constructive engagement policy, asserted that South Africa had been encouraged to resist abolishing apartheid and to delay granting Namibia its independence by the Reagan administration's insistence on linking the withdrawal of Cuban troops from Angola to Namibia's independence. He contended that the American position was as unjust as it was incomprehensible.[63]

Despite Nigeria's declaratory policies, by the mid-1980s its ability to influence change in South Africa was reduced by growing internal political and economic problems, the latter emanating principally from mismanagement of government revenues and a precipitous drop in oil prices. Unable to persuade Commonwealth members—primarily Britain—to adopt significant sanctions against South Africa, Nigeria had initially refused to participate in the Eminent Persons Contact Group that was established by the Commonwealth to make a fact-finding tour of South Africa, but changed its position under pressure from Zambia, Zimbabwe, and Tanzania.[64] Having decided to collaborate with other Commonwealth countries, Nigeria became a prominent actor in international efforts to end apartheid. Obasanjo, widely respected for the pivotal role he played in Nigeria's transition to democracy in the late 1970s, became the cochairperson of the Commonwealth Eminent Persons Group, and cooperated with Australia, Canada, and other major countries of the Commonwealth to exert pressure on Britain to take a harder line on sanctions against South Africa, albeit with limited success. Viewing Pretoria's attempts at dialogue with Zambia, Ivory Coast, Zaire, and other African countries as part of a broader strategy of weakening African solidarity against apartheid, Nigeria hardened its position on isolating South Africa and admonished OAU members that it was no longer sufficient to pass anti-apartheid resolutions and simultaneously engage in dialogue with South African officials. Nigeria also called upon African states to review their relations with the IMF, the World Bank, and transnational corporations "which had over the years weakened their capacity to effectively support the liberation struggle."[65] In addition to diplomatic pressures, Nigeria emphasized the importance of assisting the armed resistance against apartheid.

Geographically remote from South Africa, Nigeria adopted a much more militant stance than other African countries in relation to apartheid, especially when compared to South Africa's neighbors, particularly Zambia, Botswana, and Zimbabwe. Nigeria's oil wealth undoubtedly contributed to its view that it could challenge South Africa not only indirectly but also through military means. Several Nigerian generals had entertained the idea that direct military action against South Africa was necessary to protect southern African countries from Pretoria's aggression. For example, in 1977 it was suggested that Nigeria would become militarily involved in southern Africa if the various liberation groups requested assistance; if independent African countries were attacked by South Africa and called upon Nigeria to provide military support; and if a major racial conflict involving Zimbabwe and South Africa arose.[66] Furthermore, Nigeria would develop nuclear weapons to counter South Africa's military might. Although Nigeria did not engage Pretoria militarily and did not produce nuclear weapons, it usually responded favorably to requests from South Africa's neighbors for financial and material assistance. For instance, when South Africa launched military raids on several Frontline States in mid-1986, Nigeria sent the various countries approximately $15 million within forty-eight hours. And a month later, Foreign Minister Bolaji Akinyemi made an extended visit to Angola, Zambia, Zimbabwe, and Botswana, during which he pledged about $75 million to the region over a five-year period.[67] Nigeria's relations with the Frontline States were viewed as the principal motivation for unconfirmed reports at the end of 1986 of an impending South African air strike on Nigerian oil fields. It was alleged that Pretoria had established a communications center in a central African country for that purpose. When South Africa actually concluded an agreement with Equatorial Guinea to undertake a number of projects in order to improve relations between the two countries, Nigeria pressured Equatorial Guinea to cancel the agreement.[68] Lagos was determined to emphasize its regional hegemony.

Even though Nigeria did not directly challenge South Africa militarily, it provided substantial amounts of military and financial assistance to the African National Congress (ANC), the Pan-Africanist Congress (PAC), and other southern African liberation movements. Following the Soweto uprising in 1976 the Nigerian government shifted some of its resources away from the ANC and the PAC, preferring instead to support more vigorously the South African Youth Revolutionary Council (SAYRCO). Believing that younger South Africans were willing to engage in militant activities that would eventually undermine apartheid, Nigeria allowed SAYRCO to establish its headquarters in Lagos and provided both military aid and training for its members. However, Nigeria also continued to support the ANC's armed struggle.[69] Equally important, Lagos concentrated much of its diplomatic efforts on persuading international organizations, as well as individual governments, to impose stringent economic sanctions against South Africa.

Nigeria's precarious economic conditions and the divergent perspectives within the country on the effectiveness of sanctions and the costs of abiding by them ultimately eroded Nigeria's ability to obtain full compliance with its declared policy. Trade relations established with South Africa while Nigeria was under British colonial rule created bonds of interdependence, thereby making any abrupt severing of ties with South Africa difficult. Throughout much of the 1970s there were unconfirmed reports of clandestine trade between South Africa and Nigeria. For example, it was alleged that in 1975 Nigerian businessmen, with prior approval of President Yakubu Gowon, went to South Africa on a trade mission, even as Nigeria was urging other African states to isolate South Africa economically and diplomatically. Similarly, it was asserted that although Nigeria enforced an oil boycott against South Africa, it arranged with third parties to purchase food and mining equipment from South Africa. These goods were allegedly unloaded at ports of small neighboring countries and subsequently transported into Nigeria by trucks or aboard fishing vessels.[70] Even if these circumventions of sanctions imposed by Nigeria and the OAU did occur, the main thrust of Nigeria's actual South African policies was largely consistent with its strong anti-apartheid position.

From the mid-1970s to the early 1980s, Nigeria was powerful enough to implement countervailing measures against Western companies, primarily British firms, that had extensive trade links with South Africa. Widely perceived as Africa's new economic power, Nigeria attempted to isolate South Africa by forcing companies to choose between the two countries. Nigeria implemented its threat against Barclays Bank in 1976 following reports that Barclays' South African subsidiary had purchased approximately $13 million worth of South African defense bonds that were used to help fight the war against black nationalist guerrillas, many of whom were supported by Nigeria.[71] The Nigerian government nationalized Barclays Bank of Nigeria and assumed control over 60 percent of the shares. Nigeria's opposition to apartheid was strengthened when Obasanjo became president. Reiterating his country's policy on "double-dealers" doing business with both Nigeria and South Africa, Obasanjo established an Economic Intelligence Unit to recommend actions in cases where companies were involved in business transactions that were contrary to Nigeria's policy. Barclays Bank International was asked to reduce its financial stake in South Africa. When it refused, the Nigerian government withdrew its deposits from Barclays Bank of Nigeria and ordered foreign shares in the bank to be reduced from 40 percent to 30 percent. Similar actions were taken against oil companies, especially British Petroleum (BP).

Consistent with its policy of isolating South Africa, Nigeria had stipulated that its petroleum could not be shipped to South Africa. When British Petroleum violated the oil embargo, the Nigerian government expropriated BP's interests. As if to underscore its displeasure with Britain's refusal to implement significant sanctions against Pretoria, Nigeria announced its decision on British Petroleum at the beginning of the 1979 Commonwealth Conference in Lusaka, Zambia. Because Britain owned a substantial portion of BP, Nigeria's actions were taken seriously, not only by Britain but also by the United States and other Western countries. Nigeria's official reason for expropriating BP was that the British government had given formal permission to BP to export North Sea and nonembargoed oil to South Africa. From Nigeria's perspective, Britain's decision amounted to a subterfuge for making Nigerian oil available to South Africa. In other words, the release of North Sea oil to South Africa meant that more Nigerian oil was going to European countries to replace the petroleum Britain sold Pretoria. Nigeria therefore concluded that Britain could be forced to comply with the oil embargo by simply terminating BP's access to Nigerian petroleum supplies.[72] Subsequently, the Nigerian government required all companies purchasing oil to sign a Purchase Contract, under which they agreed to send a discharge certificate to the Nigerian National Petroleum Company (NNPC). The NNPC could then ascertain that crude oil had not been discharged in any South African port. Furthermore, directives were issued to the various oil companies to ensure that ships which had South Africans as crew members or crew members who had visited South Africa would not be allowed to load oil from Nigeria.[73]

Compared to the Gulf states, which did not always adhere to their own regulations concerning the oil embargo, Nigeria scrupulously enforced sanctions against South Africa. Nonetheless, Nigeria's deteriorating economy as well as its political mismanagement and instability reduced its ability to implement its broader prohibition against "double-dealers." However, Nigeria continued to pressure Britain to impose economic sanctions against Pretoria. When Prime Minister Margaret Thatcher visited Nigeria in January 1988, she was greeted by public demonstrations because of her opposition to what she often referred to as "punitive measures" against South Africa. Protestors carried placards at Lagos airport that included slogans such as "Thatcher, mother of apartheid." And trade union members burned British flags to indicate their disapproval of Thatcher's policies. But Thatcher, responding to criticisms of Britain's significant economic links to South Africa, asserted that "punitive measures would make the problems worse and multiply beyond all recognition the hardships already suffered by black South Africans and their children without ending apartheid."[74]

If Nigeria's economic problems diminished its leverage vis-à-vis Britain and prevented it from curtailing commercial activities of companies that conducted business with both Nigeria and South Africa, Lagos was able to enforce comparatively low-cost policies such as cultural and sporting boycotts against Pretoria. In 1976 Nigeria persuaded sub-Saharan African countries not to participate in Montreal Olympics, largely because New Zealand, which continued sporting ties with South Africa, had attended the Olympics. In 1978 Nigeria withdrew from the Commonwealth Games to demonstrate its opposition to New Zealand's policy of maintaining sporting contacts with South Africa. Later the same year Nigerian athletes refused to take part in the Junior Tennis Championships at Wimbledon because South Africa's athletes were allowed to attend. Reacting to South Africa's aggressive campaign to lure foreign athletes to South Africa in order to decrease the country's isolation in the sporting world, the Nigerian government decided that Nigerian passports would be invalid for travel to South Africa and that nationals of other countries who went to South Africa on social, business, and sporting visits would not be allowed to enter into Nigeria.[75]

ZAMBIA'S SOUTH AFRICA POLICIES

Compared to Nigeria, Zambia was less reluctant to engage in dialogue with South Africa. Historical ties between Lusaka and Pretoria as well as the realities of the economic interdependence of southern African countries made Zambia's relationship with South Africa extremely complex. Furthermore, many of the same economic problems that plagued Nigeria also bedeviled Zambia, thereby limiting Lusaka's ability to implement the sanctions against South Africa that it had so ardently advocated in international forums such as the OAU and the Commonwealth.

If Nigeria perceived itself as black Africa's economic and political leader, Zambia, while not vying for continental dominance, perceived itself as the African country that was clearly in the forefront of the anti-apartheid struggle. Whereas Nigeria enjoyed the luxury of geographic remoteness from South Africa and was able to formulate policies that were generally unambiguously antagonistic toward Pretoria, Zambia's geographic proximity to South Africa both heightened and modified its opposition to the apartheid regime. The essential characteristics of Zambia's foreign policy were shaped by the historical dynamics of southern Africa, President Kaunda's personality, Zambia's self-perception, South Africa's policies toward the region, and prevailing economic and political conditions within Zambia and the neighboring states.

Having inherited inextricable bonds of interdependence with South Africa as a legacy of British colonialism, Zambia exhibited many of the paradoxical behaviors that are often associated with situations characterized by dominance and dependence. On the one hand, Zambia was determined to protect its independence from South African maneuvers to undermine it. On the other hand, Zambia's economic vulnerability enhanced Pretoria's ability to compromise Lusaka's jealously guarded independence. Similarly, Zambia advocated a negotiated end to apartheid while simultaneously allowing the ANC to establish its headquarters in Lusaka. These contradictions emanated from historical and contemporary realities as well as from leadership factors. Like the other sub-Saharan countries, Zambia was preoccupied with eradicating colonialism and terminating white minority control in Africa. However, Zambia's experience in southern Africa, an area dominated by governments overtly hostile to racial equality and determined to impede independence for countries that threatened the status quo, made it painfully aware of the direct connection between apartheid's existence and the diminution of African countries' sovereignty. Furthermore, the consolidation of the apartheid regime during the zenith of Africa's movement toward independence was undoubtedly instrumental in creating an environment that was conducive to antagonistic relations between South Africa and the neighboring states. But Kaunda's personality and his own experiences during Zambia's transition from colonial rule to independence influenced him to adopt policies that contributed to diminishing the frequency and scale of regional conflicts.

Because Zambia's foreign policy was determined principally by President Kaunda himself, it inevitably reflected his personality. Deeply religious and clearly concerned about the contagious nature of apartheid, Kaunda developed an alternative philosophy, known as Humanism, that emphasized the individual's dignity and downplayed the importance of racial differences.[76] If apartheid was the embodiment of evil, Humanism would represent the virtues inherent in racial tolerance, a commitment to equality and compassion for all human beings. The moral component of Zambia's foreign policy undergirded that country's self-perception, which was largely intertwined with Kaunda's perception of himself. More akin to Scandinavia than to the United States in its acceptance of a brand of moralism that rejected violence as a primary instrument of foreign policy, Zambia attempted to portray itself as standing on the moral high ground, thereby transforming its military weakness into a political asset. Zambia's highly personalized foreign policy tried to project an image of the country, and of the president, as evenhanded. This meant that Zambia could engage in dialogue with both its anti-apartheid allies as well as with Pretoria itself, and could be an impartial broker in efforts to reach a negotiated settlement of regional disputes. Zambia's participation in international organizations such as the OAU, the Nonaligned Movement, and the Commonwealth allowed Kaunda to play an effective role as a leading African statesman, a humanist, and a peacemaker. It also provided an opportunity for him to personify a national image that he had largely shaped.[77]

This image was also a reflection of Zambia's vulnerability to South Africa's military power and its economic dependence on the apartheid regime. Unlike Nigeria and Tanzania, which were relatively isolated from southern Africa's suffering, Zambia adopted contradictory policies toward Pretoria that mirrored dilemmas arising from regional interdependence. Cognizant of the difficulties involved in assuming both a mediating role as well as that of a combatant, Kaunda adopted a tough rhetorical response to apartheid while he simultaneously avoided taking actions that could escalate into military confrontation between Zambia and South Africa. However, anxious to create schisms in the anti-apartheid coalition and to diminish its own isolation in Africa, Pretoria could not afford to completely undermine Kaunda. Consequently, Kaunda's foreign policy succeeded in keeping South Africa's military at arm's length, even though his opposition to apartheid remained strong.[78]

Pragmatic economic considerations were also at the foundation of Zambia's relations with South Africa. Although primarily reactive to South Africa's initiatives, Zambia implemented policies that did not completely jeopardize its economic interests. By supporting the objectives of the Southern African Development Coordination Conference (SADCC), Kaunda attempted to reduce Zambia's dependence on South Africa. However, personal antagonism and rivalries between Kaunda and Zimbabwe's Robert Mugabe hampered SADCC's progress toward its goal of economic independence from South Africa. Moreover, Kaunda's mismanagement of the economy, together with the costs inflicted on Zambia by South Africa's destabilization activities and Kaunda's adherence to sanctions against the white minority regime in Rhodesia, significantly weakened Zambia's ability to fully extricate itself from Pretoria's economic grip. Without appearing to compromise Zambia's determination to end apartheid,

Kaunda had to respond to increasing pressures from the country's economic and political elite to maintain mutually beneficial commercial relations with South Africa.[79] Therefore, Kaunda's principal foreign policy objective was to undermine apartheid without creating too many adverse economic consequences for Zambia. Yet the country's serious economic and political problems ultimately impeded its ability to be a significant counterweight to South Africa. These internal difficulties clearly contributed to Lusaka's reduced leverage vis-à-vis Pretoria.

Although Zambia's economic deterioration was caused largely by gross mismanagement, political stagnation, and Kaunda's personalization of power, other complex factors also contributed to the country's economic malaise. With approximately 60 million acres of prime arable land and abundant water supplies, Zambia rivaled the Sudan as a potential breadbasket for much of Africa. Yet only 5 percent of this rich agricultural land was cultivated, with the result being that Zambia, instead of being a major food exporter, was a recipient of food aid. Although Kaunda clearly saw the negative consequences of depending on foreign food supplies, his inability or unwillingness to increase agricultural production forced Zambia to accept wheat and other farm products from Canada and the United States. As was the case in the vast majority of sub-Saharan African states, artificially depressed agricultural prices eroded Zambia's ability to become self-sufficient in food. When farmers produced sufficient food for Zambia's urban residents, the mismanagement which characterized the government's bureaucracy effectively prevented agricultural supplies from reaching the market. In late 1988 Zambia produced a bumper maize crop. But due to a shortage of storage bags, tarpaulin coverings, and trucks, about 30 percent of the maize rotted in the fields and in poorly protected storage depots.[80] While administrative inefficiency, poor planning, and ineffective public policies were obviously responsible for Zambia's dismal agricultural performance, historical factors also contributed to that country's problems.

The colonial division of labor among Zimbabwe, Malawi, and Zambia, members of the Central African Federation, played a role in Zambia's food crises of the 1980s and 1990s. British economic interests, principally the British South Africa Company, which colonized the area, concentrated on developing rich copper deposits in Zambia (which was then called Northern Rhodesia) and focused on agricultural development in Zimbabwe (then known as Southern Rhodesia) where there was a large number of white settlers. Malawi (then called Nyasaland) was regarded as a source of inexpensive labor for South Africa's mines and farms. These historical factors continued to influence the economies of the three countries, to a greater or lesser extent, and partly explained Zambia's overwhelming dependence on copper for more than 90 percent of its foreign exchange, its dependence on South Africa and Zimbabwe for manufactured products, and its relative lack of interest in agricultural development. Analogous to Nigeria, where petroleum dominated the economy, Zambia's reliance on copper influenced the government to shift its financial resources away from the agricultural sector. Consequently, this policy culminated in mass migrations from agricultural areas to cities, where government subsidies were more readily available. The net result was that Zambia became the most urbanized country in sub-Saharan Africa, with a third of its 8 million people crowded into four major cities in 1991. Increased urbanization not only deprived rural areas of labor but also escalated pressure on fewer farmers to produce food for urban consumers.[81]

When copper prices plummeted in the 1970s, due to decreased demand for copper and greater industrial usage of aluminum as a substitute for copper, Zambia's economy was severely damaged. With its population growing at an alarming rate of 3.6 percent annually, Zambia faced the problem of economic stagnation and an actual decline in per capita income—from $600 in 1965 to $290 in 1989—and in the number of available jobs. It was estimated that there were 369,000 jobs in 1977, 365,290 in 1984, and 360,540 in 1986. In early 1989 Kaunda, speaking at the eighth Central Province Conference, noted that youth unemployment had reached alarming proportions. However, Zambia's precarious economic condition prevented Kaunda from moving aggressively to diffuse what he alluded to as the unemployment "time bomb."[82] In an attempt to ameliorate Zambia's economic conditions, Kaunda borrowed excessively from international financial institutions. Indebtedness became institutionalized at all levels of government and society, despite poor prospects of repayment. Consequently, external debt escalated from about $1 billion in 1974 to $3.6 billion in 1982, and climbed to more than $7 billion in 1991. Overdue payments on the national debt accumulated, despite Zambia's allocation of approximately 50 percent of its export earnings to service its debt.

Like many other African and Latin American countries, Zambia turned to the IMF for credit to repay previous debts and to maintain its much reduced imports. As a precondition for IMF assistance, the government agreed to the IMF's stringent remedies to restructure Zambia's economy. These included: (1) decontrolling prices; (2) liberalizing foreign trade; (3) reducing redundancies in the swollen bureaucracy; (4) freezing government jobs and salaries; and (5) selling Zambia's limited amount of hard foreign currency to the highest bidder.[83] These harsh measures were essentially incompatible with the fundamental realities that governed a political system based on the personalization of power.

Kaunda decided to abandon the IMF-mandated austerity program following widespread disapproval of it by Zambia's urban working class. While the government and its supporters squandered the country's financial resources, low-income families faced ever-increasing restrictions on their purchasing power. The all-items, cost-of-living index for low-income individuals doubled between 1982 and 1985, and rose an estimated 77 percent between 1986 and 1987. Scarce foreign exchange prevented many Zambians from buying basic commodities such as soap, cooking oil, and milk. IMF-mandated currency devaluations resulted in urban wages being reduced by as much as 50 percent, and the removal of price controls on breakfast meal in late 1986 induced millers to concentrate on producing breakfast meal instead of roller meal, the staple food of Zambia's poor majority. High food prices, coupled with shortages of cornmeal, eventually led to clashes between security forces and rioters, during which fifteen people were killed. These developments forced Kaunda to rescind the IMF-inspired 120 percent increase in the price of maize meal. Pointing out that the cost of subsidies would necessitate transferring resources from other programs, Kaunda nationalized Zambia's corn mills and later terminated the far-reaching reform program.[84]

Although government mismanagement, overreliance on copper, poorly implemented policies, and the neglect of agriculture were primarily responsible for Zambia's economic deterioration, racial problems in southern Africa and Zambia's efforts to end white domination in the region also contributed to the country's economic decline. Located at the crossroads of change in southern Africa and led by the United National Independence Party (UNIP), Zambia adopted an uncompromising position against Ian Smith's regime in Rhodesia. Despite being exempt from compliance with UN Security Council Resolutions mandating economic sanctions against Rhodesia, Zambia severed all commercial relations with Ian Smith's white minority regime and provided vital support for various liberation movements that were fighting for black majority rule. Declining copper prices, combined with the higher costs involved in obtaining supplies from other sources, severely weakened Zambia's economy. Confronted with the domestic consequences of his principled foreign policy—high unemployment, shortages of consumer products, inflation, and industrial strikes—Kaunda eventually reversed his decision to enforce the boycott against Rhodesia.[85]

Having gained their independence at a time when Pretoria was consolidating white control through legislating racial stratification, Zambians were acutely conscious of the deleterious effects the apartheid system could have on the entire region in general and for Zambia in particular. They also realized that their dependence on South Africa's transportation system enhanced Pretoria's leverage vis-à-vis Lusaka. Yet the basic thrust of Zambia's foreign policy made confrontation as well as cooperation with South Africa almost inevitable. Whereas Kaunda's predilection for dialogue with South Africa was conducive to relatively peaceful relations, his aversion to racial injustice propelled him toward conflict with Pretoria. By allowing the ANC to establish its headquarters in Lusaka and by leading the opposition against apartheid in international forums, Zambia exposed itself to South African retaliation. Thus, in addition to the economic costs that accrued from the embargo against Rhodesia, Zambia also experienced economic difficulties that emanated from South Africa's military actions against it.[86]

Apart from direct costs associated with attacks on Zambian civilian targets, South Africa's destabilization program resulted in many indirect costs. For example, the South African threat influenced Zambia to allocate a substantial share of increasingly scarce resources to the military. It was estimated that additional defense costs for the period from 1980 to 1988 reached $1.25 billion. Furthermore, South African–supported groups in Mozambique and Angola inflicted significant damage on transportation systems that were vital to Zambia's efforts to reduce its reliance on South Africa's railways and harbor facilities. The cost of shipping products through South Africa came to roughly $250 million over the 1980–88 period. Excluding incalculable human costs, it was estimated that South Africa's destabilization program resulted in a loss for Zambia of roughly $5 billion over eight years. The 1988 estimate alone, ranging from $450 million to $500 million, represented more than 20 percent of Zambia's GDP.[87] Although the exact costs are obviously debatable, there was sufficient evidence to suggest that Zambia had paid an extremely high price for principle. But Zambia's economic difficulties also stemmed from its deeply rooted political problems and the personalization of power, which, in turn, affected its relations with South Africa.

Although clearly occupying the moral high ground in his struggle against apartheid, Kaunda's grip on power in Zambia since that country's independence in 1964 ultimately diminished Zambia's ability to effectuate change in South Africa. Moreover, UNIP's monopoly on political power not only weakened Zambia internally but also diminished Kaunda's moral authority in relation to the minority regime in South Africa. Refusing to permit opposition parties until late 1990, Kaunda was virtually the sole decisionmaker in Zambia. He was not required by constitutional law or customary practice to consult anyone when formulating public policy; he was unencumbered in making personnel decisions; and he was largely unrestricted in his ability to reward faithful supporters. Under these circumstances, the single-party state and Kaunda's personalization of power militated against any meaningful reforms in Zambia.[88]

Even as Kaunda championed instituting democracy in South Africa, he had argued vociferously against implementing political pluralism at home. While calling on Pretoria to unban opposition groups such as the ANC, Kaunda contended that proponents of multiparty politics in Zambia were determined to destroy the country. And, similar to other sub-Saharan African leaders, Kaunda claimed that political pluralism was conducive to encouraging the pernicious effects of tribalism. Responding to widespread unrest across the country in 1987, Kaunda accused local business people of collaborating with South Africa to overthrow his government. He also arrested Alfred Musonda Chambeshi on charges of conspiring with UNITA to overthrow him. The government alleged that Chambeshi had attempted to revive the banned United Progressive Party as a guerrilla movement.[89] Throughout the late 1980s and early 1990s Kaunda was preoccupied with attempted coups as well as with threats posed to his government by efforts to restore political pluralism in Zambia. Nevertheless, significant changes in Eastern Europe and in South Africa itself provided added pressure on Kaunda to embrace democratic reforms. By late 1990 Kaunda agreed to recommend constitutional amendments that would allow multiparty competition during parliamentary and presidential elections in 1991. Moreover, when South Africa lifted its State of Emergency in 1990, Zambia was left in the awkward position of maintaining its own State of Emergency. In late 1991 the State of Emegency was quietly ended and Kaunda was overwhelmingly defeated in national elections by Frederick Chiluba. Kaunda had inadvertently participated in his own political demise.

Akin to Zimbabwe, where Mugabe allowed the State of Emergency that was implemented by Ian Smith's regime to continue, Zambia had operated under similar emergency legislation since independence in 1964, even as South Africa was urged by both Mugabe and Kaunda to terminate its emergency laws. Under the Preservation of Public Security Act, Kaunda obtained broad discretion to detain persons and restrict their movement. In contrast to South Africa, where individuals were held in detention without trial and without relatives being notified—among other basic human rights violations—persons arrested in Zambia were entitled to: (1) formal notification of the reasons for their detention within fourteen days of their arrest; (2) publication of their detention in the government gazette;

(3) access to counsel; (4) frequent visitation by family and colleagues; (5) immediate right to petition the detaining authority for release; and (6) the right to seek judicial review of the detention order by an independent and impartial tribunal after one year.[90] Despite these guarantees, the president was not legally compelled to accept the tribunal's recommendation if he believed that the detained person was a threat to what he deemed to be national security. To a considerable degree, contradictions between the basic objectives of Kaunda's South African policies and his own government's domestic behavior mirrored broader inconsistencies between Zambia's declared policy against apartheid and its actual relations with South Africa.

Zambia was simultaneously a proponent of strategies intended to effectuate change and a recipient of negative consequences accompanying the successful application of measures it vigorously advocated. Business interests in both Zambia and South Africa often conflicted with political considerations. Instead of being simply disingenuous or poorly managed, Zambia's policy toward Pretoria reflected serious dilemmas that emanated from regional interdependence. And since interdependence essentially means mutual dependence, albeit to varying degrees, Zambia's relations with South Africa were also influenced by the latter's interests, power, and strategies—a factor that further complicated Zambia's foreign policy.

Concerned about South Africa's growing international isolation, foreign policymakers in Pretoria reassessed relations with Zambia and concluded that maintaining contacts with Lusaka was an intricate component of an overall strategy to reduce their country's isolation. Improved, although vacillating, ties with Zambia provided South Africa with a measure of legitimacy in Africa and, consequently, in the international community. As a leading Frontline State, a prominent member of the SADCC, an unrelenting critic of apartheid in the Commonwealth, a respected OAU member, and as the host state for the ANC and other liberation groups fighting white domination, Zambia was perceived by South Africa as crucial to the achievement of Pretoria's foreign policy objectives.[91] Moreover, Kaunda's willingness to confront apartheid as well as to negotiate with South Africa's leaders made him both an implacable foe and a potential ally. Thus, despite antagonism between the two countries, foreign policymakers in Pretoria viewed Zambia as the political and geographic gateway to sub-Saharan Africa and, therefore, attempted to minimize inevitable tensions arising from apartheid's existence and Zambia's determination to help abolish it.

Zambia's diplomatic overtures toward South Africa were initiated by Kaunda in early 1964 when he signaled Zambia's willingness to establish diplomatic relations with Pretoria. By adopting a nonconfrontational stance toward the apartheid regime, Kaunda hoped to alleviate white South Africans' apprehensiveness about transforming their country into a nonracial democratic society. But Kaunda's proposal for an exchange of diplomatic missions was accompanied by his insistence that Zambian diplomats should be treated the same as diplomats from elsewhere. Not surprisingly, this condition was unacceptable.

If Kaunda intended to teach by example, South Africa did not perceive cooperation to be in its interest. Nonetheless, the idea of informal diplomatic ties between the two countries continued to be an important foreign policy objective in Lusaka as well as in Pretoria. Beginning in 1967, South Africa's prime minister John Vorster launched his own diplomatic initiative, known as the "outward policy," to improve relations with neighboring states. While only Malawi established formal diplomatic ties with South Africa, Vorster made considerable progress toward diminishing his country's isolation following his secret flights to West Africa to talk with the leaders of Liberia and the Ivory Coast.[92]

As the Rhodesian conflict intensified in the mid-1970s, amid the demise of Portuguese colonial control in Angola and Mozambique, South Africa and Zambia seemed to have converging interests. Ending the war was perceived as beneficial to both Pretoria and Lusaka. Cessation of hostilities would help to stabilize the region and diminish the spread of violence to South Africa itself. Moreover, by participating in peace efforts, Pretoria hoped to assist the emergence of leaders in the new state of Zimbabwe who were more amenable to South Africa's influence. Lusaka, on the other hand, would achieve its goal of removing Ian Smith's regime and would benefit from economic and political normalcy in a neighboring state.

After intense but essentially quiet diplomacy, Zambia and South Africa were able in 1975 to convene a conference between Ian Smith's regime and various liberation groups' representatives. In order to demonstrate his commitment to ending the conflict and to détente in southern Africa, Vorster claimed that Pretoria had withdrawn the police force it had sent to assist Rhodesia in 1972.[93] However, as the Angolan civil war escalated, due in part to South Africa's direct participation, and as the Rhodesian problem remained unresolved, trust between Lusaka and Pretoria deteriorated. By 1977 disagreements between Kaunda and Vorster were publicly aired. Kaunda believed that Vorster had deceived him on the issue of withdrawing the South African security forces from Rhodesia. Moreover, despite Pretoria's assurances on settling the Namibian problem, South Africa did not move decisively toward granting Namibia its independence. These perceptions, or misperceptions, undoubtedly impeded dialogue between South Africa and Zambia. Yet the convergence of their interests mitigated overt hostilities and prompted Kaunda and Vorster to maintain unofficial channels of communication.

In early 1982 South Africa's prime minister P. W. Botha and President Kaunda resumed dialogue during a meeting at Wildebeeskop on the Botswana-South Africa border. Obviously concerned about the political implications of meeting Botha, Kaunda underscored the urgency created by deteriorating relations between South Africa and the neighboring states. Asserting, as he frequently did, that South Africa faced an "unparalleled racial revolution," Kaunda contended that "speaking directly to Botha will enable us to analyze the situation in a cool and honest manner."[94] However, the other Frontline States' leaders were clearly unenthusiastic about dialogue between Kaunda and Botha. In particular, Tanzania's president Julius Nyerere, a leader who was respected throughout Africa, opposed the meeting. Although not directly criticizing Kaunda, Nyerere believed that South African leaders should give priority to talking with black South Africans, the only representatives of the country's black majority. However, since Kaunda's own agenda was much broader than his concerns about black South Africans, he continued to pursue his own initiatives. In 1984 he met with Colin Eglin and Helen Suzman, members of South Africa's opposition Progressive Federal Party, to discuss the growing violence in South Africa. When it was alleged that Kaunda's primary reason for engaging in dialogue with South African leaders was to obtain economic aid from Pretoria, the president dismissed such suggestions, and emphasized that he never discussed bilateral issues with South African leaders. Instead, he argued that Zambia's principal objective was to defuse the explosive situation in the region through "honest and truthful" methods and to assist the liberation process.[95]

Despite Zambia's commitment to the ANC, Kaunda's diplomatic efforts were motivated to a considerable extent by his apprehensiveness about the presence of large numbers of ANC members in the country. Given Zambia's precarious economic conditions, Kaunda believed that the ANC had become a threat to his government's stability. Thus, while the ANC was allowed to remain in Lusaka, Kaunda intensified his diplomatic efforts. Zambia became the meeting place for those South Africans who endeavored to secure the abolition of apartheid through negotiations. But the most significant diplomatic breakthrough came in mid-1989 when South Africa's acting president, F. W. de Klerk, met Kaunda in Livingstone, on the Zambian side of Victoria Falls. Faced with serious economic problems, partly due to international sanctions and excessive military expenditures, de Klerk took advantage of

Kaunda's predisposition toward negotiations in an attempt to diminish Pretoria's international isolation and to "clear up misunderstandings" about what was really occurring within South Africa. More importantly, both leaders were committed to breaking the costly cycle of conflict and mistrust in the region.[96] However, despite the ANC's pivotal role in regional cooperation and stability, neither de Klerk nor Kaunda discussed the liberation movement. The ANC's conditions for talks with Pretoria, adopted with much publicity at an OAU mini-summit chaired by Zambia a week before the two leaders met, were obviously excluded from the agenda, much to the ANC's chagrin. While Zambia was supportive of the ANC, the country's serious economic problems undoubtedly influenced Kaunda to compromise with Pretoria.

Pre-independence trade relations in southern Africa provided the foundation for contemporary commercial ties between Zambia and South Africa. Regional economic interdependence was often exaggerated by Pretoria in order to convince the international community that anti-apartheid sanctions were at least equally damaging to neighboring states. Nonetheless, the infrastructure built by Britain ensured that southern Africa, despite political differences among the various countries, would find it extremely difficult to escape the webs of mutual dependence. The railroads, the most obvious manifestation of Britain's colonial policy of governing the region as essentially one economic unity, also reinforced contemporary regional ties. Even though Zambia and other countries attempted to reduce their dependence on South African transportation links by finding alternative routes, Pretoria's destabilization policy and rebel group activities helped to impede the construction and utilization of roads and railways that were designed to circumvent South Africa's stranglehold. While the Tazara railway, joining Tanzania and Zambia, provided an alternative to Zambia's overreliance on South African routes, port congestion in Dar es Salaam, a shortage of engines and wagons, frequent landslides, and mismanagement combined to make that railroad unreliable.

Therefore, despite Zambia's strong advocacy of sanctions against South Africa, it remained vulnerable to Pretoria's retaliation because of its continued dependence on South Africa's transportation system. In August 1986 South African customs officials retaliated against Zambia and Zimbabwe for their prosanctions stance during a Commonwealth mini-summit a few days earlier by delaying their cargo and escalating transportation costs by conducting a "statistical survey" and by requiring cash deposits from carriers.[97] Because approximately 60 percent of Zambia's exports passed through South Africa, Pretoria was able to exercise considerable leverage vis-à-vis Lusaka. By delaying cargoes of fertilizers bound for Zambia during the planting season and by slowing down grain shipments, South Africa was in a position to make Zambia even more dependent on it. In late 1990 Zambia reopened routes through South Africa, precisely when the Tanzania Harbor Authority was seeking $100 million from the World Bank and other external sources to implement the second phase of modernizing Tanzania's port facilities. Cargo handling facilities had been recently improved at a cost of $220 million.[98]

Zambia's air transportation links with South Africa remained uninterrupted, despite the OAU's longstanding demand for African states to prevent South Africa's planes from using their airports, overflying their airspace, and serving as a link between Pretoria and other countries. In July 1987, at the height of the anti-apartheid campaign, President Kaunda acknowledged that Zambia and Zimbabwe had not felt it was feasible to sever their air links with South Africa. Nevertheless, he urged the Frontline States and OAU members to apply whatever sanctions they could against Pretoria and to intensify their efforts to obtain broader international support for sanctions.[99] But Kaunda's ambivalent and sometimes contradictory approaches to South Africa were a reflection of Zambia's significant commercial relations with South Africa, in addition to its dependence on the latter's transportation links.

Arguing that it was futile for Zambia to impose economic sanctions against Pretoria while other countries continued to trade with South Africa, Zambia's Power, Transport, and Communications minister Kingsley Chinkuli told parliament in early 1988 that trade with South Africa would continue as long as regional and international organizations lacked determination to impose mandatory sanctions against Pretoria.[100] Yet Zambia's economic conditions, not the international community's actions in relation to sanctions, were principally responsible for Zambia's economic links with South Africa. Domestic political and economic pressures, stemming in part from Zambia's poor industrial performance and its growing urban populations, also rendered a reduction in trade with South Africa virtually impossible. Zambia's policy options were severely constrained, if not altogether eliminated.

Inconsistencies between declared policy and actual practice created tensions within Zambia, especially when Kaunda's political survival appeared to be threatened. Therefore, despite Zambia's dependence on commerce with South Africa, Kaunda sometimes accused Zambians who traded with South Africa of being collaborators in the exploitation of cheap black labor. Furthermore, he asserted that Pretoria could send bombs through goods imported by greedy Zambians just as it had sent bombs that killed two people through the mail. In Kaunda's view, it was better for Zambians to starve and build on their own strength than to live and survive on the sweat of an exploited person.[101] But such rhetoric belied Zambia's reality.

As southern Africa's economic superpower, South Africa enjoyed tremendous trade advantages in relation to Zambia. Moreover, Zambia's own economic and political mismanagement contributed to its continued dependence on South African markets. Britain, Zambia's primary supplier of imported goods prior to 1982, was surpassed by South Africa. Imports included machinery, fuels, transport equipment, food, manufactured products, and chemicals. Given the region's historical ties, South Africa was clearly positioned to capture regional markets. Having better managed and comparatively more efficient industrial operations, South African exporters were able to sell their products for lower prices than Zambian firms could offer. And because many South African companies were established in Zambia, Zambian manufacturers faced well-organized and well-financed marketing operations in which the competing product lines were part of a much larger flow of imported supplies. South African–based retail stores bought their supplies directly from their home country. Furthermore, joint Zambian–South African ventures in Zambia emphasized imports instead of local production of inputs and spare parts.[102] Overall, South Africa enjoyed an advantage over other countries in the region in terms of transportation costs, delivery times, and service in a wide range of manufactured products, equipment, and spare parts. Zambia's economic inefficiency also strengthened South Africa's market position.

Unwilling or unable to allocate financial resources as an integral component of a long-term economic strategy, due partly to increasing external debt and declining revenues, Zambia frequently purchased commodities on an emergency basis. Consequently, it narrowed its buying options. Neighboring South Africa benefited from Zambia's lack of planning because it was the quickest and most reliable source of supplies. Given the prominent role of South African–based firms in Zambia's economy, the two countries were treated as one large market. Unlike other southern African states such as Zimbabwe, South Africa was able to extend credit to Zambia on relatively short notice. Ironically, even though Zambia championed the implementation of sanctions against South Africa, Lusaka required government agencies and parastatals to purchase from the cheapest source, namely, South Africa. Advanced planning and adequate financing would have enabled Zambia to buy from more distant but cheaper sources such as Japan, India, Taiwan, or Western Europe.[103] South Africa's geographic proximity and Zambia's economic problems combined to make the latter dependent on fuel supplies from the former. Even though most of Zambia's petroleum was received through a pipeline originating in Dar es Salaam, financial exigencies influenced the Zambian government to turn to South Africa for fuel supplies. Having failed to pay its debts to a consortium of London banks, Zambia's access to oil supplies originating in Tanzania was threatened in 1985. By late 1990 Zambia had decided to import refined oil from South Africa to alleviate a critical fuel shortage caused by the Persian Gulf crisis.[104]

Trade relations between Zambia and South Africa were consolidated by significant investments in the former by transnational companies and financial institutions based in the latter. Both the South African government and the various investors attempted to perpetuate Zambia's dependent relationship. However, given the divergent interests among various branches of the government and the commercial sector, close collaboration was not always feasible. Nevertheless, South African institutions generally cooperated to maintain their economic and political influence in Zambia. Historically, South African investors, particularly mining companies such as Anglo-American, expanded their operations throughout southern Africa, thereby creating webs of interdependence. Many construction, manufacturing, agricultural, and commercial ventures in the region were connected to firms based in South Africa.[105] While Zambia had nationalized many foreign companies, its deteriorating economic conditions and widespread dependence on South African expertise and equipment allowed South African firms to influence Zambia's economy. Responding to allegations that Zambia had planned to nationalize South African–owned companies, Zambia's prime minister Kebby Musokotwane stated that it would have been unfair to throw out companies originating from South Africa while they were observing Zambian law.[106] The government's commitment to encouraging South African investors to remain in Zambia was reaffirmed when a delegation from South Africa's National Federated Chamber of Commerce visited Lusaka in late 1988 to promote commercial contacts with the business community. In September 1990, it was reported, and subsequently denied by both Lusaka and Pretoria, that a South African trade mission was to be established in Zambia by the end of 1990.[107] However, significant changes in South Africa in 1990 and 1991 engendered closer commercial relations between Zambia and South Africa. By mid-1991 Kaunda was urging Zambian businessmen to take advantage of changes in South Africa for subregional prosperity.

Despite Zambia's dependence on South Africa, Kaunda remained supportive of international efforts to undermine apartheid. Yet Zambia's ability to effectuate change through its endorsement of sanctions and its assistance to the ANC was diminished by its serious political and economic problems. Furthermore, Zambia was reluctant to participate in cooperative military operations by the Frontline States to protect transportation routes from terrorist activities. Kaunda attempted to avoid military confrontations with South Africa or with groups it supported. On the other hand, the ANC's presence in Zambia demonstrated that Kaunda supported the liberation movements. Arguably, Kaunda's constant support for the various southern African liberation groups ultimately contributed to Zambia's economic deterioration.[108]

Akin to the Palestine Liberation Organization in Jordan and in Lebanon, the ANC found itself in conflict with its host country. Escalating violence among ANC members prompted the Zambian government to restrict the group's activities. In addition to shooting each other, several ANC members were accused of using their weapons during robberies. Clearly worried that his organization was abusing Zambian hospitality, ANC president Oliver Tambo urged his followers to stop killing each other and innocent Zambians. The government also reminded ANC members that their authorization to carry arms was limited. However, it rejected demands from many Zambians to force the ANC to reside in restricted areas. Alex Shapi, Zambia's secretary of state for Defence, argued that confining the organization to special areas to avoid further killing by undisciplined members would expose it to danger, presumably from South Africa.[109]

Kaunda's determination to rejuvenate dialogue between Zambia and South Africa complicated the ANC's armed struggle and essentially neutralized the organization. Although Kaunda had emphasized that the ANC was merely responding to the violent approach used by Pretoria and that it could not be expected to stop fighting because the South African government had offered it nothing in exchange for renouncing the armed struggle, his meeting with de Klerk in late 1989 weakened the ANC's argument for a violent resolution of the South African problem. Underlying the rhetoric of support for armed struggle against apartheid were Zambia's fears about the ANC's destabilizing influence. Indeed, Kaunda's desire to negotiate with de Klerk was undoubtedly prompted to some extent by his apprehensions about such a large ANC presence in Zambia. The ANC's decision to relocate approximately 5 thousand of its members to Tanzania, far away from South Africa, coincided with Kaunda's diplomatic initiatives.[110] The ANC eventually rejected the armed struggle in 1991 as its own negotiations with Pretoria progressed.

In addition to assisting the ANC, Zambia was also instrumental in mobilizing international support for implementing comprehensive economic sanctions against South Africa. From the time Zambia achieved its independence, Kaunda constantly reminded the world that apartheid was a crime against humanity, and stressed that the international community had a responsibility to try to abolish it. As chairman of the OAU in 1970, Kaunda visited Europe and the United States to persuade the various countries to terminate arms sales to South Africa. But it was in the Commonwealth where Kaunda was able to exert a modicum of pressure on Britain to adopt anti-apartheid measures. Although Prime Minister Margaret Thatcher repudiated the usefulness of sanctions in effectuating change in Pretoria, other Commonwealth members such as Canada and Australia were able to mobilize significant international support for the sanctions advocated by Zambia. Frustrated by Thatcher's resistance to measures that were detrimental to Britain's significant commercial relations with South Africa, Kaunda threatened, albeit to his own detriment, to leave the Commonwealth. Paradoxically, it was on the sanctions issue that Zambia was both strong and extremely vulnerable. While Kaunda had persuaded other countries to implement sanctions against apartheid, Zambia itself was unable to follow its own advice. In 1986, during the zenith of the anti-apartheid movement, Kaunda announced that Zambia and Zimbabwe had appointed a committee to produce a coordinated sanctions package, and asserted that severing air links with Pretoria was only a question of time.[111] The sanctions failed to materialize. Nonetheless, when the international community, particularly Britain and its European partners, terminated anti-apartheid sanctions, Kaunda admonished the world against being deceived by reforms in South Africa that did not significantly alter power distribution in that country. Even as Zambia asked other states to maintain sanctions, Kaunda was strengthening his country's commercial ties to South Africa. These obvious inconsistencies ultimately weakened Kaunda's credibility and further eroded domestic support for Zambia's foreign policy.

Unlike Mozambique and Angola, which were primary targets of South Africa's military activities, Zambia was relatively safe from attacks. Two contradictory realities, Kaunda's willingness to negotiate with South African leaders and his consistent support of the ANC, combined to produce an ambivalent South African policy toward Zambia. Zambia's decision to allow the ANC to establish its headquarters in Lusaka was generally not considered as an immediate threat by Pretoria. While South Africa engaged in a destabilization campaign against Zambia and supported and trained the Zambian dissident group led by Adamson Mushala, Kaunda's frequent assertions that South Africa had instigated antigovernment activities were generally overstated and difficult to ascertain. Moreover, opposition groups that were often accused by Kaunda of collaboration with South Africa were principally responding to the government's failed policies.[112] In other words, Kaunda sometimes emphasized South Africa's interference in Zambian affairs to divert attention from his government's dismal economic performance. Nonetheless, Pretoria's destabilization policy, especially its support of the Mozambican National Resistance Movement (Renamo), adversely affected Zambia in particular and the Frontline States in general.

Apart from the economic costs of South Africa's regional destabilization policy, confrontation militated against de Klerk's efforts to reach a negotiated settlement of his country's racial problems. Moreover, continuation of regional violence was inconsistent with South Africa's attempts to appear reasonable to its major trading partners, whose support it needed to restore its economic strength. In this endeavor, Zambia played a pivotal role. Kaunda's willingness to engage in dialogue with de Klerk created an opportunity for South Africa to diminish its isolation not only from Africa but also from the international community. Zambia's contradictory policies toward South Africa underscored both Zambia's economic vulnerabilities as well as Kaunda's belief that violent solutions to the region's problems were ultimately counterproductive and harmful to the interests of all southern African countries.

Chapter 3

Asia: India and Taiwan

Although the vast majority of Asian countries experienced either colonization or racial discrimination, and often both, apartheid did not have the same resonance in states such as Taiwan, Japan, South Korea, Malaysia, and Singapore as it did in sub-Saharan Africa. While Asian countries publicly denounced apartheid as a crime against humanity, they were, with the exception of India, generally indifferent to racial discrimination in South Africa. Moreover, because foreign policy-making was largely an elite activity throughout much of Asia, there were relatively few anti-apartheid groups and very little public interest in southern African issues. With the exception of India, Asian countries' experiences with discrimination did not influence them to mobilize international public opinion against South Africa. This comparative lack of support for anti-apartheid efforts around the world as well as in South Africa itself was a direct outgrowth of a combination of factors within Asian countries.

South Africa's racial problems, apart from being largely irrelevant to the foreign policy objectives of most Asian states, were generally not perceived with any sense of urgency in Asia because of deeply embedded cultural characteristics that were not supportive of racial equality. India, the Asian country that was most concerned about apartheid, institutionalized social, economic, and political discrimination through its caste system, which, compared to apartheid, was more deeply entrenched. In addition to caste issues, India was bedeviled by problems arising from ethnic and linguistic diversity, religious intolerance, and widespread and intractable poverty. But whereas the apartheid regime had deliberately created misery for the vast majority of South Africans, the Indian government attempted, through constitutional and social means, to alleviate some of the hardships emanating from both the caste system and from almost insurmountable poverty in the world's second most populous country. Yet India's ability to tolerate ambiguity and to manage coexistence contributed to perpetuating discrimination and inequality. Arguably, India's cultural attributes impede integration, whereas South Africa's dominant culture is more conducive to both integration and egalitarianism. However, unlike the apartheid regime, India's political system, albeit fraught with problems, was widely regarded as legitimate. Both countries were challenged to make their economic, political, and social systems more egalitarian.

If India's tolerance of ambiguity enabled it to play a crucial role in the struggle against apartheid even as its own caste system endured, Taiwan and other Asian countries were generally consistently indifferent to apartheid and uncomfortable with racial diversity. The homogeneity, xenophobia, and exclusiveness that are hallmarks of many Asian societies, militated against the emergence of genuine concerns about the negative consequences of apartheid for black South Africans. Asian countries are characterized by hierarchical structures, despite ongoing challenges to social stratification. Preoccupation with caste and racial purity are inextricably linked to how individuals perceived themselves and others. Since many Asians are more tolerant of inequalities, they were unwilling to contribute significantly to dismantling apartheid. Their general disinclination to oppose apartheid was reinforced by their perceptions of national security and their roles in the international system.

Unlike India, which viewed itself not only as a regional superpower but also as a leader of the Third World and the Nonaligned Movement, most Asian countries focused almost exclusively on domestic and regional issues. While South Korea and Taiwan attempted to achieve international legitimacy by expanding trade with most countries and by cultivating relations with Third World states, neither Seoul nor Taipei was viewed as a major Third World actor. Taiwan, in particular, was ostracized politically from much of the world community. Whereas India's historical ties to African members of the Commonwealth and its concerns about the treatment of Indians in South Africa influenced it to initiate the UN debate on apartheid, Taiwan, South Korea, and other Asian countries were geographically and politically removed from southern African problems. If domestic considerations constrained India's ability to be more actively involved in nonregional issues, preoccupation with survival concentrated Taiwan's and South Korea's attention on domestic and national security concerns. Located only 90 miles from the People's Republic of China (PRC), Taiwan regarded its survival as a sovereign state as an intensely emotional issue. Directly threatened by a country with more than a billion people, Taiwan, with approximately 20 million citizens, clearly saw apartheid as a comparatively insignificant issue. The historical experiences of both Taiwan and Korea during the critical stage of state formation had galvanized their determination to elevate national security above moral considerations. Moreover, establishing economic and political ties with as many countries as possible was viewed as being consistent with their perceptions of national security. It is within this broader context that Taiwan's relations with South Africa developed.

Converging political and economic interests augmented links between Taipei and Pretoria. Regarded as pariah states, Taiwan and South Africa increasingly relied on each other for political as well as economic support. As more countries recognized the PRC as the legitimate China, Taiwan's insistence that it represented all of China became less credible. However, Taiwan's assertion was accepted by South Africa, not so much because of its validity but largely because of South Africa's need for friends. By contrast, India, which also had its own troubles with China, very early distanced itself from South Africa. But even as Taiwan was developing closer links to South Africa, primarily because of their shared experiences with isolation as well as their mutual aversion to communism, South Africa was simultaneously encouraging its private sector to establish commercial links with China. Although both South Africa and Taiwan opposed communism, Pretoria was mainly worried about Soviet expansionism in Africa whereas Taiwan was principally concerned about China's threat to its security. India, on the other hand, was allied with the Soviet Union against China.

Far more important than ideological issues, Taiwan's economic ascendancy heightened South Africa's interest in Taipei. While much of the world focused on the United States and Western Europe as the main supporters of apartheid because their significant economic ties with Pretoria, Taiwan, like Japan, emerged as a major trading partner with South Africa. Its advanced technology essentially negated Western sanctions against Pretoria, especially in the areas of computers and electronics. However, radical changes in the international political system, especially the diminution of communism, significantly altered the environment in which relations between Pretoria and Taiwan had flourished. On the other hand, given the predominance of economic issues in the post–Cold War period, Taiwan was likely to remain a major trading partner of post-apartheid South Africa. However, trade between the PRC and South Africa was also likely to increase. Furthermore, normalized relations between Pretoria and the West will diminish the importance of Taiwan's special relationship with South Africa. India faced mounting political and economic internal problems, and was severely disadvantaged vis-à-vis Taiwan in the postapartheid society that it had helped to establish.

INDIA'S POLICY TOWARD SOUTH AFRICA

In contrast to most of sub-Saharan Africa, India's interest in South Africa predated its own independence. The quest for racial equality in South Africa and India's struggle against British colonial domination were connected by Mahatma Gandhi's activities in both countries. For more than twenty years Gandhi had attempted to influence the South African government to end discrimination against nonwhite South Africans, particularly those of Indian descent. His strategy of nonviolence, which was utilized to achieve change in South Africa, was transferred to India during his efforts to persuade the British to "walk out of India" peacefully. Consequently, the essentially nonviolent anti-apartheid movement in South Africa reminded India of its own struggle for independence. Furthermore, the color bar, which had been an integral component of British rule in India, contributed to an awareness among Indians of the deleterious effects of racial discrimination. Public facilities such as rail cars, park benches, and social clubs had been segregated. Indians were excluded from positions of leadership. Thus Gandhi's pivotal role in India's fight for independence and the fact that Indians in South Africa as well as in India itself were victims of discrimination influenced the Indian government to initiate an international campaign to terminate apartheid. When the UN General Assembly met for the first time in October 1946, India, a self-governing territory within the British Empire, introduced the issue of the unjust treatment of Indians in South Africa, thereby putting the white minority government's racial practices on the international agenda.

Apartheid's formal implementation so soon after India achieved its independence undoubtedly reinforced New Delhi's determination to make ending racial discrimination in South Africa a major foreign policy objective. And given the dominant role of the prime minister and the Cabinet in India's foreign affairs, the values of leading political figures helped to shape the country's international relations. For example, Jawaharlal Nehru, India's first prime minister, incorporated Gandhi's philosophy of nonviolence into India's foreign policy. Furthermore, widespread consensus among elite groups that their country should project moral power in international relations buttressed Nehru's position. Yet the blending of India's experiences acquired during its struggle for independence with

Hindu political culture culminated in what Lucian Pye called "a form of amoral politics carried out in an atmosphere of verbal moralizing."[1] In other words, moral considerations did not supersede realpolitik assessments. However, given India's size and large population, its leaders believed their country should assume a prominent role in world politics, particularly in relation to the Third World and international organizations. By adopting a policy of nonalignment, India not only gained flexibility vis-à-vis the superpowers during the Cold War but also strengthened its credibility as a primary advocate of Third World concerns. The very nature of colonial rule made many of the newly independent countries sensitive to South Africa's ideology and practice of racial superiority. India's early opposition to apartheid clearly enhanced its position within the Nonaligned Movement. India's policymakers consistently championed Third World interests. Although India's strategy resulted in some concrete achievements, the principal objective of India's strong moralistic stances was to enhance its image within the Third World.[2]

While apartheid remained an important issue, India was preoccupied with the security of the South Asian subcontinent, especially after the war with China in 1962. In addition to strengthening its military forces, India sought to consolidate its position in the region through cooperation with the neighboring states. But ongoing tensions between India and Pakistan, the two most powerful countries on the subcontinent, made cooperation difficult. Akin to South Africa in southern Africa, India was determined to be the regional security manager, an aspiration that resulted in continuous friction between India and its neighbors.[3] Despite the formation of the South Asian Association for Regional Cooperation (SAARC) in 1985 to overcome regional challenges that emanated from poverty, underdevelopment, low production levels, and overpopulation, India's unwillingness to eschew its tacit regional superpower status impeded cooperation and the realization of SAARC's objectives.[4] The Soviet Union's decline as a superpower and its focus on domestic economic and political problems following the end of the Cold War left India in a stronger hegemonic position. Thus, while opposed to South Africa's domination of the neighboring countries, India itself was not reluctant to use force to achieve its objectives in its own region. India's inability to project power beyond South Asia was inextricably linked to its economic and political difficulties. Similar to Nigeria, India viewed economic and political development as essential prerequisites for an enhanced international role.

Compared to sub-Saharan Africa, India's economic progress has been impressive. Its industrial development and large number of highly skilled scientists and other professionals distinguished it from sub-Saharan Africa. Unlike most African countries, where agricultural productivity declined steadily, India responded to the Bihar famine of 1966–67 and subsequent food shortages in the early 1970s with massive investments in agriculture. Enjoying greater political integration and legitimacy than the vast majority of the artificially created African states, the Indian government was better equipped to implement the far-reaching agricultural reforms that provided the foundation of the country's Green Revolution.[5] Relative bureaucratic efficiency, significant investments in infrastructure, industry, and education, and relative political stability facilitated India's economic development.

The Indian government embarked on a program of industrial development shortly after independence. Despite comparatively high growth rates in the industrial sector, protectionist policies designed to protect fledgling industries from international competition eventually restrained initiative, depressed private investments, and politicized economic decisions.[6] However, growing self-sufficiency in food, increasing exports, and the fall of Indira Gandhi's government in early 1977 paved the way for the implementation of reforms that encouraged economic liberalization. The economic turbulence created by high oil prices in the late 1970s and early 1980s forced the government to decrease imports and to stimulate domestic production of essential commodities.

Despite agricultural improvements, the industrial sector's expansion, decreased bureaucratic regulations, and the relaxation of licensing restrictions, poverty in India remained pervasive. The major beneficiaries of economic growth were urban middle class residents, about 40 million of whom had a standard of living comparable to their middle class counterparts in advanced industrial countries. Another 60 million were on the threshold of a comfortable middle class life.[7] Internal sociopolitical dynamics restrained industrial productivity, thereby making basic necessities less accessible to the country's poor majority.

Even though India attempted to attract foreign investments in an effort to spur economic growth, elite values seemed to militate against the realization of that goal. India's ruling classes, primarily the intellectuals (mostly Brahmins) and politicians (mainly Kshatriyas), have traditionally despised businesspeople (mostly Vaishays) whom they regarded as rich but socially inferior. These caste prejudices against the business class created a barrier to foreign investment.[8] India's industrialization was also impeded by government policies that consolidated the powers of domestic monopolies and cartels, promoted an antiexport bias, and neglected research and development. A World Bank study in 1989 concluded that India's licensing system, reinforced by controls on large firms and preferences for small-scale industry and public enterprises, tended to maintain a seller's market that reduced incentives for cost cutting and quality control. Moreover, the high profitability of sales in the domestic market made exporting unattractive despite export incentive programs.[9] Finally, India's external debt, approximately $72 billion in 1991, further exacerbated the country's economic problems. Interest payments alone were around $5 billion in 1991. The 1990–91 Persian Gulf crisis exacerbated India's financial difficulties by increasing the costs of the country's petroleum imports while, simultaneously, depriving it of approximately $2 billion in remittances from Indians in the Gulf and roughly $0.4 billion in exports to Iraq and Kuwait.[10] These economic realities directly affected India's ability to influence developments in South Africa. On the other hand, India's relative political stability and the survival of its democratic parliamentary system were valuable foreign policy assets.

Whereas democratic institutions in sub-Saharan Africa were short-lived, India managed to maintain a free press, a professional and apolitical military, and other aspects of democratic governance. Despite constant and widespread ethnic and religious tensions, India's leaders were able to resolve many conflicts within the country's constitutional framework.

Unlike Africa, where many small communities existed in isolation of each other, India experienced a greater sense of unity for much of its history. As a result, traditional elites in India enjoyed greater authority than their African counterparts. In India there was less of a break between the past and the present than in Africa.[11] In other words, the foundations upon which democracy could be constructed were far more secure in India than they were in Africa. Moreover, Britain dominated India much longer and to a greater extent than it ruled Africa, and Indians experienced self-government long before India achieved its independence. As early as 1909 Britain had passed the Government of India Act which enabled Indians to participate in the political process. Consequently, when India gained its independence in 1947, a well-trained group of Indians were ready to assume leadership responsibilities. These elites benefited not only from deeply ingrained British values but also from traditional Indian values. Another important factor contributing to democracy in India was the quality of political leadership during the country's formative stages. The leaders' willingness to compromise and to resolve problems principally through democratic processes established precedents for future leaders. Finally, the existence of comparatively strong bureaucratic values and a relatively effective administration contributed to India's ability to implement its public policies.[12] These factors helped to perpetuate democracy in India.

But democracy in India has always been precarious and is likely to be challenged by the forces of modernization and tradition. The Congress Party, which governed India for almost forty years, faced increasing opposition from smaller political parties. Disappointed with the Congress Party's performance, Muslims, the rural poor, and the so-called Scheduled Castes or untouchables gave their support to various groups that formed the National Front coalition government in the late 1980s and early 1990s. However, the coalition partners supported diverse and often irreconcilable policies. For example, whereas the Janata Dal Party attempted to reduce economic and political inequalities in India by implementing policies (recommended by the Mandal Commission) that increased the percentage of jobs and seats at universities for disadvantaged castes, including the untouchables and tribals, the Bharatiya Janata Party (BJP) wanted to end what it regarded as special privileges for disadvantaged groups and to deny Muslims any special treatment because of their religious beliefs or their majority status in the state of Kashmir. In a country plagued by alarming inequalities, ethnic and regional frictions, and religious violence, the BJP's commitment to Hindu secularism, which was tantamount to equating Indian culture with Hinduism, was bound to be antagonistic. The national government was increasingly unable to control the ensuing violence.[13]

Ironically, India, which had consistently opposed apartheid, was confronted with growing polarization emanating from efforts to provide equal opportunities for the Scheduled Castes and tribals just as South Africa was abolishing the legal structures of apartheid. Even though India strenuously rejected comparisons between its caste system and apartheid, widespread human rights violations and the continuing significance of the caste system made it difficult to ignore similarities between India and South Africa. Many Indians regarded caste as the most important criterion of social identification. Rigid social stratification was deeply embedded in Indian society. As K. Subramaniam, one of the five members of the Mandal Commission, put it, "caste is a reality, it exists in all groups, and it has to be given official recognition, despite it being a bitter pill to swallow for many."[14] Akin to black South Africans, lower caste Indians experienced centuries of organized oppression. While economic development and the forces of modernization contributed to the weakening of the caste system, injustices based on caste remain an integral component of India's social, political, and economic systems. Indeed, the philosophical, religious, and cultural foundations of the millennia-old caste system made it far more difficult to achieve equality in India than in South Africa, where the religious and cultural underpinnings of apartheid were more recent in origin and comparatively less secure. Furthermore, Indians' tolerance of ambiguity and their tendency to compartmentalize government from society and traditional values from Western concepts have made it possible for them to pile ideas about power upon each other without any noticeable blending or compromise.[15] Therefore, they are less vulnerable than are South Africans to the effects of cognitive dissonance.

India's caste system, rejected by the government since independence, is based on the concepts of purity and pollution and on the hierarchical and inegalitarian ranking of social groups. One's position in this highly stratified social system is determined by birth. And since one's status is a direct result of one's actions over many incarnations, one's social status is a reflection of moral justice and a well-defined religious order. Castes and everything in creation are ranked according to their relative purity or pollution. Even within the individual there is purity and pollution. For example, the right side of the body is perceived as being purer than the left side. Interpersonal relations, food, and occupations are also categorized in terms of purity and pollution. Reinforcing social stratification is the belief that birth sets only the upper limits of purity. Pollution can emanate from one's own acts, particularly selfishness and physical desire. It can also result from violations by others. Contact with people and things regarded as less pure is polluting. Thus marriage between people from different castes is viewed as impure and unnatural, and eating with lower castes is widely perceived as defiling.[16]

Whereas Americans are more comfortable with the rhetoric of equality, Indians tend to emphasize subordination and superordination. Since one's social position is not an accident of birth, hierarchical relationships are considered natural. Consequently, aspects of behavior such as seating arrangements, salutations, and deference symbolize accepted social inequality to which individuals must be constantly alert.[17] These deeply rooted practices undergird inegalitarianism and pervasive abuse of fundamental human rights. The caste system challenges Western concepts concerning the moral significance of being human, not only because it draws fundamental moral distinctions between people but, more important, because it fails to clearly distinguish human beings from other parts of creation. Within India's cultural framework, the idea of human rights is regarded as a moral outrage and an attack on natural order and justice.[18] The persistence of discrimination based on caste, despite government efforts to provide equal opportunities for disadvantaged groups, indicates that inequality in India is supported by durable cultural foundations.

India's constitution explicitly outlawed untouchability and mandates compensatory measures to assist groups classified as disadvantaged to integrate into the mainstream of Indian society. Various laws were enacted to protect them from discrimination.[19] Apart from cultural resistance to egalitarianism, programs designed to give disadvantaged groups access to education, government jobs, welfare services, and political positions have been largely ineffectual because of strong resistance to them from higher ranking castes. At the heart of the problem is a struggle to prevent significant alterations in the current distribution of power. Despite vociferous and violent opposition to government policies that reserve jobs and university seats for lower castes, there was no serious erosion of the upper castes' privileges and power. The Brahmins, for example, comprised only 3.5 percent of the population but exercised tremendous power. Brahmins controlled much of the media and most of the senior positions in government and the military. The Nehru dynasty, which governed India for most of its existence as an independent state, was Brahmin. Nine of the sixteen supreme court judges were Brahmin, as were nineteen of the twenty-six state secretaries and thirteen of the twenty-seven governors and lieutenant-governors. And 2,376 out of 3,300 officers of the elite Indian Administrative Services were Brahmin.[20] Overall, upper castes accounted for less than 20 percent of India's 840 million people but wielded significant power throughout society.

Confronted with the upper castes' continued dominance and cognizant of the social structures that perpetuated the disadvantaged position of the lower castes, Prime Minister V. P. Singh attempted to rectify the situation by implementing provisions of the Mandal Commission report that recommended reserving 27 percent of all government jobs for the backward castes who constitute approximately one-third of the country's population. This new policy reserved almost 50 percent of all government jobs for underprivileged Indians. Although quotas at both the state and national levels were rarely met—partly because bureaucrats and others responsible for their implementation were strongly opposed to them—granting relatively secure civil service jobs to particular groups in a society plagued by high levels of unemployment and limited opportunities was bound to be extremely controversial and destabilizing. Although many Indians from upper castes protested against the reservations, the most ardent opponents of the policy were Indians from the lower middle class but from caste backgrounds that did not qualify them for reserved jobs. Obviously threatened by any economic and social advances of groups immediately below them, middle class students hijacked buses, constructed roadblocks, participated in nation-wide protests, and some committed suicide by self-immolation.[21] Indians who had customarily adopted a superior moral attitude toward apartheid seemed oblivious to the similarities between apartheid and caste discrimination. And when Nelson Mandela, during his visit to India in mid-October 1990, praised the National Front coalition government for courageously implementing the Mandal Commission report, the Peoples' Union for Civil Liberties and other organizations criticized Prime Minister V. P. Singh for involving him in India's internal affairs. But Mandela's assertion that Indian reforms had struck "a responsive chord in our hearts and in the hearts of all those struggling against discrimination and domination"[22] clearly indicated that from his perspective caste problems in India paralleled apartheid in South Africa.

Ironically, international pressures against South Africa, many initiated by India, had contributed to the dismantling of apartheid precisely when greater attention was focused on India's own human rights violations. Similar to South Africa, India imprisoned thousands of political opponents without bringing specific charges against them and without trials. Under the Terrorist and Disruptive Activities Prevention Act, individuals were detained for up to a year and could obtain bail only if they could convince a magistrate that they were innocent. There were reports of torture and deaths in detention.[23] Despite India's criticism of South Africa's policies that legalized the exploitation of black labor, New Delhi came under increasing domestic and international scrutiny in the early 1990s for widespread inhumane treatment of children from backward castes who were virtually enslaved. Of approximately 120 million children who worked in shops and on farms to help their parents, an estimated 55 million were treated as slaves. Many children were branded with hot irons when they became bonded laborers. Although child labor is illegal in India, the practice was perpetuated by wealthy landlords, textile manufacturers, and other businesspersons. Police officers and government investigators were usually bribed to ignore India's numerous labor laws that purportedly protect children from hazardous occupations. Groups such as Britain's Anti-Slavery Society for the Protection of Human Rights and India's South Asian Coalition on Children in Servitude focused their campaigns against the carpet industry, the principal violator of child labor laws.[24] The horrendous working conditions became a political issue when Prime Minister Singh linked bonded labor to his controversial job reservation policy. But deeply entrenched cultural values and opposition to Singh's reforms from powerful political figures and upper class castes eventually forced Singh from office. Both India and South Africa are challenged to make their societies more egalitarian.

Despite India's internal and regional problems, apartheid was one of its major foreign policy concerns. Central to India's interest in South Africa was the harsh treatment experienced by the Indian community in Natal. British control over India and Natal provided the basis of the linkage between India and South Africa. While Britain wanted Natal to be settled by white immigrants, few English citizens were attracted to the colony, preferring instead to emigrate to Canada, Australia, and the United States. Experiencing labor shortages, Britain brought indentured Indians to Natal in late 1860 to work on plantations, in households as domestic servants, and in various government departments as lower-level civil servants.[25] Despite efforts to terminate the flow of Indians to Natal and to repatriate those already there, the Indian community continued to grow and became a major political force in South Africa. Given Mahatma Gandhi's pivotal role in the struggles for racial equality in South Africa as well as his leadership of India's independence movement, the treatment of Indians in South Africa became intertwined with Indian nationalism. Consequently, even before India achieved its independence, it brought South Africa's abusive policies toward Indians to the UN's attention. Nehru's pivotal role in India's foreign policy further strengthened the country's interest in South Africa.

But India could not effectively mobilize international opposition to the Indians' treatment without also emphasizing the plight of South Africa's black majority. Apart from the fact that the UN Charter's human rights provisions formed the foundation upon which India could construct its opposition to South Africa's racial policies, the prevailing political climate in the aftermath of the Holocaust in particular and World War II in general favored an approach that was broadly humanitarian. India, therefore, found it necessary to extend support to all groups and communities subject to racial discrimination in South Africa.[26] Furthermore, if India wanted to assume leadership of the emerging countries of Asia and Africa within the Nonaligned Movement, it had to broaden its concerns. Moreover, the dynamics of apartheid influenced Indians and blacks in South Africa to cooperate to a greater extent than previously to protect their interests. For example, passage of the Group Areas Act served as a catalyst to consolidate opposition to apartheid's legal structures. The combination of India's international efforts to dismantle apartheid during its inchoate stages and the white minority's determination to augment racial domination by legal and social means helped to unite the African National Congress and the South African Indian Congress.[27]

Yet the divisive nature of apartheid, an integral component of which was preferential treatment for nonwhite groups based on their skin's pigmentation, contributed to the existence of tensions between Indians and blacks. Within South Africa's system of racial stratification the former enjoyed greater opportunities than the latter. Apart from cultural and individual characteristics, variations in success among groups were directly related to access to education and the quality of that education, the availability of financial resources, and variations in political and legal restrictions on upward mobility. Largely middle class and urbanized, the Indian community occupied a much higher socioeconomic position than black South Africans. Indians generally got middle-management and professional positions vacated by whites. And whereas Indians were given political representation in South Africa's segregated parliament, the black majority was relegated to the status of noncitizens. Prior to reforms instituted by President de Klerk in the late 1980s and early 1990s, black South Africans were regarded as citizens of internationally unrecognized Homelands, comprising only 13 percent of the country's land. These significant economic, political, and social differences between Indians and blacks diminished solidarity between them.[28] Nonetheless, their common interests, as well as experiences Indians had elsewhere in Africa, fostered cooperation against apartheid.

India's consistent opposition to apartheid in international forums was accompanied by its tangible support for southern African liberation movements, a fact which helped to cement ties between the South African Indian and black communities. Although the Indian government was committed to nonviolence as an instrument of change in South Africa, it believed that violence used by the apartheid regime rendered the achievement of equality through peaceful means virtually impossible. From India's perspective, the fact that many of those killed and wounded during the 1976 Soweto riots were students and children not only demonstrated "the inhuman and racist character of the South African regime" but also underscored the necessity for the "freedom fighters" to resort to armed struggle.[29] Following the Soweto riots, India increased its assistance to the ANC and other liberation movements. Its contributions included arms and ammunition, military training, medical supplies, food, money, and equipment. Equally important, India established diplomatic contacts with the liberation movements.

The ANC's president, Oliver Tambo, and the South West African People's Organization president, Sam Nujoma, visited India and were met by that country's leaders. Both the ANC and SWAPO were given facilities to enable them to operate their missions in New Delhi. These ties were regarded by India as a way of demonstrating its support for equality and freedom in southern Africa, and the visits by Tambo and Nujoma were perceived as evidence of their faith and confidence in India's policy.[30] Prior to Namibia's independence in March 1990, the Indian government expressed its opposition to South Africa's illegal occupation of Namibia by allowing SWAPO to establish an embassy in New Delhi in 1986. India was thus the first country to recognize Namibia as an independent country. When Nujoma arrived in New Delhi in mid-1986 he was met by Prime Minister Rajiv Gandhi and was given a ceremonial welcome generally accorded to heads of government.[31]

India's support for southern African liberation groups was also confirmed by Nelson Mandela's five-day visit to New Delhi in mid-October 1990. Noting that India was the first country to support diplomatic and economic sanctions against Pretoria, to voice its abhorrence of apartheid to the world, and to initiate the anti-apartheid movement, which had grown into a world-wide movement, Mandela explained that his relatively late visit to India was partly due to meetings with the ANC's national executive in Zambia, and subsequent trips to other African countries, the United States, and Britain.[32] During Mandela's visit, India reiterated its stance against apartheid. Mandela was given a tumultuous welcome; held meetings with President R. Venkataraman, Vice President Shankar Sharma, and Prime Minister V. P. Singh; received the prestigious Jamnala/Bajaj award; and was given a check for $5 million as a token of solidarity between India and the anti-apartheid movement in South Africa. These actions seemed to underscore Mandela's view that India was the single largest source of inspiration to South Africa's oppressed majority and their best friend.[33]

In addition to assisting the liberation movements, India provided a modest amount of aid to the Frontline States. As a leading member of the Nonaligned Movement, India was instrumental in translating that organization's general declarations into specific programs that were directly beneficial to the Frontline States. At the Harare conference of the Nonaligned Movement in 1986, the Africa Fund was created to strengthen the economic and financial capabilities of the Frontline States, to assist them in enforcing sanctions against Pretoria, and to mitigate the effects of South Africa's retaliatory economic actions against them. To accomplish these objectives, India, as chair of the nine-member Africa Fund Committee, collaborated with the UN and its specialized agencies, the European Community, the Commonwealth, the International Labor Organization, and the Southern African Development Coordination Conference. Despite its own poverty, India gave more than $40 million to the Frontline States in medical equipment, diesel pump sets, small-scale agricultural implements, brick manufacturing plants, railway wagons, and electric motors. India also offered its agricultural expertise to southern African states and allowed students from South Africa and Namibia to obtain technical training at several of its institutes.[34] Indian leaders made numerous visits to the Frontline States to show their support for South Africa's beleaguered neighbors. For example, Prime Minister Gandhi visited Zambia, Angola,

Zimbabwe, and Tanzania in early May 1986. Similarly, President Venkataraman went to Botswana in late September 1986 to participate in that country's Independence Day celebrations in Gabarone. He was accompanied by Eduardo Faleiro, India's minister of state for External Affairs, and a high-level delegation.[35]

Another component of India's policy toward South Africa was the mobilization of international support for sanctions against the apartheid regime. India severed economic links with South Africa in 1954, thereby becoming the first country to voluntarily terminate trade with South Africa. Although the Indians in Natal had developed commercial relations with India, trade between the two countries was relatively insignificant. Therefore, the impact of India's decision was primarily symbolic. Yet it was India's ability to translate its symbolic power into tangible actions that ultimately contributed to the demise of apartheid. As a prominent member of the Commonwealth and the leader of the Nonaligned Movement, India was able to work with Britain, Canada, Australia, and Third World countries to develop a package of economic sanctions against South Africa. Like Nigeria and Zambia, India called for mandatory economic sanctions against the white minority regimes of southern Africa and appealed to the international community to increase both moral and material assistance to the region's independence movements. Collaboration between Western countries and South Africa was condemned. The Reagan administration's "constructive engagement" policy was perceived as perpetuating the status quo, and multinational corporations were generally regarded not as instruments of black empowerment but, instead, as forces that exploited black labor. Efforts to initiate negotiations between Pretoria and the ANC were viewed as meaningless. Consequently, India derided attempts by the Commonwealth's Eminent Persons Group to talk with South Africa's government. India's views were consistent with its position as the leading proponent of comprehensive mandatory sanctions against South Africa in the UN, the Nonaligned Movement, and the Commonwealth.[36] Believing that Western countries with significant economic ties to South Africa were advocating dialogue with Pretoria because they were unwilling to jeopardize their interests, Prime Minister Gandhi, as chairman of the Nonaligned Movement, argued that external economic sustenance reinforced Pretoria's intransigence. From his perspective, the only peaceful way to end apartheid was to enforce mandatory sanctions. The alternative was unprecedented violence.[37]

Gandhi's views were supported by India's anti-apartheid groups. The establishment of the Committee of Trade Unions Against Apartheid was designed to encourage consumers to boycott products of multinational corporations that operated in both India and South Africa. But, unlike Nigeria, the Indian government did not explicitly prevent companies from doing business in both countries simultaneously. Furthermore, the general population was not strongly committed to boycotting popular products. Nevertheless, groups such as the Bharatiya Mazdoor Sangh and the National Front of Indian Trade Unions supported black South African trade unions, increased pressure on companies with operations in South Africa, and raised funds for the ANC.[38]

However, the porous nature of national boundaries reduced the effectiveness of attempts to enforce trade sanctions against Pretoria. Apart from obvious difficulties involved in controlling multinational corporations' activities, smaller Indian companies also tried to circumvent economic sanctions. In 1985, at the height of the sanctions debate, the Indian government investigated approximately fifteen companies on suspicion of trading with South Africa and arrested eight persons who were accused of violating sanctions against Pretoria. South Africa's economic ties with Malawi and Mauritius also facilitated indirect trade between India and South Africa. While the final destinations of exports were often listed as Malawi and Mauritius, the products were eventually shipped to South Africa. Mauritius maintained close relations with India, partly because of family bonds created by the arrival of Indian workers over 100 years ago. When Prime Minister Gandhi visited Mauritius in 1986, he denounced racism, militarism, and tyranny in South Africa and asked Mauritius to reexamine its special relationship with Pretoria. But Mauritius remained opposed to imposing sanctions against its neighbor, and Vice-Premier Gaetan Duval argued that his country could not afford to pay higher prices for imports from the United States, Britain, and France; South Africa was the cheapest source of its imports.[39] India's decision to promote trade with Mauritius inevitably blurred its policy of not trading with South Africa.

Despite India's consistent advocacy of comprehensive sanctions against Pretoria, the country was a major beneficiary of South Africa's diamond industry. About 62 percent of the world's gem diamonds were processed in India in 1991 and over half a million people were employed in the business. In direct contradiction to India's South African policy, the largest supplier of diamonds for India's industry was the Diamond Trading Corporation, an affiliate of the London-based Central Selling Organization. Both organizations are part of South Africa's De Beers corporation, which has a virtual monopoly on the world's diamonds. In addition to private companies, De Beers' Indian customers included the Hindustan Diamond Company, half of which was owned by the Indian government. So important was cutting and polishing diamonds to India that both De

Beers and the Minerals and Metals Trading Corporation of India sought to diminish their mutual dependence by endeavoring to find alternative sources of labor and diamonds, respectively. Whereas De Beers focused on cheap labor in Thailand, China, and Sri Lanka, India looked to Africa, principally Ghana, for primary sources of diamonds.[40] To a much greater extent than Israel, India was inextricably linked to South Africa's diamond industry.

Ironically, India's exports of polished diamonds increased dramatically, from roughly 10 billion rupees in 1983 to around 50 billion rupees in 1990, at the height of India's anti-apartheid campaign. In addition to cutting and polishing diamonds, Indians were also part of a global network, with offices in the principal diamond centers of Antwerp, London, New York, and Hong Kong. These offices were usually managed by families, many of whom were members of the Palanpuri Jain community. It was estimated that out of approximately 2,400 members of the Gem and Jewelry Export Promotion Council, 95 percent were Jains. The division of labor among family members closely resembled that of the multinational corporations that were often criticized by the Indian government. After purchasing rough diamonds in London from the Diamond Trading Corporation, an Indian would send them to his brother in Bombay to be cut and polished. The finished products were then shipped to another brother in Antwerp, who instructed cousins in New York and Hong Kong to sell the diamonds to jewelry manufacturers.[41]

India's dominant position in the diamond industry as well as the central role of gold in the country's culture contributed to the importation of large amounts of gold. The Indian government itself had one of the largest reserves of gold in the world, estimated to be more than 7,000 tons. Although India produced only 3 tons of gold a year and banned imports under the Gold Control Act, about 200 tons of gold were smuggled into the country from South Africa, the Middle East, Europe, South Asia, and the United States. South Africa, which produced almost half the world's gold, was undoubtedly the principal and original source of India's imports. The high price of gold for jewelry exporters as well as the government's inability to prevent widespread smuggling led to the abolition of the Gold Control Act in early 1990. For most Indians who bought gold ornaments and jewelry for weddings and gifts, the fact that the gold and diamonds could have come from South Africa was largely peripheral. Similarly, India's Ministry of Commerce, concerned about the much needed foreign exchange generated by gold jewelry exports, supported unrestricted gold imports.[42] Thus, to some extent, India's South African policy was undermined by domestic economic and cultural considerations and the realities of the global economic system.

Consistent with its view that comprehensive sanctions would ultimately undermine apartheid, India supported the arms embargo and the cultural and sports boycott against South Africa. Although several African countries initiated resolutions in the UN Security Council that called for a mandatory arms embargo against Pretoria, their tendency to link the issue of military sales to financial assistance to and economic cooperation with South Africa reduced their chances of getting the resolutions adopted. Britain, France, and the United States generally opposed comprehensive measures that would jeopardize their interests. India's role in securing the UN Security Council resolution banning arms sales to South Africa in 1977 was pivotal. Realizing that Western countries would veto any resolution that contained economic measures, India drafted a resolution that dealt only with weapons transfers. It became the basis for the final resolution terminating arms sales to South Africa.[43] Despite India's leading role on this issue, it inadvertently violated the arms embargo. The Indian government "was deliberately tricked" into selling ninety old Centarion tanks to South Africa in 1977. India believed that Mozambique was to be the recipient. Instead, the tanks were shipped to South Africa where they were modernized. Their old 86-mm guns were replaced with 105-mm guns linked to computerized sights, and new South African diesel engines were installed.[44] Cultural and sporting links between India and South Africa were officially severed, even though India, like Britain, has family links to that country. As early as 1974 India had decided not to play against South Africa in the Davis Cup. When Britain refused to adopt economic anti-apartheid sanctions in 1986, India joined twenty-three other countries in boycotting the Commonwealth Games in Edinburgh. Prime Minister Gandhi argued that Britain had lost its leadership role in the Commonwealth because of its refusal to impose sanctions against Pretoria. The boycott of the Commonwealth Games was the first time India had not participated in an international sports event because of political considerations.[45] However, once the legal foundations of apartheid were demolished, India was the first country to play cricket with South Africa.

Despite India's seemingly insurmountable economic and social problems, it consistently opposed apartheid from 1945, when it introduced the issue to the UN, until the early 1990s, when Pretoria had dismantled the cornerstones of minority rule. Even as India continued to wrestle with its own problems, generated by inequalities among castes and efforts to address them, apartheid remained a central concern of its foreign policy.

TAIWAN AND SOUTH AFRICA

The linkage between Taiwan's domestic politics and its foreign policy was extremely strong. And to a much greater extent than in India or Nigeria, there was an overlapping of economics and politics in Taiwan. At both the domestic and international level, it was very difficult to separate political issues from economic factors. An underlying cause of this fusion between domestic economic and political factors and Taiwan's foreign policy was the country's uncertain political status within the international community. Like South Africa, Israel, and South Korea, Taiwan was considered a pariah state and, as such, was relatively isolated, at least politically, in world affairs.

Pariah states exhibit characteristics that distinguish them from most ordinary countries. They are usually small, have few close allies, and tend to be surrounded by less than agreeable neighbors. Their security problems are more acute than those of ordinary states because of their political isolation. Whereas both Israel and South Korea were supported militarily by the United States, Taiwan and South Africa could not depend on military assistance from a major power. To the contrary, their security was often threatened, or perceived to be threatened, by much more powerful states. Despite variances in security arrangements among pariahs, their common concern with survival is obvious. Ultimately, their existence depends on their own self-defence. Consequently, all pariahs are preoccupied with national security. Under these circumstances, they usually view international norms and UN resolutions as less binding on their own behavior than on that of other countries. Respect for international law is further diminished as a consequence of ideologies that accompany the siege mentality experienced by pariahs. Moral considerations, an integral component of legal systems, are secondary to military and economic aspects of national security. Finally, although some pariahs ameliorated their international environment and diminished their isolation by taking certain actions, others had little control over external forces.[46] Israel and South Africa were clearly more capable of making compromises that would reduce their neighbors' hostility than was Taiwan. In the latter's case, its pariah status, indeed its loss of sovereignty, was imposed by the dynamics of international relations. The outside world, much to Taiwan's chagrin, had determined its position in the international community. Thus, South Africa and Taiwan were isolated for very different reasons.

Unlike South Africa, whose existence was not questioned, Taiwan had to contend with its nonstate status. Whereas the former gained increased acceptance into the world community by abandoning the legal structures of apartheid, the latter was confronted with more difficult choices and, consequently, adopted foreign policy strategies that reflected its narrower options. Having embraced the view that it represented an undivided China, Taiwan's international political status was seriously undermined as the vast majority of nations recognized the PRC. In effect, they derecognized Taiwan as the legitimate representative of the Chinese people. Confronted with this reality, Taiwan modified its foreign policy strategies. Instead of breaking diplomatic relations with countries that recognized the PRC, Taiwan pursued "flexible diplomacy," in which it maintained contacts with states with which it had no diplomatic relations. Traditional diplomatic relationships were gradually replaced with "the innovative promotion of substantial relations and the internationalization of Taiwan's foreign policy."[47] In addition to accepting dual recognition (of PRC and Taiwan), Taipei focused on economic ties with other countries and used its economic power to induce smaller states in Latin America, the Caribbean, and elsewhere to establish diplomatic relations with it.

More importantly, significant changes in the international political system and the increased relevance of economic power in foreign affairs in the late 1980s and early 1990s facilitated the achievement of Taiwan's foreign policy objectives. Communism's demise in Eastern Europe and Mikhail Gorbachev's political and economic reforms in the Soviet Union greatly enhanced Taiwan's position in the world community vis-à-vis the PRC and in general. In an international environment that was relatively free of ideological polarization, Taiwan's isolation became less pronounced and its economic power was more applicable as an instrument of foreign policy. International trade and investment had long been employed by Taipei in its international relations. When Japan recognized the PRC in 1972, Taipei and Tokyo simply found new organizations to assume much of the embassies' responsibilities. Taiwan opened the Association of East Asian Relations in Tokyo and Japan established the Interchange Association in Taipei.[48] Similarly, when the United States severed diplomatic ties with Taiwan and recognized the PRC, the Coordination Council for North American Affairs of Taiwan and the American Institute in Taiwan were created as unofficial agencies to conduct relations between Washington and Taipei. Taiwan established numerous trade, agricultural, and technical missions abroad and financed international educational conferences, academic exchanges, and other activities to enhance the country's image as well as to consolidate its relations with other countries. Trade with Eastern Europe increased and most communist countries sent trade missions to Taipei. Even the PRC expanded its commerce with Taiwan.

Though neither Taiwan nor the PRC recognized each other's sovereignty and claim to represent China, and despite the former's apprehension about becoming dependent on the latter, Taiwan's remarkable economic development, which was deliberately pursued to strengthen the country against threats from the mainland, created bonds of interdependence between the two countries. The PRC, influenced both by its economic problems and a desire to eliminate barriers between Taiwan and the mainland, encouraged Taiwanese imports. But Taiwan was also interested in commercial relations with the PRC. As calls for American protectionism intensified, Taiwanese companies endeavored to reduce their dependence on U.S. markets. They also wanted to compete more effectively with Japan and Korea, an objective that influenced them to avoid rising labor costs and environmental regulations in Taiwan. Furthermore, China offered new markets, inexpensive raw materials, and attractive investment policies.[49] With foreign exchange reserves of approximately $80 billion in 1992, Taiwan saw the PRC as offering great investment opportunities. Since direct business contacts with PRC were prohibited by Taiwan, trade and investment activities were conducted through third parties, particularly Hong Kong and Singapore. Recognizing its inability to prevent economic ties between Taiwan and the mainland, Taipei lifted the forty-year ban on indirect trade in 1987. By 1990 Taiwan had become the PRC's seventh largest trading partner, with former enjoying a large trade surplus. In 1990, $2.5 billion of the PRC's $6.5 billion trade deficit, or more than a third, was with Taiwan.[50] Clearly, Taiwan's economic strength was its most important foreign policy instrument.

The circumstances under which Taiwan became a state made its existence precarious. Convinced that economic development was essential to its survival as a political entity, Taiwan focused on promoting exports and on reducing imports. Unlike Nigeria, India, and South Africa, which enjoyed widespread international recognition of their right to statehood, Taiwan faced imminent danger of invasion from the mainland, despite American military guarantees. As M. Shadid Alam observed, this reality imparted to economic development an urgency that was by no means common among developing countries.[51] Although Taiwan's rapid development cannot be attributed to any single factor, it is clear that states such as Nigeria and Zambia—which have more natural resources than Taiwan and had comparable incomes in the early 1950s—faced few external threats and, consequently, squandered their resources without fear of risking their existence as states. However, given the myriad of internal problems with which they are confronted, it is unlikely that their survival would have been possible in the face of external hostility similar to what Taiwan endured.

Confronted with stark choices, Taiwan avoided many of the development problems that characterized most Third World countries. Explicitly authoritarian, the government assumed primary responsibility for economic growth and diversification. Taiwan's politicians set the broad economic objectives and then allowed a politically neutral technocratic bureaucracy to achieve them. As Chalmers Johnson observed, in capitalist developmental states such as Taiwan, South Korea, and Japan, depoliticization of economic policy is accomplished through a covert separation between reigning and ruling.[52] While politicians protect the bureaucracy from political pressures, they do not involve themselves in the specifics of development. The government provided both political and economic stability; invested heavily in education; implemented policies that ensured equitable distribution of wealth; and fostered cooperation with the private sector. Instead of abandoning agriculture, as Nigeria did, Taiwan linked agricultural productivity to industrial development, thereby diminishing capital outflow for food imports. In addition to receiving economic aid from the United States, Taiwan encouraged privatization and domestic savings.[53] These factors, among others, assisted Taiwan's rapid industrialization.

Economic prosperity ultimately contributed to weakening the authoritarian regime that had governed Taiwan since Chiang Kai-shek retreated with his anticommunist supporters to the island in 1949. Whereas older generations of Taiwanese generally accepted political and social restrictions as necessary for economic development and national security, younger, better educated, and more affluent Taiwanese questioned emergency rule, martial law, the ban on opposition political parties, censorship, and various human rights abuses. Furthermore, they rejected the dominant role of aging former mainland Chinese in the three national representative bodies—the National Assembly, the Legislative Yuan, and the Control Yuan. Perhaps even more important, the younger generation challenged the assumption that Taiwan represented all of China, thus undermining arguments that legitimized the former mainland Chinese' claim to power.

While factors such as leadership, generational changes, and reduced preoccupation with national security may have influenced change in Taiwan, dramatically improved economic conditions undoubtedly generated demands for democracy. Even though economic prosperity may actually consolidate authoritarian rule and democracy may flourish in relatively poor countries, evidence suggests that rich countries are more likely than poor ones to be democratic. Private wealth generated by industrialization and economic expansion provided not only political autonomy for groups and individuals but also enabled them to mobilize public support for institutional reforms and greater public participation in the political process.[54]

An emphasis on economic development as a catalyst for democracy in Taiwan is not inconsistent with the view that "the analysis of democratization should focus on the origin and development of political opposition."[55] Clearly, political opposition in an authoritarian society will be challenged to find ways to circumvent formidable obstacles erected by those in power. Taiwanese opposition groups, which forced the ruling elite to institute a new set of rules, were primarily from middle class backgrounds. The education and political skills they acquired stemmed in large measure from economic prosperity. Therefore, political participation and agitation for change in Taiwan were direct consequences of the country's rapid industrialization.[56]

Improvements in human rights have also been directly attributable to economic progress. Even though Taiwanese—especially aboriginal groups such as the Ami, Tyal, and Paiwan—experienced discrimination, rapid economic growth and deliberate attempts by the government to distribute resources to underprivileged groups culminated in reduced discrimination. By contrast, India's efforts to assist the untouchables and backward castes were less successful, partly because the country's economic resources were severely limited and those needing assistance constituted a majority of the population. South Africa faced similar problems. Taiwan, on the other hand, enabled virtually all groups to share in the country's prosperity. Social programs were created to assist aborigines and to integrate them into society. They received special educational opportunities and job training and benefited from special constitutional representation and privileges.[57] Nonetheless, many aborigines continued to be socially and economically disadvantaged. While Taiwan was concerned about equality among its own citizens, it was more preoccupied with national security and economic issues in its relations with South Africa.

In contrast to India and sub-Saharan Africa, Taiwan neither criticized South Africa nor encouraged its citizens to participate in anti-apartheid activities. It took no actions to assist apartheid's victims. Yet few anti-apartheid movements in Western Europe and North America voiced opposition to the growing contacts between Taiwan and South Africa that were clearly designed to undermine Western efforts to influence change in South Africa. Taipei's overriding concern with security, its authoritarian practices, and cultural attributes of the society conspired to militate against the emergence of strong anti-apartheid organizations. Groups in Taiwan, Hong Kong, and South Korea that opposed apartheid were usually associated with Christian churches. The Presbyterian church supported domestic democratic movements as well as anti-apartheid groups. However, its human rights activities often led to confrontations with the government. For example, when the Presbyterians invited Allan Boesak, leader of South Africa's United Democratic Front, to visit Taiwan in early 1987, the Taiwanese government denied him a visa.[58] Close political, economic, and military links between South Africa and Taiwan undoubtedly affected Taipei's views and position on apartheid.

Political and ideological considerations undergirded relations between Taiwan and South Africa and overrode any apprehensions the former may have had about the latter's treatment of the black majority. Because the South African government construed challenges against apartheid as communism and viewed Soviet and Chinese collaboration with the ANC as evidence of preparations for a "total onslaught" on the country, it was relatively easy for Taiwan, directly threatened by Communist China, to cooperate with South Africa. Apart from facing a common enemy, the two states were drawn together by their growing ostracism from the international community. Moreover, southern Africa itself was perceived as a battleground by the United States and the Soviet Union. In this contest between East and West, South Africa and Taiwan were unequivocally committed to anticommunism.

Yet the complexity of great power rivalries in southern Africa ultimately complicated the Taipei-Pretoria alliance. Whereas the PRC was concerned with championing Third World causes to elevate itself to a leadership position within the Nonaligned Movement as well as to frustrate Soviet objectives and influence in Africa, the Soviet Union expressed comparatively little interest in much of Africa prior to the 1970s.[59] However, when Taiwan's relations with South Africa grew stronger in the early 1970s, Pretoria worried more about Soviet assistance to the ANC and other liberation groups than about the Chinese. If Taiwan moved closer to Moscow to take advantage of the Sino-Soviet rivalry, Pretoria believed that by consolidating ties with Beijing, albeit controversial and covert, it could diminish the Soviet threat to the apartheid regime. However, Taipei's and Pretoria's mutual dependence helped to obscure, or at least downplay, the fact that Taiwan's communist antagonist was being wooed by South Africa and, conversely, Taiwan was developing closer links with Eastern Europe and the Soviet Union.

Underlying the ideological and political kinship was Taiwan's struggle for international recognition of its claim to be the sole legitimate representative of China on the one hand and South Africa's inability to convince the world community that apartheid was legitimate and consistent with the fundamental rights and freedoms to which the West subscribed on the other.

Relations between Taiwan and South Africa began in 1949 when China was divided as a result of civil war. South Africa opposed the PRC's admission to the UN and regarded Taipei as the seat of China's legitimate government. But Taiwan's attempt to establish closer ties with sub-Saharan Africa to prevent the PRC from obtaining Third World support influenced Taipei to distance itself from Pretoria. Thus from 1949 until 1971 relations between Taiwan and South Africa were virtually nonexistent. However, as more Third World states recognized the PRC and as South Africa was increasingly isolated because of apartheid in the 1970s, the two countries strengthened their political, economic, and military links. Furthermore, the emergence of strong liberation movements in southern Africa in the 1970s and massive infusions of Soviet and Chinese assistance to them prompted Taipei and Pretoria to reassess their perceptions of each other. Diplomatic relations were upgraded from the consular level and embassies were established in 1976.[60]

Increasing Western pressures against apartheid in the aftermath of the Soweto uprising influenced some South Africans to question the wisdom of maintaining strong ties with the West. Moreover, U.S. recognition of the PRC was evidence of changing international alignments that could not be ignored by South Africa. The Soviet Union's involvement in Angola and its support for the ANC prompted the South African Department of Information to launch a covert campaign to enlist the PRC in an anti-Soviet alliance. Apart from potential economic benefits that could be accrued from improved relations with Beijing, Eschel Rhoodie and others in the Department of Information concluded that South Africa's close ties with Taiwan, despite the latter's preoccupations with threats to its security from the PRC, would not necessarily be damaged by political overtures toward the mainland.[61] Because South Africa, South Korea, and Saudi Arabia were the most important countries with which Taiwan enjoyed diplomatic relations, until Saudi Arabia recognized PRC in 1990, Taipei's leverage vis-à-vis Pretoria was limited. Therefore, despite South Africa's growing trade with and political overtures toward the PRC, its relations with Taiwan were strengthened, especially subsequent to the West's imposition of anti-apartheid sanctions.

In early 1976 Taiwanese officials visited South Africa and, from 1980 onward, South Africans went to Taiwan on official business. These trips were politically significant because of the two countries' growing isolation, a point underscored by Prime Minister P. W. Botha during his week-long official visit to Taiwan in 1980. Botha compared Taiwan's determination to survive to his own government's struggle against the anti-apartheid movement. Disappointed by the United States' growing opposition to apartheid as well as its recognition of the PRC, Botha asserted that "our two countries have experiences of the communist threat and of the transformation under pressure of fair-weather friends into vocal critics. We have seen many former allies choose to leave us to sink or swim on our own."[62] Reaffirming Prime Minister Yun-suan Sun's view that Taiwan and South Africa confronted similar difficulties due to international appeasement policies and their own strong anticommunist stance, Botha pointed out that both countries were victims of double standards. However, he maintained that they were "firmly resolved to prosper individually and in partnership."[63] In late 1989 Taiwan's vice foreign minister John H. Chang and the deputy director of the African Affairs Department of Taiwan's Foreign Ministry Du Ling stopped in Johannesburg before going to Malawi. Similarly, Liu Kou-Tsai, the speaker of Taiwan's parliament visited South Africa in January 1990 at the invitation of Louis le Grange, the speaker of South Africa's parliament. Both visits were an integral part of the broader objective of augmenting relations between the two countries.[64]

When the United States, Canada, and Western Europe increased economic sanctions against South Africa in the mid-1980s, the general assumption, nurtured by hubris, was that Western economic pressures would force the white minority to abandon apartheid. While the effectiveness of sanctions as foreign policy instruments was debated, there was comparatively little analysis of the role of newly industrialized and developing countries in assisting Pretoria to circumvent international sanctions. Akin to Japan, East Asian countries such as Taiwan, Hong Kong, South Korea, and Singapore were extremely reluctant to allow their economic interests to be negatively affected by political considerations. From their perspective, a strong economy was the most important element of national security and the foundation of not only domestic stability but also of military power. The importance of unimpeded access to critical raw materials for their technologically advanced export sectors virtually eliminated their choices in relation to imports from South Africa. To a large extent, political stability in East Asia was so intricately intertwined with strong economies that adhering to international sanctions against South Africa was tantamount to sabotaging their own national security interests. Consequently, Pretoria was able to use Taiwan as a conduit for its clandestine trade throughout the period when international sanctions were most intensely applied, thereby rendering relatively ineffective Western pressures and enhancing South Africa's bargaining leverage vis-à-vis many European countries that worried about forfeiting traditional markets, especially in electronics and computers, to Taiwan and South Korea. South African minerals and agricultural products passed through Taiwan for sale to numerous countries in Asia.[65]

Clandestine trade through intermediaries was facilitated by the proliferation of multinational corporations in a region preoccupied with commerce as well as by the very nature of international business transactions. Even countries, such as Singapore, that denounced apartheid participated in various schemes that enabled South Africa to continue trade with Asia. Hong Kong, a major financial center, maintained close economic ties with South Africa and was indifferent to that country's internal problems. Lacking significant domestic opposition to apartheid, Hong Kong was unencumbered to serve as a conduit for South African trade. Worldwide Shipping Group, based in Hong Kong, began transporting petroleum to South Africa after Denmark and Norway banned the shipping of oil to Pretoria in 1986 and 1988. Similarly, Hong Kong allowed companies based in the colony to transship South African coal to Asia. Singapore also participated in a consortium, known as Safari, that shipped cargo from several countries to South Africa. Commodities channeled through Singapore included rubber, timber, plywood, and manufactured products from Malaysia, Indonesia, and Thailand.[66] Within the region, Taiwan was second only to Japan as South Africa's most important trading partner.

Escalating international pressures against apartheid forced Pretoria to look to Taiwan for alternative markets and sources of investments. Increases in commerce between the two countries were directly associated with their growing isolation. Between 1960 and 1971 the total volume of trade between them was insignificant, rising from only $8 million to $12 million a year from the beginning to the end of that period. But in 1976 trade climbed to around $200 million, and by 1988 had reached almost $1 billion. Although these figures were relatively low compared to those for Japan, West Germany, Britain, and the United States, by the late 1980s Taiwan had become South Africa's seventh largest trading partner, due in part to the West's general compliance with international sanctions to influence change in South Africa. Whereas the United States had experienced about a 39 percent decline in imports from South Africa between 1985 and 1987, Taiwan's imports jumped by 115 percent. Similarly, while U.S. exports decreased by 31 percent during that period, Taiwan's increased by 102 percent.[67] However, given that Taiwan and South Africa conducted much of their trade covertly through third parties and stopped releasing trade figures in 1987, the full extent of commercial relations between the two countries was difficult to ascertain.

Taiwan's rapid economic development, its advanced technological base, its massive foreign exchange, and its need for raw materials provided the foundation for its commercial relations with South Africa. Taiwanese bankers, sensitive to their country's interests, played a major role in assisting South Africa to obtain credit for trade and investment. Organizations such as the National Chinese Association of Commerce and Industry also assisted the development of trade. To consolidate and expand these economic links, the South African Foreign Trade Organization opened a permanent showroom in Taipei's World Trade Center. The two countries signed several agreements. These included accords on establishing air services between Taipei and Johannesburg, fishing and navigation, taxation, agricultural and technical cooperation, and mineral and energy cooperation. Approximately nineteen such agreements were concluded by 1989. The foundation for these commercial arrangements was laid during exchange visits by the countries' leading officials.[68]

To facilitate trade, a Taiwan-South Africa Chamber of Commerce was established and the two countries held a yearly ministerial conference on economic and technical cooperation, beginning in 1979. Furthermore, Taiwan's National Science Council and South Africa's Council for Scientific and Industrial Research agreed in early 1989 to cooperate in scientific and technological areas. In light of South Africa's interest in processing more of its strategic resources, Pretoria regarded Taiwan's technological advances as an asset. The president of South Africa's Council for Mineral Technology, A. M. Edwards, viewed cooperation in manufacturing a range of platinum catalysts, chemicals, jewelry, and stainless steel as mutually beneficial.[69]

These considerations, as well as political factors, influenced the development of trade. Taiwan imported a wide variety of products from South Africa, including coal, uranium, steel, iron, maize, fruits and vegetables, base metals, wood, paper, chemical products, ferro-alloys, manufactured goods, natural clothing materials, diamonds, and gold. Its exports to South Africa were primarily manufactured products. Among them were clothing and textiles, electrical and electronic goods, machinery, tools, vehicles, transport equipment, and chemicals. Taiwan also exported advanced technology, including computers and software, to South Africa's parastatal organizations. Unlike most governments, which traded with South Africa even as they claimed to support sanctions, Taipei publicly pledged to ignore calls for restrictions on trade with Pretoria.

Political uncertainties in Asia and the Middle East contributed to Taiwan's increased imports of gold and coal.[70] Stronger currencies in Asia in general and in Taiwan in particular made gold more affordable. Taiwan rapidly expanded gold imports in 1988, partly because of inadequate investment outlets and also because it wanted to reduce its foreign exchange reserves. Moreover, Hong Kong's transition from a British colony to reintegration into the PRC in 1997, and the implications of that development for Taiwan itself, strengthened demand for gold. Similarly, political turmoil in the Middle East, even before the 1990-91 Gulf crisis, heightened Taiwan's vulnerability due to its dependence on petroleum imports. With its own coal reserves declining, Taiwan took deliberate steps toward energy diversification by increasing coal imports, by obtaining oil from a larger number of countries, and by purchasing more uranium for its nuclear power plants.

But neither political and ideological ties between Taipei and Pretoria nor the PRC's support of southern African liberation groups and the Frontline States prevented South Africa and the PRC from developing trade links. The Soviet Union had alleged in 1979 that clandestine trade, especially in weapons, was being conducted between the PRC and South Africa. By 1989, economic considerations were dominant, and the PRC's role in southern Africa significantly diminished. Under these circumstances, ideological differences were largely irrelevant. Covert contacts between South Africa and China paved the way for a contract under which the South African firm Steinmuller-Lavis supplied about 2,000 tons of fabricated structural steel for construction of the Yue Yand electric power station in the PRC. Similarly, China imported South African steam coal in 1989 to meet rising demands in its southern province of Guangdong. The coal was shipped from Maputo in Mozambique to the PRC through Hong Kong. However, exports of South African coal to the PRC were likely to be temporary because of the latter's vast reserves. Production and infrastructure problems that necessitated imports were to be solved by 1994.[71]

Commercial transactions between Taipei and Pretoria were augmented by investments. While Taiwan's growing investments in South Africa were partly motivated by its efforts to strengthen its foreign relations and to reduce its isolation, there were several economic factors that also influenced Taiwan's decision. Within the broader context of global competition, Taiwan's strategy of focusing on low-technology, labor-intensive industrial processes to increase exports was rendered virtually obsolete by its own success. A much higher level of industrialization, requiring comparatively advanced technology and less labor, was needed for Taiwanese businesses to remain internationally competitive. Given the political component of Taiwan's investment policies and the government's central role in the country's economy, South Africa was a logical investment partner. In addition to strong political ties between the two countries, South Africa's abundance of cheap labor and raw materials, labor shortages and relatively high wages in Taiwan, and the strength of Taiwan's currency vis-à-vis the South Africa's rand made South Africa attractive to Taiwanese investors. Conditions in South Africa, particularly in the "homelands," were conducive to the operation of Third World multinational corporations. Moreover, their activities were consistent with South Africa's policy of "decentralization"—encouraging investments in the homelands.[72]

Furthermore, faced with ever-increasing imports from Taiwan, Japan, South Korea, and other Asian countries, the United States and Western Europe became more protective of their own domestic industries. To counteract Western import quotas and tariffs, especially in textiles and electronics, several Taiwanese firms established subsidiaries in South Africa to circumvent U.S. and European restrictions on Taiwan's exports. Before the United States banned imports of South African textiles in 1986, the Taiwanese Chia Ho company exported flannel shirts and other apparel to America from a factory in South Africa. But after the United States adopted sanctions against Pretoria, the same company created a new factory across the border in Swaziland as the venue for a false labeling operation.[73] Many Taiwanese textile firms had established subsidiaries in South Africa to take advantage of its under-utilized export quota. Only minimal manufacturing was done in South Africa. Clothing and textiles had been virtually finished before being imported into South Africa to be assembled and labeled for export as South African products.

More importantly, Taiwan's investments in South Africa were critical to Pretoria's scheme to create independent "homelands" for the black majority and to diminish its dependence on Western technology. An integral component of the homelands policy was a decentralization program that was designed to develop industrial economies and create employment in predominantly rural areas. An underlying objective of this policy was to promote "orderly urbanization" by restricting migration from the countryside to major industrial centers within what was regarded as "white South Africa." But high unemployment levels amid serious recessionary conditions in the country frustrated the realization of this goal. Critics of industrial decentralization contended that the program was incapable of creating vibrant economies and that its impact on unemployment in rural areas was negligible.[74] Nonetheless, the government found it extremely difficult to implement alternative programs, and continued to encourage Taiwanese and others to invest in the homelands.

Incentives offered by the government's Decentralization Board to both South African and foreign firms included reduced factory rent for ten years, wage subsidies as high as 95 percent for seven years, tax holidays, reduced personal income taxes, and no real estate taxes. However, the government derived revenues from sales taxes and withholding taxes on individuals and earnings leaving the country. In addition to inducements granted by Pretoria, homeland governments also attracted investments by outlawing trade unions and providing tax havens. Wages were extremely low and companies were usually free from competition. Visits for Taiwanese investors interested in building manufacturing plants in the homelands were financed by Development Corporations, and many homeland governments were represented in Taiwan. The Bophuthatswana National Development Corporation published a color catalog written in Mandarin and offered to take potential investors from Taiwan and elsewhere on tours of the homeland.[75]

Taiwanese entrepreneurs comprised the vast majority of foreign investors and were primarily involved with labor-intensive industries that made textiles, footwear, fabricated metal goods, plastics, electronics, cutlery, and clothing. Several factories also assembled electric products and personal computer components. In 1989 Drake Networking Systems of South Africa and Superwave Systems, one of Taiwan's largest electronic component manufacturers, formed a joint venture in South Africa to produce a range of personal computer products for export. Between 1979 and 1991, Taiwanese industrialists had invested more than $300 million in South Africa, principally in the homelands. The estimated 170 small companies employed over 40,000 South Africans, the majority of whom were unskilled.[76]

Commercial and investment links between Taiwan and South Africa were reinforced by strong military ties. Arms and military technology transfers were consistent not only with overall close relations between the two countries but were also perceived by the pariah states as essential to their survival. This view, strengthened by political developments that contributed to South Africa's and Taiwan's isolation, prompted them to collaborate to lessen their dependence on traditional weapons suppliers, particularly the United States. Preoccupied with threats to its existence from the mainland, Taiwan also cooperated with Israel to obtain military technology and weapons, despite Saudi Arabia's sensitivity to contacts between them. Taiwan's cooperation with Saudi Arabia in areas such as agriculture, medicine, and electrical power generation, its dependence on oil from the Persian Gulf, and its strong diplomatic ties with Saudi Arabia complicated Taiwan's relations with Israel. However, South Africa's close military links with Israel virtually guaranteed that Taiwan would benefit not only from Israeli military technology but also from American weapons systems to which Israel had access. Furthermore, Taiwan continued to receive unofficial U.S. military advice and technology even after official arms supplies were sharply reduced. In addition to developing its own weapons, including fighter aircraft, Taiwan obtained Gabriel ship-to-ship missiles from Israel and field artillery, machine guns, automatic rifles, and missiles from South Africa.[77] Due to the covert nature and complexity of the arms trade, it was difficult to determine the exact nature of military relations among the pariahs.

Nevertheless, it was widely believed that Taiwan had acquired sophisticated weapons technology as well as the ability to produce nuclear weapons. In the aftermath of Operation Desert Storm, especially following U.S. and other coalition members' insistence that Baghdad's remaining nuclear and chemical weapons be destroyed, greater attention was given to countries such as Israel, South Africa, India, Pakistan, North Korea, and Taiwan that either possessed nuclear weapons or expressed interest in developing them. Taiwan's purchases of South African uranium for its nuclear power plants were seen as part of its broader objective of acquiring nuclear weapons. Its cooperation with South Africa and Israel, both of which developed nuclear weapons, further strengthened that view. As early as the mid-1970s it was assumed that Taiwan had made a concerted effort to obtain nuclear weapons. In addition to reprocessing spent fuel, Taipei sent military-trained researchers to the Massachusetts Institute of Technology (M.I.T.) to study ballistic missile–related technology. But U.S. intelligence and Department of State officials, concerned about this development, pressured M.I.T. to terminate their instruction.[78] Yet the large number of Taiwanese students at elite American universities as well as Taiwan's own advanced scientific base diminished the significance of this setback. Moreover, Israel, which had legal as well as illegal access to American technology, was determined to enhance its nuclear arsenal and launching systems. To achieve its objectives, Israel cooperated with South Africa and Taiwan,[79] thereby rendering U.S. restrictions on Taiwan meaningless.

Ideological bonds among the pariahs and their perception of their security interests strongly influenced them to exchange technical information and military personnel. Although Taiwanese officials denied that naval visits to South Africa had any military significance or that weapons projects were being developed in cooperation with Israel, evidence indicated otherwise. Israel helped Taiwan build missiles capable of delivering warheads; Israeli scientists worked in South Africa's nuclear energy program; Taiwan's scientists helped South Africa to produce enriched uranium; and South Africa supplied uranium to both Israel and Taiwan.[80] Furthermore, Taiwan had secretly constructed a small-scale plutonium unit, but decided to stop work on the project and to dismantle a 40-megawatt research reactor under pressure from the United States. American officials suspected that Taiwan intended to extract plutonium from the reactor's spent fuel to create nuclear weapons.[81] Both individually and cooperatively, Taiwan, Israel, and South Africa seemed determined to develop nuclear weapons to achieve their national security objectives.

As economic and military relations with Taiwan expanded, South Africa paid greater attention to the approximately 11,000 South Africans of Chinese descent. Brought to South Africa by the British in the late 1880s to work in gold mines, Chinese laborers were regarded as undesirable temporary residents. Of the more than 50,000 who came with the British, only a few thousand remained. Like their Indian counterparts, they were victims of apartheid. However, their status was elevated to that of "honorary whites" in 1985 as trade and political relations between Taiwan and South Africa improved. Similar to the Japanese in South Africa—who are also regarded as honorary whites—the Chinese were granted access to "white areas." Despite that desgination many within the Chinese community continued to experience some official discrimination until President de Klerk instituted major reforms in 1990 and 1991.

Cultural links between Taiwan and South Africa, while still comparatively limited, were fostered by the presence of the small Chinese community and by commercial interests. When President Chiang Ching-Kuo died in early January 1988, South African officials attended the funeral in Taipei. South Africa's Commission of Police General Johann Coetzee was awarded Taiwan's Yun Hai medal for strengthening friendship and cooperation between the two countries. Cultural ties were augmented through academic exchange programs and tourism.[82] Unlike India, which discouraged contact with South Africa, Taiwan had little to gain by distancing itself from Pretoria.

Chapter 4

Latin America: Brazil

In marked contrast to sub-Saharan Africa, India, and Taiwan, Latin American countries—with the exception of Brazil, Chile, and Argentina—evinced little interest in Africa in general and southern Africa in particular. Several factors account for the relative low level of interaction between South Africa and Latin America. These include different colonial heritages; Latin America's inclusion in the American and European security zones; Latin America's preoccupation with internal political and economic problems; linguistic and cultural barriers; and a general lack of significant overt racial tensions in Latin America. Consequently, South Africa's system of discrimination did not generate strong anti-apartheid feelings in Latin America.

Despite the existence of anti-apartheid movements in many Latin American countries, unlike their American and European counterparts, they remained politically marginalized and, consequently, their ability to influence their governments' foreign policies was negligible. When the Latin American Regional Conference for Action Against Apartheid met in Caracas in late 1983 and vigorously condemned South Africa, their declarations seemed to have little impact on Latin America's relations with Pretoria.[1] To the contrary, military regimes in the region were more inclined to support the apartheid regime than to permit internal anti-apartheid groups to openly oppose it. Apart from the domestic political implications of allowing vibrant political opposition groups to flourish, military leaders generally shared South Africa's antipathy toward communism, the belief that they were bulwarks of Western civilization, and a widespread disregard for fundamental human rights. Many Latin American governments practiced racial discrimination against lower classes, Indians, and blacks, and violently silenced any opposition. With the exception of Brazil, which believed that it had achieved racial democracy and which endeavored to maintain its economic links with South Africa even as it improved relations with sub-Saharan Africa, Latin America did not evince an emotive response to apartheid.

Unlike sub-Saharan Africa, where military governments attempted to eliminate internal political opposition to their policies but advocated apartheid's termination and the implementations of democratic rights and responsibilities in South Africa, Latin American governments pursued a more consistent policy of silencing domestic opposition and being virtually oblivious to developments in South Africa. Few Latin American countries experienced democracy prior to the mid-1980s, and even then they were confronted with the vestiges of authoritarian ideologies. In Argentina, where the military overthrew the government in 1930, between that time and 1985 only one freely elected government completed its term, and that was led by one of Latin America's most successful demagogues, Juan Domingo Peron.[2] But during Peron's tenure in office, the military's role in politics had increased significantly. Military leaders believed that the armed forces were the ultimate guardians of the state's internal and external security interests. In Chile they blamed that country's economic and political difficulties not only on the Marxist government of President Salvador Allende Gossens, whom they overthrew in September 1973, but also on democracy itself, which they regarded as a showcase for venal self-serving demagogues who were incapable of defending the country against leftist subversion.[3] In Chile, and throughout Latin America, military leaders suppressed political and labor union leaders, human rights organizations, university professors, and students. In Chile the military promoted market policies and the development of new enterprises. While the emphasis on economic growth may have ultimately contributed to unleashing forces that fostered the achievement of democracy in Chile, the government had persecuted groups that were closely associated with anti-apartheid activities, perceiving them as internal enemies of the state. Thus, while Latin America adopted a consistent policy of relative indifference toward South Africa, countries such as Chile, Argentina, and Brazil developed closer political ties to Pretoria. Conversely, as these countries became more democratic, they tended to distance themselves politically from South Africa.

But their preoccupations with seemingly insuperable economic problems influenced them to maintain their comparatively small amount of trade with South Africa, regardless of their internal political realities. Tangible commercial interests were less affected by political considerations. Because Latin American countries' economies are similar to South Africa's, trade relations are not very significant. Compared to Taiwan's export-oriented approach, Brazil, Argentina, and Chile were largely concerned with import-substitution strategies. With large internal markets, abundant natural resources, relatively high per capita incomes, and a growing middle class that created demands for products from industrialized countries, Latin America focused on developing industries to produce appliances, cars, and other durable consumer items. Due to these industries' lack of internal comparative advantage, a reflection of their reliance on imported capital-intensive equipment and the presence of a relatively highly paid industrial labor force, governments protected fledgling industries from lower-priced imports to ensure their survival.[4] Under these circumstances, diversifying export markets was clearly more important than expanding imports. Yet internal demands for manufactured products reduced these countries' need as well as ability to export.

However, Latin America's pattern of industrialization forced governments to borrow heavily from foreign creditors at a time when the prices of their raw material exports had declined drastically. This resulted in debt accumulation that surpassed that of the other developing regions, including Africa. Interest payments on their external debt amounted to more than one-third of their exports of goods and services.[5] Brazil, the world's largest debtor country, until the United States acquired that dubious distinction under President Ronald Reagan's administration, allocated almost half of its foreign exchange earnings to interest payments on its external debt. Faced with these difficult economic realities, Latin Americans eschewed adopting economic sanctions against South Africa.

If Latin American states seemed disinterested in forging stronger bonds with South Africa, Pretoria was not deterred from attempting to consolidate and expand its relations with countries such as Chile, Argentina, Uruguay, and Paraguay. Increasingly isolated from the world community following the Sharpeville Massacre, South Africa actively sought allies in Latin America. Its ambassadors in the region were granted considerable authority to improve relations with various countries. As a result of these efforts, the number of states with which South Africa established diplomatic ties climbed from two in 1964 to fourteen by 1975.[6]

To underscore Latin America's importance to Pretoria, Prime Minister John Vorster visited Uruguay and Paraguay in 1975, and when Paraguay's General Alfredo Stroessner went to South Africa in 1974, Pretoria rewarded him with a magnificent Palace of Justice and a headquarters for the foreign ministry. In 1983 South African Navy chief Andres Petrus Putter visited Paraguay and met with high-ranking officials. During the same year a delegation of Paraguayan legislators attended several official ceremonies in South Africa and were invited to a special session of the South African parliament. These visits were perceived as evidence of "the excellent relations between Paraguay and South Africa."[7]

Chile's pariah status under General Augusto Pinochet Ugarte facilitated South Africa's efforts to cultivate closer political, economic, and military ties to that country. Pretoria upgraded the status of its diplomatic representations by appointing General John Sutton as a full ambassador. By so doing, South Africa also terminated its practice of having its ambassador to Argentina also accredited to Chile.[8] In early 1988 South Africa's foreign minister Pik Botha visited both Chile and Uruguay.

Argentina, prior to the end of military rule, had developed close political links with the apartheid regime. Although part of Spain's empire until its independence in 1816, Argentina was strongly influenced by Britain. British investors and entrepreneurs built the country's railroads, utilities, and general infrastructure. The Argentine elite developed close cultural, economic, and political ties with Britain, France, and the United States. Partly due to Britain's control of South Africa, Argentina developed some links to the latter. South Africans of Afrikaner descent, many of whom became Argentinian citizens, form a small community in Argentina. Approximately 15,000 Argentineans resided in South Africa in 1991. Many of them were professionals who did not have strong ties to South Africa and had planned to return eventually to Argentina. Responding to internal pressures for democratic reforms as well as to calls from the Nonaligned Movement to diminish political interaction with South Africa in exchange for Third World support on important North-South issues, Buenos Aires severed diplomatic relations with Pretoria in May 1986 but maintained its modest economic links. South Africa was permitted to retain an honorary consulate in Comodoro Rivadavia to look after the interests of the small South African community there. While Argentina closed its consulate in Cape Town the following year, its consulate in Johannesburg remained open.[9] By 1986, most Latin American governments, especially those that were democratically elected, had downgraded their political ties with South Africa and, like Argentina, had adopted the view that apartheid was a threat to international peace and security. Nonetheless, their commerce with South Africa was essentially unaffected.

Although South Africa's economic relations with the region grew, special emphasis was placed on Brazil, Argentina, Chile, Paraguay, Uruguay, and Ecuador. As early as 1965, South Africa gave Ecuador approximately $50 million to modernize its railroads, and water and sewage systems, to construct bridges, and to develop its fishing industry. Paraguay received roughly $6.2 million in loans for road construction, housing, and agriculture, while Uruguay was given a $15 million loan to build a cement factory in 1975. Uruguay received additional financial assistance in 1976 for two refrigeration plants.[10]

South Africans invested in mining, hydroelectric power plants, and fertilizer factories throughout Latin America. However, most of these investments were concentrated in the largest countries. South African companies participated in joint ventures in mining agriculture, construction, chemicals, oil exploration, and fishing in Argentina. South African commercial activities in Chile were principally in the fishing industry. When President Allende nationalized foreign firms operating in Chile, South African companies that were involved in fishing left the country. However, following Allende's downfall, the Pinochet regime reversed many of his economic policies, reduced the state's role in the economy, and championed free enterprise. Ideological factors were diminished as the military attempted to separate economics from politics. Pinochet's willingness to extend economic incentives to foreign companies to invest in Chile, the increasing depletion of South Africa's fisheries and the previous experience of South Africans in Chile combined to induce South African firms to return. South Africans' expertise in canning operations enabled Chileans to maximize their profits by canning fish instead of simply processing them into less lucrative fish meal and oil. Cooperation was also beneficial to the South African entrepreneurs who provided ships, equipment, marketing channels overseas, and a major market in South Africa itself for Chile's fish products.[11] In addition to fishing companies, Shaft Sinkers, a subsidiary of South Africa's Anglo-American conglomerate, and other South African firms had investments in Chile. The state-owned enterprise Asmar (Naval Docks and Yards) and the South African company Sandock Austral formed a joint venture to construct a shipyard in Punta Arenas. As will be discussed, several South African companies also had investments in Brazil.

Trade between Latin America and South Africa was limited. Nevertheless, given the negative impact of economic sanctions on South Africa, increased exports of iron and steel to Latin America were not inconsequential. Similarly, Latin America's dire economic conditions undoubtedly influenced the various countries to regard exports to South Africa as important, especially since they generally enjoyed a trade surplus with South Africa for much of the 1980s. South Africa's exports to Argentina,

Chile, and Uruguay ranged from $0.14 million for Uruguay to $1.94 million for Chile in 1966, whereas their exports to South Africa ranged from $0.05 million for Chile and $3.32 million for Argentina during the same year. Both imports and exports grew steadily but modestly between 1966 and 1983. However, from 1983 to 1987 there were relatively sharp increases in trade between South Africa and Latin America, primarily with Argentina and Chile. After reaching a high of $41.8 million in 1980, Argentina's imports from South Africa declined to $13 million in 1983. By 1987 its imports from South Africa had climbed to $55 million. While Argentina's exports to South Africa reached $77 million in 1985, this figure decreased to roughly $49 million in 1987. Chile's imports increased to $30.6 million in 1981, dropped to $16 million in 1983, and jumped to $40 million in 1987. Chile's exports to South Africa increased from $21 million in 1983 to about $41 million in 1987.[12]

Latin American exports to South Africa included leather goods, agricultural machinery, home appliances, table sets, textiles, building materials, fish products, fats, chemicals, and various primary products. Imports from South Africa included iron, steel, manganese, asbestos, color television sets, processed foodstuffs, machine tools, home appliances, and Krugerrands. Tourism between Argentina and South Africa was facilitated by an agreement between Aerlineas Argentinas and South African Airways, which permitted direct flights between the two countries. Regular shipping services between South Africa and Argentina were provided by Argentine shipping companies.[13]

As the international anti-apartheid movement launched a concerted campaign to force South Africa to dismantle apartheid, Pretoria looked increasingly to countries that were generally regarded as pariahs to diminish its growing isolation. Chile, like Taiwan and Israel, developed close military links to South Africa, much to the chagrin of countries such as Nigeria. Chile was viewed as being instrumental in South Africa's attempts to circumvent the international arms embargo against it. Consequently, several states, especially those in sub-Saharan Africa, tried to pressure Santiago to sever its ties with Pretoria. In September 1988 Nigeria's minister of External Affairs Major General Ike Nwachukwu indicated his country's displeasure with Chile's close relationship with South Africa when he met with Chile's Foreign Minister Ricardo Garcia at the UN.[14] But Nigeria's concerns were perceived by Chile as of secondary importance. Like other pariah states, Chile viewed security issues, both internal and external, as survival interests that took precedence over moral considerations.

Naval vessels from Chile routinely called at Simonstown and its training ship, the Esmeralda, sailed to Cape Town in 1981 to participate in South Africa's Republican Festival. In early 1988 two ships from the South African navy, a logistical support ship and a missile-carrying ship, arrived in Puerto Montt to take part in maneuvers with Chile's navy during the International Air Fair. In 1981 General Cesor Mendoza of the Chilean junta visited South Africa as a guest of South Africa's commissioner of police, General Mike Geldenhuys. He was awarded a South African police medal. Similarly, in 1983 Chile's military regime received high-ranking South African military officers who visited Chile to participate in official ceremonies commemorating that country's 173 years of independence from Spanish rule. In 1988 South Africa's foreign minister Pik Botha visited both Chile and Uruguay.

Military collaboration between Santiago and Pretoria underscored the view that the partnership between the two countries was mutually beneficial. In the early 1980s Chile purchased Crotale surface-to-air missiles that were manufactured in South Africa under license from France. Throughout the period when Chile was under military rule, the South African Weapons Corporation (Armscor) transferred military technology and weapons to Santiago. Armscor's president Piet Marais, who attended the Fourth International Air Fair in 1984 that was organized by the Chilean Air Force, noted that Armscor had displayed sophisticated electronic equipment and a selection of the 143 varieties of arms it manufactured. To emphasize the close relationship between Chile and South Africa, Marais asserted that Chile was extremely interested in South African weapons because it was fighting a war against terrorism and that South Africa was prepared to share its experience with its military allies.[15] In August 1984 Chile invited the commander-in-chief of the South African Armed Forces, General Constand Viljoen, to visit the country. Clearly rejecting the international arms embargo against Pretoria, leading officials in Santiago contended that the arms trade between Chile and South Africa was lawful and consistent with trade exchanges among various nations.[16] Armscor continued to exhibit its weapons. Military cooperation between the two countries existed until Chile returned to democracy in late 1988.

BRAZIL'S POLICY TOWARD SOUTH AFRICA

Compared to the rest of Latin America, Brazil's policy toward South Africa was influenced by more complex factors. A former Portuguese colony with a large black population, Brazil endeavored to develop closer links with Angola and Mozambique after they achieved their independence from Portugal in the mid-1970s. Prior to that time, however, Brazil nurtured its traditional relationship with Portugal, a fact that complicated its policy toward the white minority regime in South Africa. Brazil's determination to play a significant role in world affairs required it to be more sensitive to Third World interests, particularly those of African states.

As a rapidly industrializing middle power that was dependent on export markets in the Third World and that relied on other countries for approximately 90 percent of its petroleum needs, Brazil believed that its national interests could be best secured through diversifying its political and economic relations. Consequently, it developed stronger links with Africa, Asia, the Middle East, and the Soviet Union.[17] Though anticommunist, Brazil's leaders avoided becoming entangled in East-West disputes and refused to allow political problems and rigid ideological alignments to influence their country's commercial relations with the Soviet Union and other states, including South Africa. Analogous to Taiwan, South Korea, Japan, Hong Kong, and Singapore, Brazil was preoccupied with economic development and regarded trade as an integral component of its security interests. In light of this perception, Brazil's commercial relations with South Africa were largely unaffected by political factors. General agreement within Brazil on the paramount importance of economic issues fostered greater continuity in that country's foreign policy than was generally the case for other Latin American nations.

Brazil's foreign-policy-making process ensured a considerable degree of consistency in its relations with Africa in general and South Africa specifically. Brazil's elites supported flexible economic-oriented policies toward other countries. In contrast to the United States, where interest groups significantly influence policy-making, Brazil's political system was not conducive to the existence of powerful political lobbies. Its decision-making processes functioned relatively independently of external pressures. A long lasting tradition of presidential control of foreign policy, especially during military rule, precluded public opinion from being a decisive factor in the formulation of foreign policy. Moreover, Itamaraty, the foreign affairs office, essentially shaped Brazil's external economic and political relations. Even when power was centralized by strong military regimes, Itamaraty played a key role in foreign affairs. Akin to Britain, where Oxford and Cambridge graduates dominate upper echelons of government, including the prime minister's Cabinet, Brazil's foreign policy was made by a largely homogeneous professional diplomatic elite. The widely held view that Itamaraty should conduct foreign relations in relative independence from political parties and interest groups further consolidated that elite's dominance of Brazil's policy toward South

Africa, thereby ensuring greater continuity than change.[18] Having decided to concentrate on economic development, Brazil's military leaders viewed foreign policy as instrumental in achieving that overall objective. Therefore, economic considerations assumed a predominant role in determining the nature of Brazil's foreign relations, especially during the period of rapid industrialization, which began in 1966. Prior to 1966 Brazil had pursued a policy of import substitution. High tariffs were imposed to exclude foreign goods from domestic markets. But the high cost of capital and the advanced technology required to achieve this policy's objectives grew too burdensome for the domestic market. The immediate result was decreased economic growth, a development that was detrimental to the continuation of what had become known as the Brazilian economic miracle. Relatively small industrial plants were often inefficient and poor investment planning led to building ahead of demand, thus creating excess capacity.[19]

Acquiring external markets was seen as essential for Brazil's realization of benefits generally emanating from economies of scale. Internal markets were too small to permit factories to operate efficiently. Rapid expansion of exports of nontraditional primary products as well as manufactured goods became a principal objective of the military regimes. Manufactured exports grew by roughly 38 percent between 1966 and 1973, thereby making Brazil's growth rate the fourth highest in the world. It was surpassed only by South Korea (50 percent), Taiwan (47 percent), and Singapore (42 percent). Brazil's GNP increased at an average annual rate of 10 percent, which was slightly lower than Singapore's 12.2 percent, South Korea's 10.7 percent, and Taiwan's 10.7 percent growth rate. Raw materials accounted for a decreasing portion of Brazil's exports, declining from 85 percent in 1964 to approximately 18 percent by 1978.[20] Brazil had clearly joined the ranks of the newly industrializing nations and was capable of supplying Third World states with a wide range of manufactured products. Commercial relations with the Soviet Union also expanded as Brazil attempted to diversify its economic links.

Because industrial growth depended on large infusions of foreign capital, Brazil's indebtedness grew from around $3.5 billion in 1965 to roughly $100 billion twenty years later. Exports had contributed to both rising incomes and employment, factors that ultimately stimulated domestic demand for many products that were originally intended for export. Furthermore, imports of raw materials needed for expanding industries grew, thereby draining off some of the country's foreign exchange reserves and worsening its balance of payments situation. What clearly exacerbated Brazil's economic problems was the quadrupling of petroleum prices in

1974 and additional increases in 1979. While the overvalued cruzeiro made Brazil's exports more expensive and less competitive abroad, oil price increases significantly compounded its debt problem. Government policies also contributed to the country's economic quagmire. In fact, government policies were principal causes of the more obvious debt problem. Brasília's decision to borrow heavily when interest rates were extremely high (around 18 percent in the early 1980s) to fund large-scale projects such as hydroelectric dams, iron mines, steel mills, and sugar cane production for alcohol to replace gasoline dealt a severe blow to the economy. The expansion of inefficient state-owned enterprises was manipulated politically, either to favor some private sector activity or in attempts to disguise inflation.[21] By 1987 Brazil had decided to suspend interest payments on its medium and long-term debt with its major creditors—U.S., Western European, and Japanese banks. Since these banks had loaned Brazil about $68 billion, that country's economic difficulties worried not only the banks themselves but also their home states.

When Fernando Collor de Mello was elected president of Brazil in December 1989 he attempted to address the problems of the 1980s. During that "lost decade," per capita income stagnated, inflation exceeded all previous records—reaching a high of 1,765 percent in 1989—and investment declined precipitously. President Collor's objectives included: (1) cutting the country's inflation rate by reducing prevalent tax evasion, eliminating half the number of ministries, and selling inefficient state companies; (2) reducing Brazil's $110 billion foreign debt by encouraging foreign creditors to exchange their debt titles for shares in Brazilian companies and to negotiate debt service payments to around $5 billion annually; and (3) restoring economic growth by making the country more attractive to foreign investments, lowering government-imposed trade barriers, and promoting greater economic integration with the Third World.[22]

Like much of sub-Saharan Africa, Brazil was apprehensive about the implications of political and economic developments in Eastern Europe for its own rejuvenation. Moreover, companies from the Pacific rim nations were making significant inroads into Brazil's foreign markets. Likewise, South Africa, following important reforms in 1990 and 1991, was increasingly perceived by Brazil as a formidable competitor in Africa, particularly in Angola and Mozambique. Believing that many of Brazil's economic problems could be alleviated if it became self-sufficient in petroleum, President Collor increased gasoline prices and encouraged Petrobrás, the state-owned oil company, to continue exploration in the

Amazon region and elsewhere. Important oil discoveries in the Amazon and off the country's southeast Atlantic coast in the early 1990s helped to reduce the oil import bill, which had climbed by approximately 14 percent prior to Operation Desert Storm. In addition to Brazil's expanding oil reserves, estimated to be 3.6 billion barrels in 1991, there were discoveries of significant gas fields. It was calculated that recoverable volumes of newly discovered gas totaled 60 billion cubic meters, enough to supply Brazil's gas needs for twenty years at 1991 consumption rates.[23]

While Brazil's preoccupation with economic development clearly influenced its foreign policy in general and its pragmatic approach to South Africa in particular, the country's relative lack of anti-apartheid fervor may have been influenced by its own serious economic and political inequalities. Brazil, which had the world's eighth largest economy in 1986, had one of the most unequal income distributions in the world. The highest 20 percent of Brazilian households received more than 60 percent of total household income.[24] More than half of the nation's population lived in households with incomes of $120 a month. Poverty was most pervasive in northeastern Brazil, where most of the country's black population lived. In that region there were 130 deaths for every 1,000 registered live births. Only one-fifth of the 35 million children had access to public education. Brazil fell into the same category as the less developed African and Asian countries when it came to social welfare indices.[25] Demands for greater social equality were virtually ignored and advocates of the poor were repressed under the military regimes. But since Brazilian elites continued to exercise power under democratic governments as they did under military rule, Brazil's transition to democracy in the mid-1980s did not alter the poor's plight. Indeed, the country's deteriorating economic conditions guaranteed that poverty would increase. Thus, similar to South Africa or India, Brazil was confronted with almost insurmountable socioeconomic problems. And the burden of poverty weighed heaviest on Brazil's black and Indian population, just as it did on South Africa's black and colored groups.

Compared to South Africa and the United States, Brazil managed to achieve a remarkable degree of racial harmony. By emphasizing class differences instead of creating a society that was rigidly stratified racially, Brazil avoided violent confrontations that have characterized race relations in the United States and South Africa. To a considerable extent, Brazil's foreign policy was a reflection of its more flexible racial attitudes. Other countries generally regarded Brazil as a model of racial tolerance. Brazilian whites, who had comprised approximately 38 percent of the population in 1870, controlled the society without resorting to legislative measures. As was the case in Angola, Portuguese settlers and African slaves produced racially mixed children, many of whom were accepted into the white community. They also served as a buffer between blacks and whites, thereby diminishing the chances of overt conflicts between the latter groups.[26]

Perceiving itself as a paragon of racial democracy, Brazil eschewed legalized racial prejudice and discrimination, a stance that enhanced its image in international affairs. As early as 1951 Brazil made racial discrimination a crime that was excluded from bail. According to Jose Augusto Lindgren Alves, Brazil's UN representative, such legislation was the natural juridical reflection of the very characteristics of a society that was conscious and proud of the different races and cultures which contributed to its formation.[27] By stressing that racial and cultural mingling was the essence of Brazil, a great degree of racial harmony was achieved.

Yet the absence of racial conflict was not matched by equal economic, political, and social opportunities for all races. Whites dominated the country's economic, social, and political affairs while blacks and Indians occupied the lowest strata of Brazilian society. The general consensus was that blacks were disproportionately concentrated in unskilled jobs and that it was increasingly difficult for them to improve their socioeconomic status.[28] Perceptions of race were closely connected to social class, with whiteness being associated with upper and middle class characteristics. Because of the more relaxed racial climate and the acceptance of the few upwardly mobile blacks into Brazil's power structure, many blacks subscribed to the prevalent view that any discrimination that existed was based not primarily on racial considerations but instead on class. However, given the overlap of race and social class, such distinctions were largely meaningless. Africans, particularly Nigerians and Angolans, consistently criticized Brazil's racial policies. They were concerned about the exclusion of blacks from political office, the military officer corps, business, and other important decision-making positions.[29]

Another factor that may have influenced Brazil's foreign policy was the widespread abuse of human rights in that country. Military restrictions on free speech and political activities were not removed until the late 1970s. Brazil's preoccupation with urban terrorism and political repression facilitated the security apparatus' persecution of students, intellectuals, journalists, and others perceived as subversive. Paramilitary and private vigilante groups, off-duty police officers, and Sao Paulo's infamous death squads assumed responsibility for eliminating persons they viewed as enemies of the state. Between 1987 and 1991 more than 7,000 homeless children were killed by death squads. The National Conference of Bishops, the Catholic Church, journalists, lawyers, and others challenged the government's human rights record. While never reaching the magnitude of human rights violations in Chile and Argentina, human rights abuses in Brazil clearly demonstrated the government's failure to be politically accountable and responsive to public demands for the protection of the individual's fundamental rights.[30] Despite democracy's advent, torture and ill treatment of criminal suspects and prisoners, so prevalent under the military regimes, continued virtually unabated.

Similarly, Brazil's indigenous population were frequently victims of the country's economic expansion and individuals' greed. Deteriorating economic conditions and a rapidly growing population prompted private groups and the government to more aggressively exploit the country's natural resources. But progress for the ranchers, miners, and logging companies was tantamount to the destruction of various Indian groups' way of life. Indigenous people suffered violent attacks by those who claimed their property. In the Territory of Roraima, for example, the Yanomami ethnic group was violently attacked by armed gold prospectors. And the government seemed indifferent to their plight. Little progress was made in the investigations of the deaths of about twenty-five Yanomami Indians in 1987 and 1988. However, in late 1991 Collor demarcated a 36,000 square mile area as a homeland for the Yanomamis.[31] Given Brazil's own human rights record and its policy of separating economic interests from political considerations in its relations with other countries, its failure to do more than issue anti-apartheid declarations was consistent with its domestic realities and its overall pragmatic approach to foreign affairs.

Characterized by flexibility, deftness, and commitment to national interests, Brazil's South African policy was influenced by economic imperatives, by Brazil's self-perception as a racial democracy in which diverse cultures harmoniously blended, and by its efforts to improve political and commercial relations with sub-Saharan Africa. Although Brazil's foreign minister Saraiva Guerreiro argued that his country's relations with South Africa were determined by apartheid and not by Pretoria's links with other African countries, Itamaraty was nonetheless cognizant of how developments in southern Africa could moderate relations between Brasília and Pretoria.[32] While not allowing political factors to affect its small but important trade with South Africa, Brazil also avoided actions that would antagonize sub-Saharan Africa, especially Nigeria. Thus, like Zambia, Zimbabwe, and many other countries, Brazil condemned apartheid but maintained its economic ties.

Brazil's acceptance of its African heritage, its desire to increase its markets, its determination to pursue a more independent foreign policy, the emergence of newly independent African states, and growing Third World nationalism and confrontation with the former colonial powers influenced Itamaraty to move closer to Africa in the late 1950s and early 1960s. Supported by intellectuals and lower class Brazilians, who had played a pivotal role in his election, President Jânio Quadros stressed the importance of identifying Brazil with developing countries' aspirations for independence. Concerned that Brazil had been relegated to an obscure position in the international economic and political system, Quadros wanted his country to be more assertive in foreign affairs. He focused on Africa, Asia, and the communist bloc—in addition to traditional partners such as the United States, Western Europe, Latin America, and Canada.

Stressing that Brazil was linked to Africa by its ethnic and cultural roots, Quadros departed from traditional Brazilian foreign policy by emphasizing the African dimension of the country's foreign relations. Writing in *Foreign Affairs*, Quadros stated that:

It is precisely in Africa that Brazil can render the best service to the concepts of Western life and political methods. Our country should become the link, the bridges between Africa and the West, since we are so intimately bound by both peoples. In so far as we can give the nations of the Black continent an example of complete absence of racial prejudice, together with successful proof of progress without undermining the principles of freedom, we shall be decisively contributing to the effective integration of an entire continent in a system to which we are attached by our philosophy and historic tradition.[33]

Apart from political and social considerations, Quadros accentuated economic and technological components of Brazil's relations with Africa. Improving Africans' living standards was perceived as inextricably intertwined with Brazil's own economic well-being. Apartheid was undesirable not only because it was morally repugnant but also because it threatened Brazil's economic objectives. From Quadros' viewpoint, the exploitation of Africans by European capital was detrimental to Brazil's economy because inhumane practices gave South Africa and other countries operating there unfair advantages in international markets. In other words, unfair competition, based in part on paying low salaries to black workers, was facilitated by apartheid's existence. Therefore, apartheid ultimately threatened Brazil's democratic government. In light of rapid population growth and increasing demands by the middle class for improved government services and consumer items, democracy's existence depended on the country's ability to expand its export markets. Thus economic competitiveness outweighed ideological considerations in Brazil's policy toward South Africa. As Quadros put it, "material interests know no doctrine."³⁴

But Brazil's shift toward sub-Saharan Africa, despite the fact that it did not alter the country's relations with South Africa, clearly worried the military, conservative elites, the "Americanists" in Itamaraty, the large Portuguese immigrant organizations, and many white cosmopolitans who strongly identified with Western Europe and the United States. If Quadros believed that by adopting an anticolonial position and by stressing Brazil's African heritage he would bolster Brazil's prestige internationally, most Brazilians did not share his view. Although Quadros, under pressure from Portugal, had refused to support UN resolutions condemning Portuguese control of Angola and Mozambique, his rhetorical support for African nationalism angered many Brazilians who equated the struggle for independence with communism.

Nevertheless, following Quadros' presidency, which lasted less than a year, his successor João Goulart (1961–64) continued to identify Brazil with Africa's emerging states. Brazil cast its first UN vote against Portugal in 1962 on a resolution supporting Angola's right to self-determination. However, military officials, regarding the demise of Portuguese colonial rule as remote and perceiving Brazil's new orientation as supplanting close relations with Washington, launched a successful coup on April 1, 1964. The new president, Hamerto Branco, renewed the country's political alignments with the West and its support for Portugal's policies in Angola, Mozambique, and Guinea-Bissau. Yet he maintained the commercial component of his predecessors' African policy.³⁵ Simultaneously, Brazil's political links with South Africa were consolidated, even as apartheid was strongly condemned.

As Portugal's colonial wars escalated amid political turmoil in Portugal itself, Brazil's military regime gradually recognized the necessity of moderating its support for minority governments in southern Africa. Pragmatically inclined and committed to Brazil's elevation of economic interests above all others, the military rulers were cognizant of their nation's vulnerability to any termination of petroleum supplies. OPEC's embargo against the West, the concomitant quadrupling of oil prices, and the Africans' new alliance with the Arabs against Israel, South Africa, and Portugal underlined Brazil's susceptibility to external pressures and concentrated its leaders' minds on the need to adjust their foreign policy toward Africa in general and southern Africa specifically. Consequently, the initial policy of consistently backing Portuguese colonialism shifted adroitly to one of attempting to mediate between Portugal and the various liberation movements in Angola and Mozambique to achieve a negotiated settlement of the colonial wars. Brazil's proposed solution was to grant Portugal's colonies independence within a larger Afro-Portuguese-Brazilian community. Brazil would use its multiracial experiences to improve race relations.[36]

With Nigeria's power on the ascendancy—due to its huge petroleum reserves and its OPEC membership—and Portugal's political system disintegrating, Brazil responded to the imminent collapse of Portugal's colonial rule by publicly condemning Portugal's policies. In a joint declaration with Nigeria, Brazil supported the African states' right to self-determination and repudiated apartheid, colonialism, and all forms of discrimination. While Brazil's declaratory policies had little impact on its substantive interests in South Africa, its stance resulted in promises of cooperation with the Nigerian National Oil Company as well as the opening up of greater commercial opportunities in western Africa for Brazilian subsidiaries of foreign transnational corporations and Brazilian firms.[37] Affirming its policy shift, on November 10, 1975—the day before Angola's formal independence was announced—Brazil declared its intention to recognize the Popular Movement for the Liberation of Angola (MPLA) and promised noninterference in Angola's internal affairs. Although Brazil's new policy was clearly inconsistent with South Africa's opposition to the MPLA and its military support for the MPLA's rival, the National Union for the Total Independence of Angola (UNITA), Brazil's early recognition of the MPLA, sooner than any other Western country, was not aimed against South Africa but was instead part of a pragmatic policy that safeguarded Brazil's economic interests.

Yet Brazil's stronger identification with sub-Saharan Africa and its transition from authoritarianism to democracy in 1985 culminated in a modification in its political relations with South Africa. Responding to developments in South Africa and to an assertive international anti-apartheid movement, Brazil's new civilian president, José Sarney, scaled down diplomatic relations with Pretoria. While South Africa maintained an embassy with an ambassador in Brasília and consular posts in Rio de Janeiro and São Paulo, Brazil reduced its diplomatic representation in South Africa to a charge d'affairs in Pretoria. Brazil's foreign minister Abreu Sodre eschewed completely severing diplomatic ties with Pretoria. He believed that even a second-level mission enabled Brazil to directly observe the South African situation and to communicate with local opposition groups.[38] However, there was no evidence to suggest that Brazil was actively engaged with anti-apartheid forces in South Africa or elsewhere. Nevertheless, Brazil's strong condemnation of South Africa's destabilization policies in southern Africa, its criticism of U.S. military assistance to UNITA, its view that Cuban troops were legitimately operating in Angola because they were invited by the government, and reports that Brasília had volunteered to send its own troops to fight UNITA and its South African ally enhanced Brazil's position in sub-Saharan Africa.[39] An indication of Brazil's credibility in Africa was that it was the only Latin American country that was invited to Zimbabwe's independence ceremonies in 1980.

By consistently defending Angola's sovereignty, Brazil strengthened its political role in southern Africa. When the U.S.–brokered negotiations between Angola and South Africa resulted in an agreement to end hostilities, Brazil praised the development and expressed its hope for regional peace as well as for Namibia's independence. Similarly, when American diplomatic efforts led to the signing of accords that provided for the withdrawal of all Cuban troops from Angola by mid-1991 and Namibia's independence from South Africa in early 1990, Brazil was selected to head an international commission composed of Norway, Spain, India, the Congo, and Yugoslavia to verify compliance with the peace accords.[40]

Whereas Brazil adopted an anti-apartheid stance on political issues, it carefully protected its commercial interests in South Africa and in sub-Saharan Africa. Within Africa, Brazil initially had two trading partners, South Africa and Morocco, which accounted for more than half of its exports to that continent.[41] But trade between South Africa and Brazil has always been relatively minor. However, given Brazil's massive foreign debt problem and its preoccupation with economic expansion on one hand and South Africa's need for external markets both for economic and political reasons on the other, commercial ties between them were not insignificant. Yet their economic similarities seemed more conducive to competitive than to cooperative trade relations.

Both countries dominated their respective continents in terms of economic productivity, industrialization, market size, and economic prosperity. They also contained populations whose extreme poverty tarnished their image as newly industrializing states. This also meant that their internal markets were still largely underdeveloped, thus reducing their need to export, especially when compared to Taiwan. Furthermore, opportunities for regional expansion were abundant. South Africa's neighbors, confronted with what appeared to be insurmountable economic and political problems, provided markets for its manufactured products. Brazil's Amazon region, larger than the Indian subcontinent, was sparsely populated and virtually unexplored. Containing gold, hardwood trees, sizable deposits of bauxite, manganese, nickel, copper, and tin as well as diamonds, the Amazon was the country's new frontier. Yet neither South

Africa nor Brazil was completely self-sufficient in raw resources, a factor which necessitated trade. And because their domestic industries were comparatively inefficient and their markets too small to provide economies of scale, both countries had to export low-level manufactured products to the Third World. Therefore, African markets became important to Brazil and South Africa, a reality that engendered competition between them.

Furthermore, there were few historical links between Brazil and South Africa. While the former enjoyed close relationships with Portugal and its African colonies, the latter was historically closely connected to Britain, Germany, and the various southern African states, including Mozambique. Consequently, trade patterns tended to follow historical ties. This factor, together with underlying economic similarities between Brazil and South Africa, impeded the expansion of their commercial relationship. Despite South Africa's attempts to encourage exports to Latin America in general, the business community seemed reluctant to respond. Though relatively close geographically, there were few transportation links between Latin America and South Africa. Moreover, financial services essential to promote trade were severely limited. To improve the investment climate for entrepreneurs, the South Africa Reserve Bank purchased bonds issued by the Inter-American Development Bank (IDB) in late 1968. By so doing, South African contractors and exporters could participate in development projects funded by the IDB. However, private businesses did not cooperate with the government's export program.[42] Instead, they continued trade with industrialized countries and Africa. Brazil also focused on Africa as an outlet for its manufactured and agricultural products. Nonetheless, both Brazil and South Africa maintained their limited but important economic ties. The closure of Brazil's Office for Trade Promotion at the embassy in Pretoria in 1978 did not adversely affect trade.

South Africa's exports to Brazil grew steadily from 1966 to 1980, declined sharply in 1980, but increased gradually until limited sanctions were imposed by Brazil in 1985. In 1966 South African exports amounted to $0.36 million. That figure increased to $9.0 million in 1973; $15.90 million in 1975; and $130 million in 1980. By 1981, however, the value of South Africa's exports to Brazil had declined to $70 million, reflecting not only Brazil's burgeoning foreign debt—which dampened demand for imports in general—but also the country's self-sufficiency in phosphoric acid, the principal South African export. From 1983 through 1985, exports hovered around $22 million. Although international sanctions helped to diminish South Africa's exports to its major trading partners between 1986 and 1988, Brazil's imports from South Africa rose to $60 million in 1986, and to $71 million in 1987. Preliminary trade figures for 1988 indicated a continuation of this trend.[43]

Brazil enjoyed a trade surplus with South Africa from the beginning—a major disincentive for severing economic links with Pretoria. Brazil's exports grew steadily from 1966 to 1983, but dropped for the period from 1984 to 1986. The value of exports stood at $8.66 million in 1966; $12.20 million in 1970; $22 million in 1972; $31 million in 1978; $77 million in 1980; $131 million in 1981; and $148 million in 1983. During South Africa's economic downturn in the mid-1980s, Brazil's exports plummeted to around $53 million in 1985. Other factors that contributed to this decline were Brazil's own economic problems, declining productivity, and increased domestic consumer demand for products that were usually exported. By 1987, however, as both economies showed signs of recovery, Brazil's exports had increased to roughly $90 million, which resulted in a trade balance of $19 million in Brazil's favor.[44]

Trade between Brazil and South Africa consisted primarily of raw resources and some manufactured products. South Africa's exports included phosphoric acid, fertilizers, uranium, steel, asbestos, glass, nickel, copper, iron, newsprint, zircon, chromite, combed wool threads, synthetic paraffin, corn, agricultural seeds, plastic pens, and bags. Leading Brazilian exports were soy meal, organic chemical products, shelled corn, cocoa butter, leaf tobacco, printing and writing paper, glazed and ornamental tiles, wood, leather, shoes, refined soya oil, chestnuts, insecticides, tractors, sewing machines, car parts, and kitchen ovens. While Brazil's economic relations with South Africa were important, they were relatively minor when compared to its trade with the rest of Africa. Partly due to Brasilia's decision to downplay trade with South Africa, while simultaneously making a concerted effort to find new markets elsewhere on the continent, by 1978 its trade with the other African countries had reached more than $1 billion.[45]

Commercial ties between Brazil and South Africa were accompanied by growing South African investments in Brazil's mining industries. South African mining companies, particularly Anglo-American Corporation, had considerable expertise, capital, and influence in precious metals markets. Even South Africa's most vociferous African critics recognized that cooperation with Anglo-American was a necessary, if painful, compromise. Unwilling to confront obvious contradictions in their own South African policies, they refrained from drawing attention to South African investments in Brazil. Since it was clearly in Brazil's interest to maintain a low profile in its economic dealings with Pretoria, Brasilia quietly allowed South African companies to invest in the country.

By 1973 Anglo-American Corporation had established a subsidiary called Anglo-America do Brasil (Ambras) and had created two firms in partnership with Industria e Commercio Mineiros SA of Brazil and Bethlehem Steel of the United States to explore for precious as well as base metals in Brazil. Ambras expanded its holdings by purchasing a 49 percent share of the Morro Velho gold mining group, 40 percent of Unigeo (another gold mining company), and 30 percent of Brases, an explosives firm.[46] These acquistions made Anglo-American the largest foreign holder of prospecting rights. Only two state-owned enterprises had more dominant positions in Brazil's mining industry. Following the common practice employed by transnational corporations to disguise their holdings, increase their leverage vis-à-vis governments, and reduce their tax burdens, Anglo-American registered Ambras' holding companies in Panama, Bermuda, and Liberia, thereby shedding its subsidiary's South African affiliation. This decision also permitted Brazil to claim, if necessary, that there were no South African investments in the country. Likewise, the South African government could deny participating in Brazil's mining sector. Indeed, Donald Klopper, the South African mining attaché in Rio de Janeiro, stated that Pretoria would not become directly involved in any mining project.[47]

However, as the Brazilian government encouraged gold prospecting, South Africa's role expanded. Two South African firms, General Mining Company and Goldfields, joined Anglo-American in Brazil. Furthermore, private Brazilian gold prospectors deepened South Africans' involvement in the industry by requesting their assistance. About 80 percent of Brazil's gold was produced by local prospectors, many of whom were illiterate and had little technical knowledge. More than 2,000 mines in the Amazon forests resulted in severe pollution of surrounding streams and rivers. Tributaries of the Amazon River were highly contaminated with mercury used by miners to separate gold from other deposits. This process not only polluted the environment but was also very inefficient; almost half the gold was lost. To modernize their production techniques and simultaneously reduce pollution, prospectors invited a team of South African gold mining specialists to Brazil on a fact-finding tour. Because the Brazilian government had made gold mining a national priority, this development also had political connotations. Pretoria, cognizant of the political and economic implications of assisting Brasília, sponsored several visits by leading Brazilian gold prospectors to South Africa. However, as South Africa's ambassador to Brazil, Alex van Zyl, put it, the Brazilians wanted to "keep things low-key, and we try to keep a low profile."[48]

If relations between Pretoria and Brasília were generally cool, that was partly because the latter had developed close trade and political links with sub-Saharan Africa that it did not want to jeopardize by overly and unnecessarily embracing the white minority regime. Clearly worried by the deleterious effects of the sudden and unprecedented oil price increases following OPEC's oil embargo for Brazil's economy, the country's new leader and former head of Petrobrás, General Ernesto Geisel, decided to improve economic relations with Angola, Nigeria, Mozambique, and other African states in an attempt to safeguard his nation's access to oil supplies. Geisel offered financial and technical assistance to Angola and Mozambique, and Petrobrás became involved in oil exploration and production in Angola. Brazil also wanted to export more of its manufactured products to Africa. While there was no evidence that clearly linked these developments to Brazil's policy of politically distancing itself from South Africa, Itamaraty was certainly aware of the growing importance of Brazil's Third World markets as well as sub-Saharan African views on apartheid.

During the period from 1966 to 1969 South Africa went from being Brazil's main African market to its fifth largest, having been surpassed by Nigeria, Angola, Algeria, and Zaire. But trade between Brazil and South Africa had also grown during that period. In promoting commerce with Africa, Brazilian officials downplayed economic relations with South Africa and emphasized their nation's historical and cultural affinity with Africa, the exemplary nature of Brazilian race relations (contrasted to apartheid), Brazil's expertise in appropriate tropicalized technology, the suitability of its exports for African countries, and the relatively advantageous financial arrangements that Brazil could offer its African customers.[49] As part of the effort to improve economic relations, Brazil's foreign minister Gibson Barbosa visited several African states in 1972. In November 1983 President João Fegueredo, the first Brazilian president to visit Africa, spent ten days in Nigeria, Guinea Bissau, Senegal, Cape Verde Islands, and Algeria.

Brazil established strong commercial ties with many African countries and sold a variety of products. These included automobiles, ceramics, shoes, meats, and agricultural products. Brazilian experts were involved in road construction in Mauritania, in soybean cultivation in Ivory Coast, and in building tile and brick factories in Ghana. Nigeria and Angola were particularly important because of their petroleum resources and large markets, and because of Brazil's desire to increase sales to oil-producing states with which it had large trade deficits.

Due to the production of similar agricultural products in Africa and Brazil, 88 percent of Africa's purchases from Brazil were manufactured and semimanufactured goods. Manufactured products accounted for 99 percent of Nigeria's purchases in 1981 when its economy was rapidly expanding.[50] Volkswagen do Brazil depended on Africa, primarily Nigeria, for about a third of its foreign trade. Autoparts from Brazil were used in the Volkswagen assembly plant in Nigeria—a joint venture between Volkswagen of West Germany and the federal government of Nigeria—as well as in Mercedes and Scania heavy vehicle assembly plants. Nigeria also imported iron rods and bars, hardboard, plywood, glass, ceramics, wood and aluminum door and window frames, asbestos sheets and cement, tractors, equipment for sausage making and cassava processing, cold storage plants, milling and meat-processing machines, and other food-processing equipment. Under civil engineering contracts with Brazil, Nigeria imported a wide range of construction machinery: road rollers, graders, earth moving and asphalting equipment, concrete pipe-making equipment, and brick and tile-making machinery. Brazil also exported frozen meat and chicken, rice, soy oil, sugar, tea, tomato paste, animal feed, and corned beef as well as consumer products—air conditioners, refrigerators, freezers, footwear, sewing machines, bicycles, furniture, laboratory instruments, and petroleum products. Brazil, the sixth largest arms exporter, agreed in 1984 to sell Nigeria its Tucano trainer aircraft, a development that demonstrated growing military cooperation between the two states.[51] By 1981 Nigeria had become Brazil's second largest trading partner. The United States remained its most important market.

Most significant for both Brazil and Nigeria, given their dependence on oil imports and exports respectively, several arrangements were made relating to petroleum. Petrobrás, the Nigerian government, and Cotia Comercio Exportacao—the trading company that dominated Brazilian trade with Nigeria—concluded an agreement in 1984 that allowed Nigeria to supply Petrobrás with $500 million worth of oil annually. The payment, which was deposited in an escrow account with the United Bank for Africa in New York, could only be used by Nigeria to purchase Brazilian products. This form of barter characterized Brazil's commercial relations with many developing countries.

Brazil's Portuguese and African heritage was instrumental in creating strong bonds with Angola. Linguistic and cultural links facilitated close cooperation in several areas. Brazilian teachers, researchers, administrators, technicians, and other experts played a major role in Angola's educational system. The Brazilian government supplied books, records, films, and related teaching materials. Brazilian management specialists worked with state-owned people's stores, and Brasília provided food aid to Angola. Between 1975 and 1979 trade between the two countries escalated from $4 million to $400 million.[52] Petrobrás and the Angolan government participated in joint ventures, and Brazil was a major importer of Angolan oil. As it did in Nigeria, Petrobrás worked out barter arrangements with the Angolan state oil company, Sonangol. When Cuban troops began their withdrawal from Angola in 1988, the Angolan government agreed to purchase Brazilian trucks and jeeps for military use. The Brazilian firm, Engesa, built a truck assembly plant in Angola that used Brazilian components. The company also wanted to modify Soviet-made trucks to improve their reliability and fuel efficiency.[53]

Both Nigeria and Brazil were forced to adopt austerity measures to protect their economies from world recession. Nigeria saw the price of oil plummet from around $38 a barrel to under $10 a barrel in less than two years. In an effort to cut imports by around 33 percent, ambitious projects were delayed, luxury car imports were prohibited, and tariffs were increased on imports such as Brazilian refrigerators. The sharpest decline was in Brazilian exports to Angola, approximately 57 percent.[54] Financial difficulties in Angola, caused partly by a war between South African–backed UNITA guerrillas and the Angolan government, led to the cancellation of the Kapanda hydroelectric project. Brazil's demand for Angolan and Nigerian oil diminished as offshore oil discoveries were made in Brazil and its own huge gas reserves were more fully exploited. Furthermore, greater use of alternative fuels and improved conservation also contributed to a decline in petroleum imports. Brazil's imports plunged from a high of $23 billion in 1980 to less than $14 billion in 1984.[55]

Despite a trade surplus of $6 billion in 1983, Brazil offered exporters incentives in order to achieve a surplus of around $20 billion by 1990. To stimulate foreign sales, it devalued the cruzeiro by 30 percent in relation to the U.S. dollar, earmarked $4.5 billion for export credit through its Export Finance program, and implemented a special Program of Fiscal Benefits for Exports. Under this scheme companies were given an export target ($35.6 million worth of exports between 1983 and 1991) in exchange for rights to import duty-free inputs and parts for their plants.[56] The enterprises most interested in this program, principally automobile manufacturers, were looking for markets in Africa.

Brazil's economic relations with sub-Saharan Africa, among other factors, influenced its leaders to eschew military contacts with South Africa. Brasília refused to participate in a proposed South Atlantic Treaty Organization (SATO) that was strongly favored by Pretoria as well as by the Reagan administration. South Africa's persistent promotion of SATO reflected its desire to portray itself as the protector of Western interests in the South Atlantic and southern Africa from the dangers of Soviet-Cuban expansion. While Brazil shared South Africa's aversion to communism, it had divergent perceptions of the nature of the Cuban-Soviet threat. Equally important, Brazil believed that an integral component of Pretoria's defense strategy against what it regarded as the "total onslaught" was to attempt to utilize SATO to gain allies as well as respectability in the West, to diminish the country's growing isolation, and to defuse the widespread antipathy of apartheid.[57] But Brazil's relations with Angola, Nigeria, and other African countries as well as its desire to project an image of itself as a model of racial harmony and multiculturalism undoubtedly militated against its involvement in any alliance with South Africa, despite Brasília's own concerns about South Atlantic security issues.

Domestic politics also influenced Brazil's decision. The primary advocates of a SATO were naval officers. However, under military rule, naval chiefs were checked by the president who was either an active or retired member of the army. The army, which dominated the military, was more preoccupied with internal security than with foreign threats. Therefore, Brazil's presidents were unwilling, and perhaps unable, to increase the navy's power. Such a development would have weakened their position and harmed their supporters' interests. Furthermore, economic constraints shifted the nation's attention away from expanding the navy to industrialization and other economic issues. Finally, many Brazilian leaders believed that SATO's existence would have contributed to militarizing the South Atlantic and engendering the escalation of superpower rivalry. Ultimately, the alliance with South Africa would have inadvertently eroded the region's security, which many felt was adequately safeguarded by the Rio Treaty. Brazil's pragmatic approach to South Africa was further demonstrated by its choice of strategies for effectuating change in Pretoria. Brazil employed foreign policy instruments vis-à-vis Pretoria that were very similar to those preferred by the United States and Western Europe, countries with considerable trade and investment ties with South Africa. Apart from Brazil's tendency to follow the United States' lead in foreign affairs, the legalistic nature of Brazil's foreign service establishment precluded the adoption of comparatively strong measures to influence Pretoria to abolish its apartheid system.

Unlike India, which initiated anti-apartheid resolutions on behalf of South Africa's Indian community, Brazil perceived racial discrimination as primarily an internal matter. Thus any attempt to ameliorate conditions for oppressed South Africans was regarded as excessive interference in a sovereign country's affairs. When India introduced resolutions in the UN that appeared to abrogate South Africa's sovereignty, Brazil mobilized Latin American states to defeat them. Moreover, Brazil's foreign minister

Oswaldo Aranha, in his capacity as president of the UN General Assembly session in 1947, blocked India's modified resolutions. Although Brazil denounced apartheid and emphasized the multiracial harmony that arguably characterized its own society, it voted against concrete measures that might have hastened apartheid's demise.[58] But, also relying on legal principles, Brazil opposed South Africa's control of Namibia and strongly supported UN resolutions that upheld UN authority over Namibia.

Instead of the punitive anti-apartheid sanctions advocated by the Afro-Asian group of states, Brazil favored measures that would later be euphemistically called "constructive engagement" by the Reagan administration. While declaring its opposition to apartheid, Brazil argued that isolating South Africa would be counterproductive. Especially prior to radical political changes in southern Africa and escalating oil prices in the mid-1970s, Brazil's military rulers and Itamaraty believed that reforms in South Africa could be encouraged through commercial relations, communication with the white minority regime, and the creation of an anti-apartheid world public opinion through education. Yet when South Africa's prime minister John Vorster suggested upgrading relations between the two countries, Brazil declined the offer.[59] This seemingly contradictory stance of advocating communication with Pretoria while simultaneously downgrading formal diplomatic relations with it was observable in other aspects of Brazil's relations with South Africa.

Having organized the UN Human Rights Seminar on Apartheid and after agreeing to host it in Brasília, Brazil arranged for South Africa's foreign minister Hildgard Muller and its minister of Economic Affairs H. Kotzemberg to visit the country in 1966 for trade discussions two months prior to the seminar. Though economic links with South Africa were consistent with Brazil's general policy of not allowing political factors to influence trade, it had recently voted for a UN resolution that discouraged states from establishing closer business links with South Africa.[60] Similarly, while publicly advocating greater international opposition to apartheid, Brazil's military leaders attempted to eliminate all dissent, including anti-apartheid activities, within the country. It was not until after Brazil's transition to democracy in 1985 that the Brazilian Committee on Solidarity with South Africa and Namibia was established and allowed to launch information campaigns against apartheid.[61]

Similar to many countries, Brazil opposed sanctions on the grounds that it was illusory to expect South Africa's major trading partners to deprive themselves of strategic mineral supplies by severing economic links with Pretoria. As if to underscore their country's commitment to free trade and its disapproval of using economic sanctions as foreign policy instruments, the military leaders ignored a request by the UN's Special Committee on the Policies of Apartheid to cancel weekly flights by South African Airways and Varig, the Brazilian airline, between Johannesburg and Rio de Janeiro. In early 1969, Brazil sent a high level delegation, which included the minister of Commerce and Industry Edmundo Macedo and the minister of Planning Helio Beltrao, on Varig's inaugural flight to South Africa.[62] Varig also scheduled regular flights to Lagos and Dakar. However, due partly to Third World pressure, Varig stopped flying to South Africa in 1979.

Beginning in 1975 there was increased African pressure on Brazil to implement its strong anti-apartheid declarations. Nevertheless, apart from supporting the ban on military sales to South Africa, Brazil remained reluctant to adopt policies that would adversely affect the nonpolitical aspects of its policy toward Pretoria. In 1977 Itamaraty officially recognized and celebrated the Anti-Apartheid Day in March. But on substantive issues such as sporting contacts with South Africa, Brasília remained apprehensive. Eventually it decided to terminate sports and cultural exchanges with the minority regime. Although transfers of military weapons were prohibited by the government, Itamaraty defended the sale of light arms, hunting guns and ammunition, and small caliber revolvers, contending that such sales did not violate the UN Security Council arms embargo.[63]

Mounting international pressures against apartheid, South Africa's declaration of a State of Emergency in 1985, modifications in Western policies toward Pretoria in response to domestic as well as international anti-apartheid activities, and Brazil's democratization influenced Brasília to change its stance on sanctions. On August 9, 1985 Brazil's president José Sarney signed a decree that prohibited cultural and sports exchanges, exports of oil and petroleum products, and arms sales and related materials.[64] These particular actions, however, were symbolic because they were already in effect. But the decree also marked an unprecedented step away from previous policy: it banned commercial relations with Pretoria that were contrary to UN resolutions. While modest compared to standards adopted by the Scandinavian countries, Canada, and the United States, this step was significant within the Brazilian context. Until that time the government had only advised private firms that did business with South Africa to discontinue trade relations. The companies themselves had been responsible for the final decision in compliance with the government's recommendation. Equally important, the decree explicitly stated that apartheid contradicted Brazil's democratic principles and racial coexistence.

Yet Brazil's actions and strong condemnations of apartheid did not radically alter its modest economic relations with South Africa. Government regulations did not prohibit imports of South Africa's agricultural products, uranium, coal, or products of parastatals. Furthermore, Brazil allowed computer and software products to be sold to Pretoria, despite widespread international concern that computers were essential to apartheid's elaborate surveillance practices. But the presence of Taiwanese computer companies in South Africa and Taipei's refusal to implement sanctions against Pretoria vitiated arguments against Brazil's commercial ties with South Africa.

Chapter 5

The Middle East: The Arab States, Iran, and the PLO

Geographically and culturally remote from southern Africa's turbulence, Middle Eastern states, with the exception of Israel, were largely indifferent to the harmful consequences of apartheid prior to the intensification of the Arab-Israeli conflict in the late 1960s and early 1970s. Israel's existence as a sovereign state and the Arabs' determination to destroy it served as a catalyst for the development of the Arabs' newly found interest in black South Africans. But most Middle Eastern countries were not primarily concerned with apartheid's demise or the implementation of democratic principles in South Africa; their principal objective was the restoration of Muslim and Palestinian control over Palestine. To achieve this, they attempted to enlist the support of sub-Saharan African countries, the vast majority of which viewed ending apartheid as a cardinal foreign policy goal. Growing Arab wealth and mounting sub-Saharan African economic problems, caused partly by higher oil prices charged by OPEC, engendered closer collaboration between the two regions and facilitated political exchanges and the convergence of interests.

However, Afro-Arab cooperation would have been greatly diminished had it not been for Israel's changing relations with sub-Saharan Africa following the Six Day war in 1967. Israel's occupation of Arab lands conquered during the war; its annexation of the West Bank and Gaza; its foreign policy blunders—especially in relation to its involvement in the Nigerian civil war; its broad national security concerns that emanated partly from the Arab states' refusal to recognize its right to exist; its deteriorating economic conditions; the growth of Jewish fundamentalists;

the emergence of the Likud and small conservative religious political parties in the aftermath of the 1973 war; and Israel's emerging military, political, and economic linkages with South Africa contributed to the consolidation of Arab-African ties and the simultaneous weakening of relations between Israel and sub-Saharan Africa. Changing African perceptions of Israel and growing sympathy for the Palestinians, who were widely regarded as victims of Israeli aggression following Israel's spectacular victory in 1967, were an underlying component of Africa's shift toward the Arabs.

By adopting terrorism as a strategy to dramatize their grievances and change international public opinion in their favor, the Palestinians influenced even moderate Israelis to see the terrorist activities of the Palestine Liberation Organization (PLO) within the context of the Holocaust, the tragic event that fundamentally shaped Israel's self-perception. Yet from the Africans' viewpoint, the PLO's struggle for a Palestinian state was not significantly different from their own wars of liberation from colonial domination in southern Africa. This realization created opportunities for the PLO to collaborate with southern African liberation movements. Israel's Western orientation and its close connections with Pretoria, added credence to the PLO's assertion that its struggle was similar to those of the ANC and SWAPO. While the complex problems of the Middle East conflict, more than any direct concerns about apartheid, shaped that region's policies toward South Africa, other factors also played an important role and created obvious contradictions in the Arabs' relations with Pretoria. These included sub-Saharan Africa historical experiences with the Arab world; the foreign policy-making process within various Arab states; the political aspirations of particular Arab leaders; the absence of democracy and widespread human rights abuses in virtually all the Middle Eastern countries; many Arabs' aversion to communism; close links that Saudi Arabia, the Gulf states, and Egypt had with the West; and intraregional conflicts such as the Iran-Iraq war during the 1980s.

Though many Middle Eastern states shared Africa's experience with colonialism and foreign domination to varying degrees, Africans were also aware of their own negative historical relations with the Arabs. Many black Africans were enslaved by the Arabs long before the Europeans had colonized North and South America and had inaugurated the trans-Atlantic slave trade. While slaves in the Arab world were generally integrated into society after a certain period of time and the legal category of slave was not identified with any particular race or occupation as it was in the United States, South Africa, Brazil, and throughout the Caribbean, black slaves in the Middle East were usually associated with menial roles and low status.¹ The fact that the Arabs enslaved Europeans, Africans, Asians, and even fellow Arabs distinguished them from West Europeans who concentrated on enslaving Africans. However, the majority of the male slaves in the Arab world came from sub-Saharan Africa. But unlike Europeans, Arabs were comparatively less preoccupied with race and pigmentation. Consequently, they avoided many of the serious racial problems with which many Western countries, particularly the United States and Britain, are afflicted. On the other hand, the equivalent of the American or British abolitionist movement was nonexistent in the Arab world. On the contrary, Saudi Arabia, for example, did not emancipate slaves until the 1960s, approximately a century after the United States outlawed slavery. Despite official disapproval of slavery, several Middle Eastern states continued to enslave Africans.² Numerous foreign workers in Saudi Arabia, Kuwait, and other Gulf countries were treated as slaves, even after the United States launched Operation Desert Storm in 1991 to terminate Iraqi occupation of Kuwait. Government censorship in most Arab states and the West's unwillingness to jeopardize its oil supplies by publicizing events that the Saudis and others might have found offensive diminished the possibility of having any significant discussion of allegations of slavery in the Middle East.

Arab political and religious domination of parts of sub-Saharan Africa, together with the long history of slavery, helped to shape Arabs' and Africans' perceptions and misperceptions of each other. Furthermore, negative historical memories were reinforced by what many Africans viewed as Arab cultural and racial arrogance. Despite the absence of widespread discrimination against blacks in the Arab world, there were instances of overt racism. In countries such as Senegal, black Africans, aware of the Arabs' discriminatory practices against blacks in neighboring Mauritania, underscored the underlying tension between the two groups in 1989 and 1990 by randomly attacking and killing Arab Mauritanians who had lived peacefully in Senegal for many years. Similar conflicts erupted in Zanzibar in 1964. The small Arab elite, widely resented by the black majority, was eventually attacked and many of them were killed. These problems occurred not just because of Arab discrimination and feelings of cultural superiority vis-à-vis black Africans but also because many of the latter regarded the former as untrustworthy and cunning.³ These deeply rooted attitudes undoubtedly influence contemporary political ties between Arabs and Africans. Yet the convergence of African and Arab interests moderated latent antagonisms and contributed to an uneasy African-Arab collaboration on foreign policy issues.

Preoccupied with domestic problems, security issues, and Israel's occupation of Arab lands, including East Jerusalem where the Dome of the Rock—the third holiest site in Islam after Mecca and Medina—is located, foreign policymakers in Saudi Arabia, Egypt, Iran, and the Gulf states lacked visceral feelings about apartheid. Furthermore, the process by which foreign policy was made and implemented virtually guaranteed that only those issues the ruling elites considered important would dominate the foreign policy agenda. Consequently, anti-apartheid groups, where they existed, were essentially ineffectual.

Even in countries with institutional veneers of shared power, the rulers are principally responsible for articulating external affairs. Individual leaders enjoy preponderant influence precisely because many Middle Eastern states have weak institutions that are unable to exercise countervailing powers. Lacking broadly based political legitimacy, most leaders retain control over those areas of government that are essential to their own survival and maintenance of power. In many cases, leaders rely on their personal attitudes and charisma instead of on established customs and institutional processes to buttress their political authority. Under such circumstances, a country's foreign policy is closely intertwined with its leader's personal preferences. Egypt's Gamal Nasser surrounded himself with unquestioning allies. His cabinet was therefore unlikely to openly disagree with his foreign policies. This homogeneity enabled Nasser to act independently. Successive Egyptian presidents followed the precedents Nasser established and continued to dominate the formulation of foreign and defense policies.[4]

Saudi Arabia's foreign policy was the product of consultation and consensus among leading male members of the royal family, various religious authorities, and foreign policy and defense bureaucrats. Until Iraq's invasion of Kuwait in mid-1990, Saudi officials relied on a low-key, behind-the-scenes, patient style of diplomacy and bribes to achieve their foreign policy aims. They seemed comfortable with mediating and bargaining to obtain consensus on issues that could undermine the elites' solidarity. Complex family relations and traditions inevitably militated against reaching decisions quickly. Ultimately, the techniques of consensus building, essential to both foreign and domestic policy-making, ensured the survival and continued control of the Saudi royal family. Consquently, Saudi Arabia's foreign policy behavior was characterized by indecision, delays, and a failure to follow through, especially when controversial issues had to be decided.[5]

In addition to how policies were made, other factors helped to determine the Arab countries' relations with South Africa. Egypt's, Algeria's, and

Libya's membership in the OAU imposed greater restraints on their behavior than on Saudi Arabia's; Riyadh had relatively few significant institutional connections with sub-Saharan Africa. Egypt's leadership role in both the Middle East and Africa and Nasser's view of his country as a model for Arab and African states attempting to gain their independence made Cairo more sensitive to sub-Saharan African concerns about apartheid. But Sadat's recognition of Israel and subsequent Arab efforts to isolate Egypt improved Cairo's relations with Israel and the United States on the one hand but weakened them with sub-Saharan African states on the other. Egypt's lower profile on African liberation issues stood in sharp contrast to Libya's increased interest in sponsoring international terrorism and its strong support for the ANC and the PLO. Mu'ammar Qaddafi's self-perception as Nasser's heir as far as revolutionary activities were concerned, his strong anti-Israeli and anti-American stance, and his aspirations for leadership within the Arab world as well as in the Nonaligned Movement helped to influence Libya's approach to apartheid. Saudi Arabia's role as the guardian of Islam's holy places, its concern with national security and containing the Soviet Union's activities in the Middle East, and its close military ties with the United States made its position on South Africa more complex and contradictory than that of Libya or Egypt.

Pervasive human rights violations and the lack of democratic freedoms throughout the Arab world and in Iran further diminished the various leaders' enthusiasm for racial equality in South Africa, despite declaratory policies to the contrary. Tradition-bound and inward-looking, Middle Eastern countries continued to eschew democratic values even subsequent to Operation Desert Storm and President George Bush's assertion that out of the horrible consequences of war a new "world order" had been created. State power, largely monopolized by founding families, was far more extensive and intractable in the Arab states than it was in South Africa under apartheid. Governments in Saudi Arabia, Kuwait, Iraq, and elsewhere exercised extensive economic power due to their control over employment. Chief executives were the ultimate arbitrators—almost gods—and were protected by numerous layers of secret police. They were obeyed largely out of fear or desire to secure individual advantage.[6]

But revolutionary changes in Eastern Europe, the collapse of communism, the political fragmentation and demise of the Soviet Union, war in the Gulf, and, to some extent, the abolition of the legal framework of apartheid emboldened advocates of democracy and human rights in Kuwait, Egypt, Saudi Arabia, and Jordan to demand political changes. Arab human rights groups called on governments to terminate press censorship, to stop torturing their citizens, to refrain from arbitrary arrests and unfair trials, and to end their corrupt practices and abuse of power. Kuwait, radically altered by the ravages of war, came under increased pressure from advocates of democracy—especially those who remained in the country when Iraq invaded—to institute democratic reforms. However, significant departures from the status quo were resisted by Sheik Jabar al-Ahmed al-Sabah, Kuwait's ruling emir. Nonetheless, the worldwide momentum toward the empowerment of the individual and respect for fundamental rights and freedoms rendered maintaining the status quo extremely difficult.[7] In Egypt, groups supporting democracy campaigned against government corruption, mismanagement, and police brutality, and pressured President Hosni Mubarak to call for a referendum in late 1990 to dissolve parliament and for free elections. Yet meaningful steps toward democracy remained elusive. There were more hopeful signs in Jordan: King Hussein ibn Talal legalized opposition political parties in mid-1991. Given their domestic political realities, Arab countries and Iran were not genuinely interested in restoring human rights or ending racial discrimination in South Africa.

Unlike India, whose leadership on apartheid was a direct response to pernicious discrimination against Indians living in Natal, Middle Eastern states had few tangible connections to South Africa. Apart from a small Iranian community, there were no significant groups of Middle Eastern people in South Africa. The Iranians had established relatively close ties with South Africa after it granted Reza Shah refuge in 1941 following British and Soviet occupation of Iran. Accused of collaborating with the Nazis, Reza Shah remained in South Africa until his death in 1944. Analogous to the Japanese and Taiwanese, Iranians in South Africa were regarded as "honorary" whites, a designation that indicated the extent of their identification with white South Africans. Iranians' special status also underlined South Africa's dependence on Iranian petroleum. By contrast, the majority of South African Muslims, though generally respected by whites, identified with the black majority. Originating in India and elsewhere in Asia, the Muslims were largely ignored by the Middle East. Whereas Saudi Arabia demonstrated its interest in strengthening its religious ties to the Muslim community in South Africa by creating an Islamic Development Bank, Arab countries—with the exception of Egypt, Libya, and Algeria—were indifferent to South Africa's problems. The brutality of apartheid was relevant only within the larger Arab anti-Zionist campaign.[8]

Algeria's anti-apartheid stance was a direct outgrowth of its experiences with South Africa during its war for independence from France between 1954 and 1962. Confronted with the escalating guerrilla activities of the

National Liberation Front, led by Ahmed Ben Bella, France enlisted South African support. Believing that South Africa's experiences gained from fighting the ANC and other liberation movements and from suppressing the black majority could be applied to Algeria, France invited South African officials to Algeria to share their expertise on dealing with guerrilla warfare and domestic uprisings. France's ruthless application of its military might against the Algerians—which caused the deaths of approximately 250,000 Algerians, the wounding of about half a million, and the uprooting of another 2 million—sufficiently impressed Pretoria to influence it to send a delegation to Algeria to learn from France's experiences.[9] Ultimately, however, France left Algeria. But South Africa's collaboration with France to abort Algeria's quest for self-determination left an indelible imprint on Algeria's policies toward the apartheid regime. Opposition to apartheid became an integral component of Algeria's foreign policy and was enshrined in its constitution and national charter. The latter, in particular, emphasized Algeria's commitment to "fulfill its duty to eliminate the after-effects of colonial and racial domination in Africa." Article 92 of the constitution proclaimed that the struggle against colonialism, neo-colonialism, imperialism, and racial discrimination was basic to the revolution. Algeria's solidarity with all the peoples of Africa . . . in their fight for political and economic liberation . . . was an essential part of national policy.[10] Algeria's actual policies were generally consistent with these declarations.

While Egypt shared Algeria's antipathy toward apartheid and European colonialism, its South African policies under Nasser were also influenced by the Arab-Israeli conflict. Nasser's major foreign policy objectives were to isolate Israel, which included attempts to impede its diplomatic and economic relations with the newly independent African countries, and to render political and material assistance to anticolonial movements in the Middle East and Africa. Nasser supported the anti-apartheid struggle by training members of southern African national liberation movements and by giving them military equipment. Egypt also provided educational opportunities and scholarships for many African students. This level of involvement prompted Pretoria to view Nasser as a direct threat, a suspicion that was undergirded by the strong support evinced by black nationalist movements in South Africa for Egypt during the 1956 Suez crisis. Many nationalists perceived Nasser as the standard-bearer of their emancipation from white oppression and racism.[11]

But whereas Egypt had succeeded in establishing strong political links with sub-Saharan Africa in general and the liberation movements in Rhodesia (Zimbabwe), Angola, and South Africa in particular, it failed to frustrate Israel's economic and diplomatic efforts in Africa. The emerging African states had positive attitudes toward Israel and were impressed with its achievements. Most African leaders identified with the fledging state of Israel and were cognizant of world-wide discrimination against Jews and its horrible consequences. The Holocaust, the catalyst for the founding of Israel, also had profound implications for Africa. It was the international response to Germany's aggression and the belief, in the war's aftermath, that racial discrimination and violations of fundamental human rights were incompatible with international peace and security that facilitated Africa's independence. Thus, Africans and Jews shared an affinity that was based on endemic discrimination against both groups. Furthermore, Africans did not have the negative historical experience with Jews that they had with Arabs. Israel was not a colonial power; it was certainly too small to seriously threaten African states' independence and its mixed economy appealed to many erstwhile colonies that equated capitalism with racial, political, economic, and cultural subjugation. Consequently, Israel managed to develop good relations with Ghana, Liberia, Ethiopia, Nigeria, Sierra Leone, and Senegal between 1948 and 1961, despite Egyptian efforts to foster anti-Israeli sentiments in Africa.[12]

Both Israel and Egypt opposed apartheid while Nasser was in power. In July 1961 Israel joined Upper Volta (Burkina Faso) in issuing a statement strongly condemning apartheid and, shortly thereafter, Israel and the Netherlands were the only Western countries that voted to censure South Africa's foreign minister Eric Louw for a speech in the UN General Assembly, which they deemed to be offensive. When Israel, itself embargoed by the Arab states, voted for sanctions against South Africa in 1961, Pretoria retaliated by terminating approval of routine transfers of South African Jewish donations to Israel. Nevertheless, Israel supported additional sanctions in 1962, and in 1963 it withdrew its ambassador from South Africa and downgraded its representation to the consular level. Israel's relations with Pretoria were further strained when it voted with a UN majority in 1966 to revoke South Africa's mandate over Namibia.[13]

Although Israel had successfully outmaneuvered Egypt in Africa by adopting a consistently strong anti-apartheid position, its brilliant military performance in the 1967 Six Day War, paradoxically, weakened its connections with sub-Saharan Africa and ultimately provided opportunities for Arab states to expand their influence in Africa. Between 1967 and 1973 the interplay of developments in the Middle East and Africa culminated in reduced Israeli criticism of apartheid and greater Arab interest in supporting southern African liberation movements. Created to promote African solidarity, the OAU was pressured to adopt resolutions against

Israel following its seizure of Arab territory during the Six Day War. Simultaneously, Israel's covert involvement on behalf of the secessionist movement during the Nigerian civil war in 1967 also proved detrimental to its relations with Africa. Perhaps more important than the actual assistance rendered to the breakaway region, known as Biafra, was the fact that Portugal, Rhodesia, and South Africa had also supported Biafra. Coinciding with South African overtures toward Israel, Israel's actions were clearly detrimental to its standing in Africa as a whole. External interference in Africa's affairs was not tolerated. Yet many African States were reluctant to entangle themselves in the Middle East's quagmire or to publicly criticize Israel. Nonetheless, in order to protect significant benefits which emanated from their ties with Israel, African states endeavored to initiate a Middle East peace process in 1972. However, these efforts were frustrated not only by the complexities of the Arab-Israeli conflict but also by South Africa's diplomatic overtures toward Israel.

Feeling the deleterious effects of its growing international isolation, South Africa perceived emerging strains between Israel and sub-Saharan Africa as providing an opportunity for it to improve its own relations with Israel. Pretoria permitted South African Jews to send an additional $20.5 million to Israel, and supplied various weapons to Israel following France's decision to implement an embargo on arms shipments to that state. Israel adopted an ambiguous policy toward South Africa. While evincing reduced enthusiasm for supporting apartheid resolutions, it continued to assist southern African liberation movements until 1971, when its financial contributions to the OAU's Liberation Committee were refused.[14] Simultaneousely, Arab states became more active within the UN on southern African issues but did not require Africans to reciprocate on the Arab-Israeli conflict. Another important development that directly influenced the Middle East's relations with Africa in general and with South Africa specifically was the Palestinians' determination to dramatize their grievances by escalating terrorist attacks on civilian airlines, on Israeli settlements and schools, and against private Israeli citizens. Thus, a fundamental shift in the Arab states' South African policies was already materializing before the war erupted in 1973, a watershed event in the Middle East's relations with South Africa.

Israel's seizure of Egyptian territory forced many African states to abandon their cautious approach to the Arab-Israeli struggle and to support Egypt. Aware of their own national boundary problems and irredentist claims, African countries could not condone Israel's use of force to acquire Egyptian land. Another factor that drew the Arabs and Africans closer together politically was Portugal's decision to allow American planes that were transporting military supplies to Israel during the 1973 war to land in the Azores. Given Portugal's own war against Angolan and Mozambican independence movements, Arab leaders had little difficulty in convincing the Africans that Israel was cooperating with white minority regimes in southern Africa. This perception was reinforced by South Africa's overt political support for Israel, the participation of approximately 8,000 South African Jews in the war, and by the fact that the South African Jewish community had raised more money per capita for Israel than any other Jewish community in the world.[15] Paradoxically, as Israel became stronger militarily, it was more vulnerable politically. Africans grew more sympathetic to the Arabs, particularly the Palestinians.

Arab countries took advantage of the growing schism between Israel and Africa and used their newly acquired economic and political power derived from the OPEC's success in increasing the price of oil and controlling the availability of supplies. The Arab League threatened to retaliate with an oil embargo against African countries that refused to ostracize Israel and offered financial incentives to those that adopted a pro-Arab stance. But the Arab states also became more actively involved in the anti-apartheid struggle. They agreed to financially support the liberation movements and to implement an oil embargo against South Africa in exchange for OAU backing. This tradeoff was at the heart of the Middle East's policies toward South Africa.

To consolidate this marriage of convenience, the Arabs drew parallels between Jews whom they regarded as Zionist settlers in Israel and the white settlers of South Africa, the implication being that both were colonial powers. Collaboration between Israel and South Africa, partly in response to Israel's growing isolation and its preoccupation with the military component of national security, seemed to corroborate the view that both countries intended to dominate their regions and to oppress the indigenous inhabitants. Arab states consistently labeled Israel and South Africa as common enemies of both Africans and Arabs. The emergence of the New Zionism in the mid-1970s, articulated by Jewish fundamentalists, increased Israel's rigidity in its dealings with the Palestinians, thereby inadvertently giving credibility to Arab claims.

Stung by the infamous 1975 UN resolution that equated Zionism with racism and by persistent Arab efforts to demonstrate similarities between Israel and South Africa, the Israeli Foreign Ministry expressed concern about the "odious comparisons" between the two states and instructed Israeli representatives abroad on how to respond. The following distinctions were emphasized: (1) in Israel the principle of equality governs the status of Arabs within the Green Line; (2) Israel has no intention of ruling over the inhabitants of the territories and wants to negotiate a political solution; (3) the conflict with the Palestinians, as opposed to the white-black conflict in South Africa, is not an internal problem but connected to the Arab-Israeli conflict as whole; and (4) unlike South Africa, Israel does not deny basic human rights to the Palestinians.[16] Yet Israel's brutal treatment of the Palestinians in the Occupied Territories, its reluctance to trade land for peace, and its strong military links to South Africa reduced the effectiveness of the Foreign Ministry's campaign.

Although Israel's foreign policy blunders, its retreat into isolationism, and its disregard for the UN contributed to the Arabs' achievement of their foreign policy objectives, Middle Eastern countries adopted varying and sometimes contradictory approaches to South Africa, a reality that created an uneasiness in the Arab-African alliance. The oil boycott against Pretoria was extremely porous and conflicting national interests of the various states often resulted in cooperation between the Arab countries and South Africa. But the general thrust of the Middle East's relations with Pretoria was no more inconsistent than that of many sub-Saharan African states. The gap between declaratory policy and practice emanated partly from domestic and regional realities. Egypt's policy toward South Africa demonstrated this connection.

Following Nasser's death in 1970, Egypt's commitment to ending racial domination in southern Africa was markedly reduced. Lacking Nasser's enthusiasm for revolutionary causes, Anwar al-Sadat steered his country toward a more moderate course in regional as well as international affairs. Whereas Nasser had pursued policies that brought Egypt closer to the Soviet Union during the East-West struggle, Sadat abrogated various agreements with Moscow in 1976 and ordered the Soviets to leave the country. Realizing that wars with Israel had resulted in devastating consequences for Egypt, Sadat decided to focus on nonviolent strategies to achieve his nation's objectives. In a radical departure from Arab policy toward Israel, Sadat accepted Menachem Begin's invitation to visit Israel, thereby initiating a peace process that culminated in the Camp David peace accords and diplomatic ties between the two states. While this revolutionary step strengthened Cairo's relations with Washington, Arab countries adamantly opposed any unilateral recognition of Israel's right to exist. Consequently, Egypt, confronted with a concerted Arab attempt to isolate it, was excluded from membership in both the Arab League and the Islamic Conference subsequent to the Camp David accords. Sadat's moderate policy toward Israel and his willingness to cooperate with the United States, Israel's principal supporter, affected Egypt's South African policy. Pretoria, sensing Egypt's willingness to settle conflicts through negotiations, launched its own diplomatic initiative. The Department of Information sent representatives to Egypt, Jordan, and Morocco in an attempt to improve relations with those countries. As a result, covert links between Egypt and South Africa were established.[17]

Nevertheless, Egypt, which retained its OAU membership, continued to oppose apartheid and to support the liberation movements, albeit to a lesser extent than under Nasser. In late 1979 Egypt's minister of state for Foreign Affairs Boutros Ghali, who became the UN's secretary general in 1992, reiterated his country's commitment to the national liberation movements. Emphasizing Cairo's historical opposition to apartheid, Ghali promised to extend material and political support to the liberation movements to enable them "to achieve the legitimate goals of their struggle, rid their countries of racist regimes, and achieve true independence embodied by a transfer of power to the majority."[18] Egypt continued to approve international measures, including sanctions, against South Africa. A significant factor influencing Cairo's policy was the Arabs' effort to isolate Egypt from Africa. By stressing its determination to oppose racial discrimination, Egypt strengthened its position in Africa.

After Sadat was assassinated in October 1981 by Muslim extremists during a military review in Cairo, Hosni Mubarak, Egypt's new leader, maintained Sadat's approach to South Africa. Anti-apartheid delegations from South Africa were invited to Cairo and Egyptian officials were sent to southern Africa to reassure the Frontline States and various groups of Egypt's commitment to their struggle against the South African government. They also stressed that comprehensive mandatory sanctions were needed to persuade Pretoria to abolish apartheid. However, Egypt also permitted South Africa, Cuba, Angola, and the United States to meet in Cairo to discuss the Angola-Namibia issue. But Egypt denied that it had been contacted by the South Africans to arrange the meeting. Cairo insisted that Chester Crocker, the assistant U.S. secretary of state for African Affairs, and the American Embassy in Cairo had made the plans.[19] Yet Egypt's collaboration with the United States and South Africa to overthrow the Angolan government pointed to strong covert political links between Cairo and Pretoria.

Misgivings about the intensity of Egypt's support for radical movements in southern Africa enabled Libya and Algeria to assume anti-apartheid leadership roles. Both countries attempted to enforce the Arab oil embargo against South Africa and Libya provided military training for ANC members. Compared to Egypt, Libya, and Algeria, Iran adopted a more conciliatory policy toward South Africa. Determined to circumvent the Arab oil embargo, Pretoria concentrated on creating strong diplomatic links with Iran, a non-Arab state. In mid-1970 two Iranian diplomats visited South Africa and by November of the same year the two countries had established consular relations. Muhammad Reza Shah Pahlavi viewed economic sanctions as useless and vowed to maintain direct contacts with South Africa, despite his government's condemnation of apartheid.[20] Apart from sentimental reasons, due to Pretoria's decision to grant the Shah's father refuge, Iran's political alliance with South Africa was based on pragmatic strategic considerations. Believing that his country's navy could play an important role in impeding Soviet expansion in the Indian Ocean, the Shah perceived South Africa—which was also staunchly anticommunist—as a bulwark against Moscow. Simultaneously, however, he channeled funds to the OAU's Liberation Committee.[21] In the aftermath of the Islamic revolution in Iran in 1979, which led to the Shah's political demise, the Shah was invited to settle in Transkei, one of South Africa's unrecognized "homelands."

Iran's Revolutionary Council, formed by Ayatollah Khomeini and controlled by Islamic fundamentalists, repudiated many of the Shah's foreign policies, including his close relationship with South Africa. The provisional government publicly declared its abhorrence of apartheid, expelled Pretoria's representative from Tehran, and imposed a total oil embargo against the minority regime. But not all political ties were severed. South Africa maintained an unofficial consulate in Tehran and Iran retained diplomatic ties with South Africa through the Swiss Embassy. Iran's representative in Johannesburg, M. A. Bastani, traveled on a diplomatic passport and held the rank of vice consul.[22] While many governments which do not wish to have direct diplomatic links with a particular country ordinarily have their interests in that country represented by a third state, Iran's decision to allow Bastani to remain in South Africa seemed to be inconsistent with its strong opposition to apartheid. However, leading Iranian officials visited the Frontline States in 1986 and offered military assistance to enable them to counter South Africa's destabilization policy. Economic aid was also promised.[23]

Despite the Middle East's anti-apartheid rhetoric and putative alliance with sub-Saharan Africa, many countries maintained economic links with South Africa. Considering the importance of petroleum to any modern society, especially one with as extensive an industrial base as South Africa's, denial of oil supplies would have been a most effective sanction. During the Arab Summit Conference in Algiers in November 1973, the Arab League expressed its appreciation of the African "attitude" and pledged its support for African struggles for national liberation and economic progress and against imperialism and racism. More significantly, the Arabs offered tangible evidence of their anti-apartheid stance by imposing a "strict oil embargo" on South Africa, Portugal, and Rhodesia.[24] But the Arabs' decision was not undergirded by any moral convictions about apartheid's oppressiveness. Instead, it was in response to OAU calls for reciprocity. Having broken diplomatic relations with Israel because of its occupation of Arab lands and its treatment of the Palestinians, the vast majority of sub-Saharan countries called on the Arabs to use the "oil weapon" against the southern African white minority regimes until they had complied with UN decolonization resolutions.

In 1973 South Africa purchased approximately 90 percent of its petroleum imports from the Arab states and Iran. Any interruption in oil supplies seriously threatened South Africa's well-being. Consequently, Pretoria was determined to circumvent the embargo. Because secretiveness was essential to achieve this, the government made disclosing information about which countries supplied petroleum to South Africa a crime punishable by seven years in prison. Although many Arab oil-exporting countries were concerned about negative publicity about violating their own boycott, they conspired to secretly ship oil to South Africa.

Several factors rendered an effective embargo against South Africa virtually impossible. Many of Pretoria's neighbors' economies were so closely integrated into that of their political nemesis that ending oil shipments to South Africa was tantamount to imposing sanctions against the entire region. Furthermore, their oil supplies were shipped through South Africa, a reality that highlighted the problems involved in utilizing economic sanctions as instruments of foreign policy in an economically interdependent region. Another factor that directly affected the Arab oil embargo's efficacy was Iran's decision to continue selling oil to South Africa. As Arab countries reduced oil shipments, Iran increased its petroleum exports. Whereas Iran had provided about half of South Africa's oil supplies in 1973, it provided approximately 90 percent of South Africa's oil needs in 1974 and 85 percent in 1975.[25] African appeals to Iran to join the embargo were ignored. But South Africa's dependence on one country for its petroleum prompted Pretoria to diversify its suppliers to diminish its vulnerability to sudden oil price rises or reduced exports from Iran. This apprehension was strengthened by Iran's desire to maintain its position as a leading Third World state, growing unrest in Tehran, and the Shah's stipulation against sending Iranian oil to Rhodesia. The Iranian revolution clearly confirmed Pretoria's worst fears. Strikes by oil workers in 1978 decreased Iran's oil production and Khomeini called for a ban on oil exports in an effort to undermine the Shah. Equally important, he admonished the Shah's allies that Iran would stop selling them oil.[26] South Africa's position was clearly precarious.

But the embargo's tightness, essential to squeezing Pretoria, was jeopardized by the very nature of the oil industry and the pivotal role of transnational petroleum companies in it. Numerous independent oil companies involved in shipping oil were difficult to control. Oil was easily purchased on the spot market and resold to South Africa. Moreover, multinational oil firms with operations in South Africa simply shifted oil from some countries to others or decreased production in one region and increased it in another. Their leverage vis-à-vis Third World oil-exporting countries was considerable. Oil could be transferred from one ship to another on the high seas or a ship could simply change its stated destination. Since supertankers had to sail around South Africa, because they are too large to navigate the Suez Canal, they could easily stop in Cape Town to deliver petroleum. Furthermore, escalating oil prices induced industrial countries to search for alternative sources of oil as well as to develop alternative energy technologies. Major petroleum discoveries in the North Sea, Alaska, and Mexico weakened the Arabs' bargaining power while simultaneously enhancing South Africa's ability to obtain oil. And because of South Africa's abundant coal and uranium reserves it became an important player in the development of nonpetroleum energy supplies. After 1974 South Africa made access to its coal and uranium conditional on guarantees that petroleum companies, many of which were involved in developing alternative energy sources, would continue to supply it with oil.[27]

Furthermore, Arab countries responsible for implementing the embargo against South Africa were generally reluctant to monitor oil transfers and to punish violators. In 1975 the OAU issued a report that asserted that Arab states had continued to supply significant amounts of oil to South Africa. The OAU reiterated those allegations in 1981. Indeed, as Iran's exports to South Africa diminished, Arab oil producers became more entangled in dealing with Pretoria, much to the dismay of sub-Saharan Africa. In response to the embargo's failure, Arab states passed a resolution in 1981 calling for tighter monitoring and control of petroleum exports to limit the quantity of oil reaching South Africa.[28] But the complexities of international trade essentially vitiated the Arabs' declaration, even if they had intended to comply with it. Without comprehensive international standards and cooperation, the Arab embargo was bound to leak. National interests influenced countries to engage in semantics to circumvent enforcing the embargo. While prohibiting the exports of their own oil, many states permitted oil from elsewhere to be shipped to South Africa. Other countries cleverly differentiated between petroleum and petroleum products, thereby permitting themselves to sell the latter to South Africa and remain, in their view, in compliance with the embargo.

In light of the clandestine nature of oil shipments to South Africa, the precise extent of the Middle Eastern states' complicity in disimplementing the embargo was difficult to determine. Nonetheless, careful analysis of oil supplies to South Africa by the Shipping Research Bureau in Amsterdam indicated that between 1979—shortly after Iran officially stopped exporting oil to South Africa—and 1990 approximately 441 tankers were known to have delivered petroleum to South Africa. About 309 of them sailed from the Middle East and carried roughly 79 percent of the total volume identified. While the United Arab Emirates was by far the principal violator of the Arab oil embargo, others included Qatar, Oman, Iran, Saudi Arabia, Kuwait, and Egypt. Egypt allegedly concluded oil sales agreements with both Israel and South Africa even before signing the peace treaty with Israel.[29] The United Arab Emirates consistently sold oil to South Africa through intermediaries in the Netherlands. Several oil tankers sailed directly from the Fateh oil terminal in the United Arab Emirates to South African ports throughout the 1980s. Some tankers stopped at terminals in several countries to obtain petroleum for South Africa. Other ships, such as the Salem and the Berge Enterprise, took on cargoes of crude oil from the Gulf for delivery to Italy and Singapore, respectively, but instead diverted them to South Africa.[30] Allegations concerning Saudi Arabia's significant oil trade with South Africa were buttressed by Sam T. Bamieh's testimony before the U.S. Congress in 1987. Bamieh was approached by Prince Bandar Bin Sultan, the Saudi Ambassador to Washington, in February 1984 at the Majestic Hotel in Cannes to establish an offshore company to supply oil to South Africa and various goods and services to anticommunist movements in Angola and elsewhere. Under the proposed scheme, the company would purchase oil from Saudi Arabia for resale to South Africa.[31] This was part of a larger Saudi plan to obtain U.S. advanced radar-equipped reconnaissance aircraft, known as AWACS.

Government officials from states identified as violators of the Arab League's oil embargo denied any involvement by their countries in selling oil to South Africa and reiterated their observance of all anti-apartheid sanctions. While admitting that Saudi Arabia had no arrangements with other oil exporting countries and shipping states to ascertain compliance with the embargo and that the government did not maintain a list of companies that violated their contracts by supplying oil to South Africa, the Saudi Ministry of Petroleum and Mineral Resources asserted that South Africa did not obtain a "single drop" of Saudi Arabian oil. To prevent oil from reaching South Africa, the Saudi government required all tankers waiting to be loaded to specify their destination.[32] Although Saudi officials claimed that they made sure the oil reached its stated destination, they were unable or unwilling to prevent other nations or companies from selling the oil once the tankers were beyond Saudi Arabia's jurisdiction. Other Middle Eastern governments emphasized their legislative and administrative efforts to ensure compliance with the embargo. Qatar, which established a Boycott Office in the Ministry of Economy and Trade, included destination restrictions and end-user clauses in its contracts with oil companies and shipping firms. Based on information collected on breaches of these agreements, Qatar advised oil terminal operators to embargo Berge King, Staland, and Neptune World for transporting petroleum to South Africa. But most Middle Eastern countries seemed to subscribe to the view, articulated by Egyptian officials, that since they were unaware of buyer's violations of end-user clauses, "therefore no Egyptian petroleum was being exported to South Africa."[33] However, despite Arab denials of selling oil to South Africa, it was obvious that the Arab League's oil embargo was not scrupulously enforced.

In addition to directly or indirectly allowing oil to reach South Africa, some countries had other economic links with the apartheid regime. Although the Khomeini regime had eschewed any contacts with South Africa and Teheran had dismissed reports that it traded with Pretoria as part of "the international propaganda plot against the Islamic revolution," Iran maintained economic relations with South Africa. Faced with American sanctions and European reluctance to trade with the Khomeini government while it held American diplomats hostage, Iran continued to import industrial plastics, construction steel, vehicles, plate glass, and food grains from South Africa through intermediaries operating in neighboring Swaziland.[34] Similarly, despite the Arab League's embargo in 1973, following a private visit to Saudi Arabia by South Africa's ambassador to London, Carel de Wet, the Saudis sent a trade mission to South Africa to negotiate gold purchases. Saudi Arabia also imported food, electric resistance welded steel pipe, and prefabricated building materials from South Africa. In 1985 the Saudi government allowed South African Airlines to commence flights from Johannesburg and the nearby Comorro Islands to Jiddah, ostensibly to facilitate South African Muslims' obligatory pilgrimage to Mecca and Medina. However, these flights were terminated when they became a public embarrassment.[35] Dubai, Bahrein, and Abu Dhabi also traded with South Africa. The United Arab Emirates and Saudi Arabia bought significant amounts of South African gold. Analyzed within the broader international context, the Middle East's South African policies were similar to those of many sub-Saharan African and Latin American states. Declaratory policies were rarely matched by the actual practices.

Analogous to Israel, which was routinely castigated by the Arabs for collaborating militarily with South Africa, many Middle Eastern states established military links with Pretoria. Tensions in the Middle East, the Iran-Iraq war during the 1980s, the region's insatiable demand for weapons, and closer Egyptian and Saudi cooperation with the United States directly influenced the Middle East's military connections with South Africa. Prior to the Iranian revolution, the Shah's interests in containing Soviet expansion converged with South Africa's desire to maintain the status quo domestically and to prevent the "total onslaught" spearheaded by the communist-supported ANC. In June 1972 the head of the Imperial Iranian Navy, accompanied by two warships, visited South Africa. Shortly thereafter South Africa selected a senior military officer to serve as consul-general in Iran. Underlying this emerging alliance was the shared perception that both countries could play a crucial role in impeding Soviet expansion in the Indian Ocean.[36] Iran, a pivotal pillar of America's containment policy, was viewed as possessing sufficient military power to defend the northern entrance to the Indian Ocean. South Africa would safeguard the southern Indian Ocean route, which is generally regarded by the West as strategically significant because much of its Middle Eastern oil supplies are transported by supertankers that use the Cape route.

During the Iran-Iraq war South Africa supplied weapons to both belligerents in exchange for petroleum. Because Iraq's oil production was reduced by the war, Saudi Arabia, by supplying Iraq with oil, was indirectly providing petroleum for South Africa. The Iraqis received approximately 100 heavy-caliber howitzers as well as howitzer shells. Iraqi military links with South Africa became more apparent following Iraq's invasion of Kuwait. When the United States responded first with Operation Desert Shield, purportedly to protect Saudi Arabia from an Iraqi invasion, and then with Operation Desert Storm, ostensibly to liberate Kuwait, both American and South African complicity in arming Iraq with sophisticated artillery was revealed. Despite America's commitment to the arms embargo against Pretoria, the U.S. Central Intelligence Agency (CIA) participated in a clandestine operation that involved International Signal and Control Corporation, a firm in Lancaster, Pennsylvania, which supplied South Africa with advanced anti-aircraft missile technology and cluster bomb fuses. These were transferred to Iraq, the U.S. ally throughout the war with Iran. Ironically, the United States was threatened by its own weapons during Operation Desert Storm.

Saudi Arabia was indirectly involved with South Africa through its military assistance to Jonas Savimbi and the National Union for the Total Independence of Angola (UNITA), the group that fought the Soviet-backed Angolan government. Rendered vulnerable by Angola's independence and the subsequent presence of about 50,000 Cuban troops and their Soviet advisors, Pretoria decided to undermine the Angolan government by supporting UNITA. The United States also aided UNITA militarily until prevented from doing so, legally, by the Clark Amendment in 1975. Obsessed with fighting communism, the Reagan administration circumvented U.S. law by enlisting Saudi Arabia's help. Crown Prince Fahd, who later became Saudi Arabia's king, eagerly cooperated with the United States, partly to obtain U.S. AWACS. At CIA Director William Casey's behest, Saudi Arabia, Morocco, and Egypt contributed roughly $70 million per year to UNITA on behalf of the United States.[37] The Saudis, collaborating with the CIA, also assisted the notorious guerrillas of the Mozambican National Resistance Movement, or Renamo, who were strongly supported by South Africa. The Saudis used the Comorro Islands to transship supplies to Renamo.

Following the Camp David peace accords, Egypt received substantial amounts of U.S. military and economic assistance. Cairo distanced itself from Moscow and moved closer to Washington. The Middle East's political dynamics and Sadat's lack of enthusiasm for Nasser's revolutionary policies combined to alter Egypt's southern African policies. Working with Morocco's King Hassan, who received weapons from the United States and South Africa to fight the Polisario national liberation movement in Western Sahara, Sadat assisted U.S. and South African efforts to overthrow the Angolan government. Contrary to OAU policy, Egypt allowed South African planes to fly American weapons from Egyptian airbases to UNITA, which had its headquarters in southern Angola.[38] UNITA guerrillas were trained in Morocco, but not in Egypt.

Whereas Saudi Arabia and Egypt had indirect military links with South Africa, Jordan was one of the principal channels of illicit arms shipments to South Africa. European arms merchants began funneling weapons through Jordan to South Africa in the early 1970s. The British Foreign Office confirmed that during the mid-1970s Jordan resold a consignment of forty-one British Centurion tanks and a Tiger-cat missile system to South Africa.[39] During the 1980s Jordanian military attachés in Europe functioned as intermediaries between European arms manufacturers and the South African government. They persuaded European officials that the weapons were intended for Jordan's army or for the Iraqi army. Arms were shipped to Pretoria both from Jordan as well as directly from Europe. In some cases, Jordanian weapons dealers used the Gulf states as transshipment points. It was estimated that between 1972 and 1987 Jordanian officials and private dealers sold more than $3 billion worth of arms to South Africa.[40] These transactions occurred despite the lack of diplomatic relations between Amman and Pretoria. Jordan's official boycott of all commerce with South Africa was clearly ignored.

Compared to the Arab states and Iran, the PLO's position on apartheid was less ambiguous. While the Middle East's policies toward South Africa were influenced by the Palestinian-Israeli conflict, the PLO itself developed ties with sub-Saharan Africa and the southern African liberation movements in an attempt to counter Israel's influence in Africa and its military collaboration with the South African government. A principal Arab objective was to portray Israel as a colonial state with expansionist ambitions and to emphasize similarities between Israel and South Africa to weaken Israel's positive image in sub-Saharan Africa. The Arab states also wanted the Palestinian problem to be perceived as a colonial issue. If this could be accomplished, the Palestinian cause would be integrated into the Nonalignment Movement's anticolonial agenda.[41] Israel's strong Western cultural and political identification undoubtedly added credence to the Arab states' propaganda.

Inadvertently, Israel, more than the Arab countries, was responsible for the significant shift in African attitudes toward the PLO. The Six Day War in 1967 resulted in not only a humiliating military defeat for the Arabs in general and Nasser in particular but it also left Israel in control of all of Palestine, the Sinai Peninsula, the Gaza Strip, the West Bank, and the Golan Heights. The Palestinians' plight was highlighted by Israel's refusal to return conquered Arab territory. The vulnerable emerging African states began to perceive the Palestinians as victims of Israeli military might and drew comparisons between their own anticolonial struggles and the Palestinian problem. Furthermore, Israel's involvement in Nigeria's civil war on behalf of Biafra—which was also supported by southern African minority regimes—consolidated the African view that Israel's ambitions were similar to those of Portugal, Rhodesia, and South Africa.

Moreover, the Palestinians, frustrated by the Arab states' inability to defeat Israel with conventional armies, embraced terrorism to recover their homeland just as the Irgun and the Stern group had done to achieve a Jewish state. Although most African countries gained their independence relatively peacefully, several of them fought France, Portugal, and, to a lesser extent, Britain to end colonial rule. By resorting to violence to dramatize their cause, the Palestinians had accomplished the broader Arab objective of trying to convince the Third World in general and Africa specifically that their problem was similar to those of southern Africa's black majorities. Thus, the foundation was established for closer PLO cooperation with the African states and the ANC. However, many African countries regarded Israel as an ally and strongly supported its right to exist. But they believed that Israel should withdraw to its pre-1967 boundaries.

Devastated by escalating oil prices, committed to defend Egypt within the OAU, and determined to enlist the Arab oil weapon against southern Africa's minority governments, many sub-Saharan African countries decided to supported Algeria's contention that the Palestinian struggle was intertwined with African efforts to terminate colonialism and imperialism on the continent. But developments within Israel also contributed to Africa's changing perceptions of and relations with the PLO. Egyptian and Syrian surprise attacks on Israel in 1973 led to investigations of Israel's pre-war military intelligence and preparedness, and prompted senior military officers to resign. When Prime Minister Golda Meir resigned in April 1974, she was succeeded by Yitzhak Rabin, the first professional soldier to lead Israel. Rabin, who had advocated lowering Israel's high costs of developing weapons by exporting arms to South Africa and elsewhere, met South Africa's prime minister John Vorster during his visit to Israel and signed an agreement promoting closer cooperation between the two countries. A joint ministerial committee was formed to oversee implementation of the pact.[42]

Growing political influence of Jewish fundamentalists, the Likud's refusal to recognize Palestinians' legitimate grievances, and a heightened preoccupation with national security were instrumental not only in moving Israel closer to South Africa but also in reinforcing African perceptions that the PLO's struggle was analogous to the ANC's. The OAU endorsed resolutions supporting Palestinian self-determination. Africans also supported resolutions giving the PLO UN observer status. Furthermore, the OAU's Council of Ministers stated that Palestinians were entitled to use force to regain their usurped rights and strongly condemned "the unholy alliance between the Zionist regime in Israel and the racist regimes in South Africa, Zimbabwe, and Namibia."[43]

But Israel's increasing isolation only helped to influence its leaders to consolidate the country's military, economic, and political connections with South Africa, a development that bolstered PLO linkages with African states and the ANC. By 1987 Israel had diplomatic relations with only seven African countries, whereas the PLO had full diplomatic ties with thirty-five of them and lower-level relations with those states that maintained diplomatic links with Israel.[44] When the PLO declared the formation of a Palestinian state, the Africans recognized it.

Many African states supported PLO assertions that Israel's behavior was similar to South Africa's. PLO chairman Yasir Arafat had argued that Israel viewed Arabs as inferior, discriminated against Palestinians, and was engaged in settler colonialism. Moreover, "settler colonization in southern Africa and Zionist settler colonialism in Palestine were strategically and organically linked."[45] Israel's cooperation with South Africa and its abuse of Palestinians in the Occupied Territories buttressed the PLO's assertions and influenced greater PLO-ANC collaboration. However, the PLO's assumption that apartheid's demise was inextricably linked to Israel's destruction was obviously unrealistic.

Cold War rivalries also facilitated the PLO-ANC alliance. In an environment where questioning the wisdom of U.S. foreign policy was often perceived as anti-Americanism and tantamount to communism, countries critical of Israel as well as America's approach to the Arab-Israeli conflict were regarded as pro-Soviet. Middle Eastern and southern African liberation movements were seen by the United States not only as challenging its interests, which often depended on perpetuating the status quo, but also as abetting communist expansion.[46] Soviet military assistance to both the PLO and the ANC was perceived by Israel, South Africa, and the United States as evidence of Moscow's grand strategy to undermine Western security. Soviet support for the PLO, influenced partly by Moscow's deteriorating relations with Egypt, occurred precisely when Israel was augmenting its relations with South Africa. The Soviet Union's decision to recognize the PLO as the Palestinians' sole legitimate representative and to grant diplomatic status to the PLO's office in Moscow, combined with the Kremlin's increased assistance to the ANC, undoubtedly influenced Israel's alliance with South Africa as well as the PLO's collaboration with the ANC.[47]

As early as 1966 the Palestine National Conference had emphasized that cooperation between Palestinians and African liberation movements was essential to the success of their respective struggles. Lacking the international legitimacy and recognition that African anticolonial groups enjoyed, the PLO endeavored to be perceived as a genuine liberation group. To accomplish that objective, it established close links with the ANC, the Pan-African Congress, and SWAPO. There were regular contacts between the PLO and the ANC. They shared information, participated in each other's meetings, consulted each other to develop common strategies, and issued declarations of mutual support.[48] When Israel invaded Lebanon in 1982 and Palestinians were massacred in the Shatila and Sabra refugee camps, the ANC and SWAPO sent a joint message of condolence and support to Arafat and the PLO. Similarly, the PLO condemned Pretoria's internal repression and advocated sanctions against South Africa as well as Israel.[49]

African leaders such as Robert Mugabe and Kenneth Kaunda, leading proponents of change in South Africa, also developed strong ties with the PLO and generally viewed Israel's treatment of the Palestinians as virtually identical to the South African government's oppression of the country's black majority. When Arafat visited Zambia in April 1987 he was greeted by President Kaunda, various cabinet ministers, members of the Central Committee of the UNIP, and several Arab ambassadors. Addressing Arafat, Kaunda declared that Palestinians were fighting for a just cause and that Zambia would not restore diplomatic relations with Israel until it recognized the Palestinians' rights to repatriation and an independent state. In response, Arafat not only praised Kaunda for his courage and support but also compared developments in southern Africa to Israel's occupation of the West Bank and Gaza and its military raids on Palestinian refugee camps in Lebanon. He stated that Palestinians in the Occupied Territories "suffered under the yoke of occupation and faced an enemy that expropriated property, made arrests, and violated the sanctity of Islamic and Christian holy places in Palestine."[50] Following his meeting with Kaunda, Arafat attended the Nonaligned Movement's Summit in Zimbabwe.

In addition to its significant political links with southern African states, or because of them, the PLO also collaborated militarily with southern African liberation movements. Nigeria provided military training for SAYRCO members, and facilitated cooperation between SAYRCO and the PLO. ANC members were trained by the PLO in Lebanon as well as in Africa. As Egypt's support for Africa's liberation movements declined, Libya increased its involvement with the ANC. Qadhafi's relationship with Abu Nidal, an extremely ruthless PLO terrorist, heightened Pretoria's concerns about Libya's activities. Qaddafi openly advocated violent revolutionary change in South Africa, offered the Frontline States weapons to counteract Pretoria's destabilization policies, and financed anti-apartheid meetings held in Tripoli.[51]

ANC-PLO collaboration and Nelson Mandela's embrace of Arafat and his undaunted support for the PLO following his release from prison in February 1990 clearly worried the American Jewish community. Although American Jews were among the staunchest advocates of anti-apartheid sanctions, many believed that Mandela should not have equated the Palestinian problem with the anti-apartheid struggle. Leaders in the African-American community, cognizant of their strained alliance with Jewish Americans, attempted to allay Jewish fears. Harry Belafonte, an ardent advocate of racial equality and human rights in South Africa, proposed a meeting between leaders of the ANC and various American Jewish organizations. Although Mandela stressed that Israel had a right to exist within secure boundaries, he also emphasized that Israel's borders did not extend beyond its pre-1967 territory. Furthermore, he viewed Israel's occupation of the West Bank and Gaza as a source of continued conflict and was critical of Israel's refusal to negotiate with the PLO, as the ANC was doing with the South African government.[52] The strength of the PLO's ties with the ANC was indicated by Mandela's refusal to repudiate connections between the two groups, despite his apparent sensitivity to Jewish concerns.

Chapter 6

Post-Apartheid Challenges

Converging revolutionary changes in Eastern Europe, the Soviet Union, and in South Africa itself radically transformed the international political environment in which the Third World countries had formulated and implemented their policies toward South Africa. The end of the Cold War, German unification, Western Europe's decision to forge a Single Market, and the emergence of a multipolar world rendered concepts such as nonalignment and the Third World essentially irrelevant. By removing most of apartheid's legal underpinnings by June 1991, with the notable exception of black voting rights, South Africa had made a major and largely unanticipated first step toward creating a relatively egalitarian and nonracial society. The overwhelming white support in the March 1992 referendum for de Klerk's reforms underscored the commitment to change. Dismantling the more intractable social and economic components of a legal system of racial domination into which all South Africans had been socialized for almost half a century was clearly a more herculean endeavor. Nonetheless, the vast majority of South Africans had embraced a hopeful but uncertain future.

For those countries that spearheaded international opposition to apartheid, developments in South Africa, inadvertently, helped to intensify many of their own problems. The changes also created opportunities for greater economic and political freedom within their own boundaries. The objectives outlined in the *Manifesto for the New South Africa*, which included commitments to creating a free and democratic political system, and an equitable social system, were clearly consistent with the foreign policy aims that many Third World countries had pursued in relation to South Africa.¹ The abolition of apartheid's legal framework had profound ramifications for the Third World, especially the sub-Saharan African states. By succeeding in convincing industrialized countries to impose sanctions against South Africa, and by taking their own actions against Pretoria, Third World countries were instrumental in influencing far-reaching changes in South Africa. However, the Third World's success, together with significant changes in the international political environment, focused attention on the failure of many developing countries to practice what they wanted South Africa to do, namely, to grant their own citizens political and economic freedoms.

The prolonged Third World campaign against the brutality of apartheid strengthened the view that countries' internal human rights practices were not beyond the international community's scrutiny. No longer could the nebulous concept of sovereignty be utilized by governments to justify violations of their citizens' fundamental freedoms. By succeeding in operationalizing international provisions on human rights, many of which are included in the UN Charter and the Universal Declaration of Human Rights, Third World states had, paradoxically, also increased domestic as well as international pressures on themselves to observe the indivdual's fundamental rights and to move toward political and economic liberalization. In sub-Saharan Africa in particular, the abolition of apartheid's legal underpinnings focused greater public attention on unfulfilled promises and expectations of independence and reinvigorated internal struggles for Africa's second independence. Reformers in sub-Saharan Africa alluded to progress in South Africa to persuade African governments to implement overdue political and economic changes. African autocrats could no longer justify internal oppression and undemocratic practices by blaming apartheid's existence or Pretoria's destabilization policies. Confronted with this new reality, Zimbabwe and Zambia ended their own emergency legislation in July 1990 and in September 1991, respectively. Greater cooperation between the ruling Zimbabwe African National Union (ZANU) and the former opposition Zimbabwe African People's Union (ZAPU) undoubtedly contributed to that decision. Imposed in 1965 by the Ian Smith regime, Zimbabwe's State of Emergency had been renewed semi-annually since independence in 1980, ostensibly to curtail South African aggression. But it was used most frequently against domestic opposition groups.²

As South Africa was being reintegrated into the international community, the Third World was buffeted by criticism and threats of reduced Western economic assistance. When the United Nations Development

Program, through which industrialized nations had channeled roughly $1.4 billion in 1990 to developing countries, published a new index indicating that the world's poorest countries were also the least free, many Third World states responded by drafting a resolution to ban further publication of the human-freedom index.[3] While it is generally agreed that economic development is conducive to the realization of greater political and social freedom, what really disturbed Third World leaders was what they perceived as interference in their internal affairs—a position embraced by South Africa when it was besieged by relentless criticism from developing countries. But poorer countries were also apprehensive about how rich countries would utilize the index, fearing that it would encourage donor states to link development assistance to the recipients' human rights records.[4] However, prior to publication of the index, many industrialized countries had decided to reevaluate their criteria for giving poor states economic aid. For South Africa's neighbors, which usually based their requests for foreign assistance on the negative consequences of South Africa's destabilization policies specifically and apartheid's existence in general, the freedom index was another discouraging development. Faced with demands for investment capital by Eastern Europe and the former Soviet Union amid an economic recession, Western Europe and the United States were disinclined to continue providing aid to African countries that were becoming marginalized in world affairs without requiring them to adopt political and economic reforms.

External pressures on Third World countries, particularly those in Africa, to democratize directly challenged the pervasive personalization of political power as well as the tendency of the state to dominate economic activities. Faced with a multiplicity of ethnic groups, many leaders sought to maintain national cohesion by aggregating power and suppressing political opposition. Akin to South Africa, sub-Saharan African countries will have to allow different ethnic groups to participate in the political process. They will also have to observe human rights and demonstrate their commitment to democratic reforms to the international community. But unlike South Africa, many sub-Saharan African states lack both deeply rooted democratic traditions and leaders who embrace liberal political and economic values. Consequently, impetus for change will most likely continue to originate at the grassroots level and from the international community. As Larry Diamond observed, international condemnation of and even sanctions against human rights violations can certainly help.[5] Yet sanctions that are not carefully fine-tuned and judiciously applied could exacerbate the almost insurmountable problems confronting Africa and render the achievement of democratic reforms virtually impossible. On the other hand, it is unlikely that African leaders will abandon authoritarian rule in the absence of concerted international and domestic pressures. Ironically, by helping to dismantle apartheid, African leaders inadvertently initiated movement toward greater freedom within their own societies and, ultimately, contributed to their own demise.

Because apartheid was largely a symbolic issue and was peripheral to most Third World countries' interests, its abolition is unlikely to have a significant impact on states beyond Africa. Economic relations between South Africa and Taiwan will be relatively less important than they were when South Africa was a pariah state. With greater South African access to Western capital and the replacement of the decentralization program, which encouraged Taiwanese to invest in small factories located in the "homelands," by a new regional development program, South Africa will lessen its dependence on Taiwan. Furthermore, the growing importance of economic power in international relations and improved relations between the People's Republic of China and Taiwan could contribute to Taiwan's political reintegration in the world community. And South Africa's increasing trade with Eastern Europe, the former Soviet Union, and China is likely to contribute to the diminution of Taiwan as a trading partner. On the other hand, South Africa's need for foreign capital and China's reluctance to abandon communism or to recognize Taiwan as a separate state could influence Taiwan and South Africa to maintain close ties. Furthermore, Washington is likely to continue to pressured Taipei to reduce exports to the United States. Under these circumstances, Taiwan's investments in South Africa would enable it to circumvent American trade restrictions.

Although India initiated international efforts to dismantle apartheid and consistently supported southern African liberation movements, its relationship with post-apartheid South Africa was likely to be insignificant. India's main interests were limited to Asia. Moreover, India was preoccupied with its domestic problems, many of which were exacerbated by Rajiv Gandhi's assassination in 1991. India continued to suffer from severe political unrest and ethnic conflict. The caste system, which is deeply embedded in all facets of Indian society, essentially guaranteed continuing turmoil. Furthermore, India's declining economy, due in part to excessive bureaucratic controls on foreign investments and widespread corruption, made it more difficult for lower castes to improve their standard of living and to avoid what amounted to servitude. Yet India's human rights abuses are unlikely to engender a widespread emotional international response. Given India's close links with both South Africa's Indian community and the black majority, New Delhi and Pretoria were likely to enjoy close diplomatic relations. Increased communication and travel between India and South Africa could be conducive to trade, especially in diamonds and gold.

Latin America, marginally involved in southern African politics, was clearly least affected by developments in South Africa. Brazil's interests in developing export markets in Africa continued. Its trade with South Africa, always compartively insignificant, was not affected by apartheid's abolition. However, given the similarities between the South African and Brazilian economies, competition between the two countries for African markets was likely to intensify. The democratization of Latin America, however uncertain, reduced the need for military cooperation with South Africa. Both Chile and Argentina have deliberately reduced support for the military and have placed a greater emphasis on economic and political development.

Similarly, the Middle East's relations with South Africa were influenced primarily by regional developments. The Arab states' interest in apartheid was clearly intertwined with their efforts to undermine Israel's influence in Africa and to regain control over Palestine, or at least to secure a homeland for the Palestinians. Yet both Israel and the PLO posed challenges for the Arab countries. Thus when Yasir Arafat was perceived as supporting Iraq following its occupation of Kuwait, Arab support for the Palestinian cause declined precipitously and many Palestinians in the Gulf were persecuted by Kuwaitis and others. Decreased Arab interest in the Palestinians occurred precisely when South Africa had greater access to oil. In light of the abolition of apartheid's legal structures and diminished Arab interest in the Palestinian cause, the marriage of convenience between the Middle East and sub-Saharan Africa was no longer workable. But the PLO's close links with the ANC and Israel's collaboration with the apartheid regime posed challenges for South Africa's foreign policymakers. Peace in southern Africa reduced the need for South Africa to cooperate militarily with Israel and the ANC's collaboration with the PLO created a reservoir of black South African sympathy for the Palestinians. On the other hand, a negotiated settlement of the Arab-Israeli conflict would remove the dilemma that a post-apartheid South Africa faces in relation to Israel and the PLO.

Most of the challenges for South Africa emanate within the country itself. Apartheid created serious social, economic, and political problems that will actually be highlighted by the absence of apartheid's legal structures. Continuing discrimination by provincial governments, cities, neighborhoods, and various organizations threatened to undermine national efforts to create a nonracial society. If the United States' experience is any guide, legislative changes in South Africa will proceed much faster than behavioral changes. U.S. state and local anti-apartheid groups are likely to concentrate on the latter, thereby making it more difficult for American companies to reinvest in South Africa, despite Washington's decision to lift economic sanctions.

But the removal of all economic sanctions cannot repair the serious damage inflicted on South Africa by apartheid. Pernicious economic apartheid continues and the economic gap between whites and blacks seems virtually unbridgeable. Almost half of all South Africans are living in poverty and conditions in many parts of the country are as bad as those found elsewhere in Africa. Unemployment remains extremely high and the psychological scars left by apartheid are likely to negatively affect South Africa's overall economic performance. Apart from increased ethnic conflicts and rapidly rising crime rates, South Africa was confronted with problems common to all African countries. Overpopulation, inadequate educational opportunities, the lack of housing, and the spread of AIDS are challenges confronting the new South Africa. It is estimated that between 1.3 million and 7 million South Africans could die from AIDS-related illness by the year 2000. This means that the country's health system could collapse under the accumulating weight of AIDS victims.[6] If economic conditions deteriorate significantly and violence escalates, many white South Africans are likely to emigrate, thereby exacerbating the problems.

To begin to rectify apartheid's legacy, the government will have to allocate substantial resources to education, housing, social services, and infrastructural projects. As President F. W. de Klerk stated, "economic growth and constitutional reform have to be mutually reinforcing. Unless the pressing problems of poverty and unemployment are alleviated, constitutional models will be of little avail to us."[7] Thus, economic and social problems present formidable challenges for post-apartheid South Africa.

Despite the inevitable difficulties spawned in part by apartheid, ending the legality of apartheid produced positive consequences. The high cost of maintaining racial domination will be eliminated. The bureaucratic maze associated with enforcing the myriad of apartheid legislation will be unnecessary, thereby allowing the government to reduce expenditures. On the other hand, individuals and companies that benefited from officially sanctioned racial discrimination will undoubtedly regard the legislative changes as undesirable and costly. But for the country's majority, the abolition of apartheid's legal framework opened up numerous opportunities and removed unnecessary burdens from their daily lives. Reduced travel costs as well as commuting time, more efficient utilization of human and material resources, greater competition among individuals, and increased cooperation between South Africans from different racial and socioeconomic backgrounds will contribute to the country's economic resurgence. Dismantling the security apparatus will allow more resources to be allocated to address a plethora of social needs. The removal of economic sanctions reduced imports' costs and increased export earnings. It was conservatively estimated that sanctions, and South Africa's attempts to circumvent them, deprived the country of more than $2 billion annually.[8]

Sub-Saharan Africa, especially the southern African countries, will experience significant challenges as well as opportunities as South Africa is reintegrated into the continent's political and economic affairs. Changes in South Africa, the settlement of the Angolan conflict, and Namibia's independence undermined sub-Saharan African leverage vis-à-vis Pretoria and facilitated greater African acceptance of South Africa. President de Klerk and his foreign minister, Pik Botha, visited Mozambique, Zaire, Zambia, Namibia, Ivory Coast, Senegal, Madagascar, Morocco, Cape Verde, Swaziland, Kenya, Nigeria, and other African states following de Klerk's decision to dismantle apartheid. Kenya and Nigeria, two of Africa's leading states and staunch opponents of the apartheid regime, supported normalizing relations with South Africa.

Confronted with the stark realities of economic decline, political disintegration, and marginalization in international politics and economics, African countries adjusted their South African policies. Nigeria, facing major economic challenges, saw South Africa as a potential trading partner as well as a source of technological expertise. Similarly, Pretoria was cognizant of the political and economic benefits of developing economic links with Nigeria.[9] Yet the acceptance of South Africa as a legitimate member of and a participant in the community of African states challenged Nigeria's leadership role in sub-Saharan Africa. As a member of the OAU, South Africa will undoubtedly dominate discussions of the continent's future.

During his visit to Kenya, de Klerk emphasized his country's role in stabilizing Africa and in assuring progress and prosperity. Referring to South Africa as the "Japan of Africa," de Klerk advocated closer collaboration between South Africa and the rest of the continent in trade, industry, and agriculture.[10] Analogous to Brazil in South America, South Africa's economic power posed serious challenges for Africa. South Africa's access to the European Community (EC) as a member of the African, Caribbean, and Pacific (APC) countries could make it a formidable competitor in the areas of trade and economic assistance. Given its great economic potential, South Africa is likely to attract much of the foreign investment as well as loans extended by multilateral development institutions such as the World Bank and the IMF.

Normalization of relations between sub-Saharan Africa and Pretoria facilitated trade and prompted South African officials and business people to meet with their counterparts on the continent. Concerned about its reliance on distant sources for petroleum supplies, South Africa approached Angola in late 1990 about oil sales. The Angolan government, facing dire economic difficulties that stemmed partly from a civil war that was prolonged and intensified by Pretoria's direct participation in it and its support for UNITA, concluded an agreement that enables South Africa to purchase approximately 100 million barrels of petroleum yearly.[11] Pretoria established trade missions in numerous African states and De Beers Consolidated Mines obtained prospecting rights in several countries, including Tanzania. Due to South Africa's ability to produce consumer items that were difficult to obtain in sub-Saharan Africa, more than 240,000 Zimbabweans applied for short-term visas to go to South Africa to buy consumer products for resale in Zimbabwe. Nigerians, Kenyans, and others also viewed access to South African goods as a solution to their countries' inability to provide consumers with basic products. Consequently, between 1989 and 1991 South Africa's trade with the rest of Africa doubled, reaching about $4 billion annually.[12] To reverse their economic decline, improve their political conditions, and avoid being marginalized in the international system, African states are likely to cooperate economically with South Africa. However, by doing so they risk being influenced politically by Pretoria, a situation few governments find acceptable. The challenge for sub-Saharan Africa will be to minimize their dependence on South Africa.

Achieving economic and political autonomy will be more difficult for South Africa's neighbors. Because of Pretoria's aggression and its determination to apply sanctions against its neighbors selectively and strategically, the European Community, Canada, and the United States had responded favorably to requests from the Frontline States for assistance to develop an infrastructure to give southern African states alternatives to South Africa's roads and railways. But as apartheid was being abolished, international interest in the Frontline States—a designation that was anachronistic in light of changed South African policies—declined. The Europeans focused on Eastern Europe and the former Soviet Union. The EC and international institutions such as the World Bank paid greater attention to South Africa's problems. More importantly, South Africa's pending membership in SADCC raised serious challenges for its smaller neighbors. These concerns prompted SADCC to study the impact of South

Africa's membership on the organization. In early 1991 the ANC sat as a full SADCC member during an annual consultative conference with donors in Windhoek, Namibia. But the donor countries were clearly concerned about SADCC's decision to confine discussions on a future South Africa to the liberation movements.[13]

How SADCC will respond to the post-apartheid South Africa became a pressing foreign policy issue. The nature of the power-sharing arrangements under a new South African constitution would undoubtedly influence relations between SADCC and Pretoria. However, equally important was how SADCC would be affected by the removal of the South African threat. Cohesion among members, which was sometimes difficult to achieve even during South Africa's destabilization efforts, will be harder to maintain. Whereas Zambia is likely to embrace South Africa, Zimbabwe, which will lose its dominant position in SADCC, is likely to remain apprehensive about South Africa's regional ambitions. Because South Africa is the locomotive for regional development, it will attract much of the foreign investments. This means that inefficient industries in Zimbabwe, Zambia, and elsewhere will find it harder to compete with South African firms. That problem will be exacerbated by the greater access of neighboring states to South African products and by domestic pressures within South Africa to encourage exports.[14] To improve their ability to compete with South Africa, SADCC members—individually and collectively—can either engage in protectionism or reduce government interference in the economy and encourage more economic and political liberalization. However, given the porousness of national boundaries, protectionism would be counterproductive. Without adopting serious political and economic reforms, the southern African states cannot hope to become a counterweight to the post-apartheid South Africa.

Because South Africa itself will be confronted with numerous challenges emanating from rising expectations and the legacy of apartheid, greater regional cooperation seems to be an approach that will be in the interest of South Africa as well as its neighbors. Cooperation will require South Africa to consult with Zimbabwe, Zambia, and other states instead of trying to control them. An emphasis on finding solutions that are generally beneficial to the region is also an integral component of a collaborative approach. Cooperation can result in sharing resources in a way that results in a more efficient utilization of them. The rich agricultural lands of Zambia, Mozambique, Zimbabwe, and Angola could provide food not only for the region but also for much of Africa. Commercial forestry plantations in the Transvaal that require much water could be shifted onto Mozambique's coastal plains. Greater use of Angola's and

Mozambique's abundant hydroelectric potential could reduce the pollution in South Africa that is caused by a heavy reliance on coal.[15]

The challenge for African states in particular and the Third World in general is to replace policies of confrontation with policies that emphasize cooperation with South Africa. But this is only possible if a post-apartheid South Africa respects its neighbors and adjusts to the emerging international system in which force is of marginal utility. Cooperation, consultation, and negotiations will be generally beneficial to all states.

Notes

CHAPTER 1: THE THIRD WORLD AND SOUTH AFRICA

1. See Richard J. Payne, *The Nonsuperpowers and South Africa: Implications for U.S. Policy* (Bloomington: Indiana University Press, 1990).

2. Alan Tonelson, "The Real National Interest," *Foreign Policy*, no. 61 (Winter 1985–86):49.

3. James N. Rosenau, "Introduction," in *The Domestic Sources of Foreign Policy*, ed. James N. Rosenau (New York: Free Press, 1967), 2.

4. John J. Stremlau, "The Foreign Policies of Developing Countries," in *The Foreign Policy Priorities of Third World States*, ed. John J. Stremlau (Boulder, Colo.: Westview Press, 1982), 2.

5. Charles W. Kegley, Jr., and Eugene R. Wittkopf, "Introduction," in *Domestic Sources of American Foreign Policy*, eds. Charles W. Kegley, Jr., and Eugene R. Wittkopf (New York: St. Martin's Press, 1988), 2.

6. See Department of Foreign Affairs, *Mini Atlas of Southern Africa* (Pretoria: Department of Foreign Affairs, 1990), 15.

7. Commonwealth Committee of Foreign Ministers on Southern Africa, *South Africa: The Sanctions Report* (London: Penguin Books, 1989), 214–215.

8. John Day, "A Failure of Foreign Policy: The Case of Rhodesia," in *Constraints and Adjustments in British Foreign Policy*, ed. Michael Leiter (London: Allen and Unwin, 1976), 150.

9. Robert L. Rothstein, *The Weak in the World of the Strong* (New York: Columbia University Press, 1977), 105–106; and Olatunde Ojo, D. K. Orwa, and C. M. B. Utete, *African International Relations* (New York: Longman, 1985), 47.

10. Mohamed El-Khawas, "The Third World Stance on Apartheid: The UN Record," *The Journal of Modern African Studies* 9, no. 3 (October 1971):444.

11. See Newell M. Stultz, "The Apartheid Issue at the General Assembly," *African Affairs* 86, no. 342 (January 1987):31; and The Commonwealth Office, *Commonwealth Statement on Apartheid in Sport: The Gleneagles Agreement* (London: The Commonwealth Office, 1977), 1.

12. See Jacques Delors, "Europe's Ambitions," *Foreign Policy*, no. 80 (Fall 1990):14–15.

13. Charles F. Herman, "Changing Course: When Governments Choose to Redirect Foreign Policy," *International Studies Quarterly* 34, no. 1 (March 1990):5.

14. Ibid, 12.

15. David Beresford, "Reforms Herald a New Era in South Africa," *Guardian Weekly*, February 11, 1990, 7; and Alan Cowell, "African National Congress Suspends Its Guerrilla War," *The New York Times*, August 7, 1990, A2.

16. See Payne, *The Nonsuperpowers and South Africa*, 20–23.

17. South African Reserve Bank, *Annual Economic Report 1990* (Pretoria: South Africa Reserve Bank, 1990), 65.

18. Robert Graham, "Comecon's Uncomradely Threat to Cuba," *Financial Times*, March 21, 1990, 9.

19. Patrick Moberly, "The World and South Africa: A New Perspective," *The World Today* 46, no.6 (July 31, 1990):3.

20. Christopher S. Wren, "Moscow Circus, in a Thaw, to Tour South Africa," *The New York Times*, July 31, 1990, A3.

21. Diana B. Henriques, "Soviets to Sell Diamond Stockpile Through a Subsidiary of De Beers," *The New York Times*, July 26, 1990, A1.

22. "Horn, Botha Exchange Views," *FBIS-EEU*, January 5, 1990, 49.

23. "ANC's Nzo Criticizes Botha's Visit to Budapest," *FBIS-EEU*, January 8, 1990, 59.

24. "Dubcek, Ministry Comment on Mandela Release," *FBIS-EEU*, February 15, 1990, 23; "Maksic on Future of South African Relations," *FBIS-EEU*, February 15, 1990, 75; and "Applications to Immigrate to South Africa Increase," *FBIS-EEU*, March 16, 1990, 41.

25. Michael Manley, "Southern Needs," *Foreign Policy*, no. 80 (Fall 1990):41.

26. Crawford Young, "Beyond Patrimonial Autonomy: The African Challenge," in *Beyond Autocracy in Africa: Working Papers for the Inaugural Seminar of the Governance in Africa Program* (Atlanta, Ga.: The Carter Center, 1989), 21.

27. Colin Legum, "The Coming of Africa's Second Independence," *The Washington Quarterly* 13, no. 1 (Winter 1990):129.

28. Robert Fatton, "Liberal Democracy in Africa," *Political Science Quarterly* 105, no. 3 (1990):456.

29. Samuel P. Huntington, "Will More Countries Become Democratic?" *Political Science Quarterly* 99, no. 2 (Summer 1984):206.

30. Claude E. Welch, "Human Rights as a Problem in Contemporary Africa," in *Human Rights and Development in Africa*, eds. Claude E. Welch and Ronald Mettzer (Albany: State University of New York Press, 1984), 13.

31. J. F. Ajayi, "Expectations of Independence," *Daedalus* 111, no. 2 (Spring 1982):5.

32. John A. Wiseman, *Democracy in Black Africa: Survival and Revival* (New York: Paragon House Publishers, 1990), 18.

33. Huntington, "Will More Countries Become Democratic?" 199.

34. Meddi Mugyenyi, "Development First, Democracy Second," in *Democratic Theory and Practice in Africa*, eds. Walter O. Oyugi, et al. (London: James Currey, 1988), 179.

35. Huntington, "Will More Countries Become Democratic?" 199.

36. Ibid., 204.

37. Ibid., 217.

38. Naomi Chazan, et al., *Politics and Society in Contemporary Africa* (Boulder, Colo.: Lynne Rienner, 1988), 102.

39. Donald Rothchild, "State and Ethnicity in Africa: A Policy Perspective," in *Ethnic Preference and Public Policy in Developing States*, eds. Neil Nevitte and Charles H. Kennedy (Boulder, Colo.: Lynne Rienner, 1986), 15.

40. Jane Perlez, "East-Bloc's Admirers in Africa Draw Line at Multiparty Politics," *The New York Times*, April 22, 1990, A11.

41. Robert I. Rotberg, "Outlook Brighter for Democracy in Africa," *The Christian Science Monitor*, October 29, 1990, 19.

42. Jan Raath, "Mugabe Plan for One-Party State Suffers a Setback," *The Times* (London), September 26, 1990, 11.

43. Kenneth B. Noble, "Zaire Leader Invites Dialogue and Reaps a Harsh Review," *The New York Times*, April 14, 1990, A1.

44. Costas Christ, "The Boiling Point Nears in Kenya," *The New York Times*, July 23, 1990, A13; and Jane Perlez, "Archbishop Warns Kenyans on Graft," *The New York Times*, August 13, 1990, A6.

45. Richard Joseph, "Glasnost for Africa," *The New York Times*, December 28, 1989, A23. See also Hari Sharan Chhabra, "East Europe Has an Impact on Africa," *The Times of India*, May 23, 1990, 8.

46. Roy Laishley, "Gulf Crisis Threatens Further Setbacks to African Economies," *Africa Recovery* 4, no. 2 (July–September): 19.

47. Richard Joseph, "Support Africa's Move Toward Democracy, Too," *The Christian Science Monitor*, June 4, 1990, 19.

48. Jane Perlez, "U.S. Legislators Warn Kenya Rights Record Endangers Aid," *The New York Times*, November 16, 1990, A7; and Peter Grier, "U.S. Rethinks Africa Aid," *The Christian Science Monitor*, July 12, 1990, 7.

49. Marvine Howe, "Kenyan Human Rights Lawyer Urges Economic Sanctions by U.S.," *The New York Times*, July 29, 1990, A19.

50. Peter Norman, "Major Warns of Stricter Control on Third World Aid," *Financial Times*, May 9, 1990, 8; and Mary Brasier, "Attack on Third World Spending," *Guardian Weekly*, May 20, 1990, 7.

51. Rone Tempest, "Aid Conditions Frustrate Africans," *The Philadelphia Inquirer*, June 24, 1990, 11A.

52. Salim Lone, "Donors Demand Political Reforms," *Africa Recovery* 4, no. 2 (July–September 1990):3.

CHAPTER 2: SUB-SAHARAN AFRICA

1. Robert Jackson and Carl Rosberg, "The Marginality of African States," in *African Independence: The First Twenty-Five Years*, eds. Gwendolen Carter and Patrick O'Meara (Bloomington: Indiana University Press, 1985), 51.

2. Leroy Vail, "Introduction: Ethnicity in Southern African History," in *The Creation of Tribalism in Southern Africa*, ed. Leroy Vail (Berkeley: University of California Press, 1989), 2.

3. Colin Legum, "Democracy in Africa: Hopes and Trends," in *Democracy and Pluralism in Africa*, ed. Dov Ronen (Boulder, Colo.: Lynne Rienner, 1986), 180.

4. Donald Rothchild, "Hegemony and State Softness," in *The African State in Transition*, ed. Zaki Ergas (New York: St. Martin's Press, 1987), 126.

5. Thomas Callaghy, "The State as Lame Leviathan: The Patrimonial Administrative State in Africa," in *The African State in Transition*, 87–116.

6. Samuel Decalo, *Psychoses of Power: African Personal Dictatorships* (Boulder, Colo.: Westview Press, 1989), 187.

7. Jackson and Rosberg, "The Marginality of African States," 52.

8. The World Bank, *Sub-Saharan Africa: From Crisis to Sustainable Growth* (Washington, D.C.: The World Bank, 1989), 2.

9. Richard Sandbrook, "Taming the African Leviathan," *World Policy Journal* 7, no. 4 (Fall 1990):674.

10. The World Bank, *Sub-Saharan Africa*, 20.

11. R. Stephen Brent, "Aiding Africa," *Foreign Policy*, 80 (Fall 1990):125.

12. The World Bank, *Sub-Saharan Africa*, 3.

13. The World Bank, *World Development Report 1990* (New York: Oxford University Press, 1990), 140.

14. John Ravenhill, "Reversing Africa's Economic Decline," *World Policy Journal* 7, no. 4 (Fall 1990):710.

15. Benjamin D. Myers, "African Voting in the United Nations General Assembly," *The Journal of Modern African Studies* 4, no. 2 (October 1966):214.

16. Douglas G. Anglin, "Zambia in Southern African Detente," *International Journal* 30, no. 3 (Summer 1975):476–477.

17. UN Center Against Apartheid, *Declaration on the Question of South Africa by the Ad-Hoc Committee on Southern Africa of the Organization of African Unity* (New York: United Nations, 1989), 2.

18. Ibid., 4.

19. Adekunle Ajala, "The OAU and Southern Africa," in *Southern Africa in the 1980s*, eds. Olajide Aluko and Timothy Shaw (London: Allen and Unwin, 1985), 4.

20. Amadu Sesay, et. al., *The OAU After Twenty Years* (Boulder, Colo.: Westview Press, 1984), 30; and A. Bolaji Akiniyemi, "Africa—Challenges and Responses: A Foreign Policy Perspective," *Daedalus* 111, no. 2 (Spring 1982):249.

21. Council of Ministers, "OAU Resolution on South Africa," in *Africa Contemporary Record*, ed. Colin Legum (New York: Africana Publishing Company, 1977), C6.

22. Agrippah Mugomba, *The Foreign Policy of Despair: Africa and the Sale of Arms to South Africa* (Nairobi: East African Literature Bureau, 1977), 138.

23. Zdenek Cervenka, "The Organization of African Unity in 1976," in *African Contemporary Record*, ed. Colin Legum (New York: Africana Publishing Company, 1977), A69.

24. Ajala, "The OAU and Southern Africa," 5.

25. I. William Zartman, "The African States as a Source of Change," in *South Africa in the 1980s*, eds. Richard E. Bissell and Chester A. Crocker (Boulder, Colo.: Westview Press, 1979), 111.

26. Olusola Ojo, "Oil Sanctions and South Africa," in *Southern Africa in the 1980s*, 236.

27. "Excerpts from the Declarations and Resolutions Adopted by the Foreign Ministers of the Nonaligned Countries at the Eighth Nonaligned Summit, Harare (Zimbabwe), August 28–September 7, 1986," in *Africa Contemporary Record*, ed. Colin Legum (New York: Africana Publishing Company, 1988), C38-C39.

28. See Richard J. Payne, *The Nonsuperpowers and South Africa* (Bloomington: Indiana University Press, 1990), chapters 2 and 7.

29. Colin Legum, ed., *Africa Contemporary Record* (New York: Africana Publishing Company, 1984), B198.

30. Colin Legum and Marion E. Doro, eds., *Africa Contemporary Record* (New York: Africana Publishing Company, 1989), B68.

31. Kenneth B. Noble, "Zaire's Trade with South Africa Is Becoming More Widespread," *The New York Times*, December 5, 1989, A10.

32. "Agreement Signed by Delegation from Angola, Cuba, and South Africa in Brazzaville, Congo, December 13, 1988," reprinted in *International Legal Materials* 28, no. 4 (July 1989):9; and "Four Steps on the Road to Peace in Southwestern Africa," reprinted in *International Legal Materials* 28, no. 4 (July, 1989): 947–948.

33. Christopher S. Wren, "Ivory Coast Welcomes de Klerk with Full Pomp," *The New York Times*, December 3, 1989, A8; and Colin Legum, "The Southern African Crisis," in *African Contemporary Record*, eds. Colin Legum and Marion E. Doro (New York: Africana Publishing Company, 1989), A7.

34. "African Groups Agrees to Pretoria Contacts," *The New York Times*, March 20, 1990, A3.

35. Busari Adebisi, "Nigeria's Relations with South Africa, 1960 to 1975," *Africa Quarterly* 16, no. 3 (January 1977): 72.

36. Ibrahim A. Gamari, *Theory and Reality in Foreign Policy Making: Nigeria after the Second Republic* (Atlantic Highlands, N.J.: Humanities Press International, 1989), 5.

37. "Concert of Medium Powers: The Lagos Forum," in *Africa Contemporary Record*, eds. Colin Legum and Marion E. Doro (New York: Africana Publishing Company, 1989), C55.

38. Larry Diamond, *Class, Ethnicity, and Democracy in Nigeria* (Syracuse, N.Y.: Syracuse University Press, 1988), 291.

39. William Keeling,, "Religious Tensions Behind Challenge to Babangida," *Financial Times*, April 23, 1990, 3.

40. "Civilian Rule Postponed to 1992," *Africa Research Bulletin-Political Series*, August 15, 1987, 8567.

41. "Nigeria: First Step to Civilian Rule," *Africa Research Bulletin-Political Series*, January 15, 1988, 8725.

42. Anthony A. Akinola, "A Critique of Nigeria's Proposed Two-Party System," *The Journal of Modern African Studies* 27, no. 1 (March 1989):109–110.

43. "Civilian Rule Postponed to 1992," 8567.

44. "Nigeria: First Step to Civilian Rule," 8725.

45. Akinola, "A Critique of Nigeria's Proposed Two-Party System," 122.

46. "Nigeria's Case for Relief," *Financial Times*, April 25, 1990, 14.

47. Richard Joseph, "Class, State, and Prebendal Politics in Nigeria," *Journal of Commonwealth and Comparative Politics* 21, no. 3 (1983):26.

48. Ibid, 32.

49. Michael Holman, "Nigeria: A Question of Debt Relief," *Financial Times Survey*, March 19, 1990, 1; and P. Chudi Uwazurike, "Confronting Potential Breakdown: The Nigerian Redemocratization Process in Critical Perspective," *The Journal of Modern African Studies* 28, no. 1 (March 1990):73.

50. Kenneth B. Noble, "Nigeria's Economic Plan Falters," *The New York Times*, June 19, 1989, D10.

51. The World Bank, *Sub-Saharan Africa*, 28.

52. Tony Hawkins, "Africa May Come Second," *Financial Times Survey*, March 19, 1990, 4; and Jato Thompson, "Shuttle Diplomacy Brings Home the Bacon," *African Business*, April 1990, 37.

53. Brian Pinto, "Nigeria During and After the Oil Boom: A Policy Comparison with Indonesia," *The World Bank Economic Review* 1, no. 3 (1987):432.

54. Jato Thompson, "Can This Farm Plan Stay the Course?" *African Business* April 1990, 41.

55. Holman, "Nigeria: A Question of Debt Relief," 1.

56. U.S. Department of State, *Country Reports on Human Rights Practices for 1988: Reports Submitted to the Committee on Foreign Relations, U.S. Senate, and Committee on Foreign Affairs, U.S. House of Representatives* (Washington, D.C.: U.S. Government Printing Office, 1989), 267.

57. Amnesty International, *Amnesty International Report 1989* (London: Amnesty International Publications, 1989), 76.

58. Ibid., 77.

59. Busari Adebisi, "Nigeria's Relations with South Africa, 1960–1975," *Africa Quarterly* 16, no. 3 (January 1977): 80.

60. "Lagos Apartheid Conference Adopts Communique," *FBIS-AFR*, November 18, 1988, 44.

61. Kenoye K. Eke, *Nigeria's Foreign Policy Under Two Military Governments 1966–1979* (Lewiston, N.Y.: The Edwin Mellen Press, 1990), 66.

62. Adebisi, "Nigeria's Relations with South Africa," 77–79.

63. Alhaji Shehu Shagari, "Nigerian Policy Toward Southern Africa," *Africa Report* 27, no. 1 (January-February 1982):21.

64. Colin Legum, ed., *Africa Contemporary Record* (New York: Africana Publishing Company, 1987), B135.

65. "Lagos Apartheid Conference Adopts Communique," 44; "African Leaders Hosting Botha Criticized," *FBIS-AFR*, November 9, 1988, 22; and "Babangida Opens Lagos Apartheid Conference," *FBIS-AFR*, November 10, 1988, 23.

66. Colin Legum, ed., *Africa Contemporary Record* (New York: Africana Publishing Company, 1978), B748.

67. Colin Legum, ed., *Africa Contemporary Record* (New York: Africana Publishing Company, 1988), B121.

68. Colin Legum, ed., *Africa Contemporary Record* (New York: Africana Publishing Company, 1989), B755.

69. Olajide Aluko, "Nigeria and Southern Africa," in *African Independence: The First Twenty-Five Years*, eds. Gwendolen Carter and Patrick O'Meara (Bloomington: Indiana University Press, 1985), 143; and "ANC Aid Pledge," *Africa Research Bulletin-Political Series*, January 15, 1987, 8327.

70. F. R. Metrowich, *South Africa's New Frontiers* (Sandton, South Africa: Valiant Publishers, 1977), 46; and "No Color Bar in South Africa's Trade," *U.S. News and World Report*, April 10, 1978, 32.

71. Business International South Africa, *Apartheid and Business: An Analysis of the Rapidly Evolving Challenge Facing Companies with Investments in South Africa* (Pretoria: Business International South Africa, 1980), 445.

72. Colin Legum, "The Diplomacy of Tory Pragmatists," in *Africa Contemporary Record*, ed. Colin Legum (New York: Africana Publishing Company, 1980), A130.

73. United Nations, *Report of the Intergovernmental Group to Monitor the Supply and Shipping of Petroleum Products to South Africa* (New York: UN General Assembly, 1987), 33.

74. "Thatcher Visits Nigeria," *Africa Research Bulletin-Political Series*, February 15, 1988, 8762.

75. United Nations, *Policies of Apartheid of the Government of South Africa: Concerted International Action for the Elimination of Apartheid* (New York: UN General Assembly, 1987), 22; and Ihebom Egedo, "Nigeria and Apartheid," *The Round Table*, no. 301 (January 1987):38.

76. Kenneth Kaunda, *Humanism in Zambia: A Guide to the Nation* (Lusaka: Government Printer, 1967); and Douglas G. Anglin and Timothy M. Shaw, *Zambia's Foreign Policy: Studies in Diplomacy and Dependence* (Boulder, Colo.: Westview Press, 1979), 40.

77. Stephen Chan, "Zambia's Foreign Policy—Elitism and Power," *The Round Table*, no. 302 (April 1987):230; and Douglas G. Anglin, "Zambia in Southern African Detente," *International Journal* 30, no. 3 (Summer 1975):474.

78. Stephen Chan, *Exporting Apartheid: Foreign Policies in Southern Africa* (New York: St. Martin's Press, 1990), 80.

79. Marcia M. Burdette, *Zambia: Between Two Worlds* (Boulder, Colo.: Westview Press, 1988), 144.

80. "Update: Zambia," *Africa Report* 34, no. 1 (January-February, 1989):12.

81. Payne, *The Nonsuperpowers and South Africa*, 207–208.

82. Kenneth Good, "Zambia and the Liberation of South Africa," *The Journal of Modern African Studies* 25, no. 3 (1987):531; and "Kaunda Notes Youth Unemployment Time Bomb," *FBIS-AFR*, April 28, 1989, 29.

83. Christopher S. Wren, "Even the Best of Times are Tough in Zambia," *The New York Times*, May 29, 1989, A36; Kenneth Good, "Debt and the One-Party State in Zambia," *The Journal of Modern African Studies* 27, no. 2 (1989): 298–300; and Jurgen Wulf, "Zambia Under the IMF Regime," *African Affairs* 87, no. 349 (October 1988):580.

84. Jennifer Seymour Whitaker, *How Can Africa Survive?* (New York: Council on Foreign Relations Press, 1988), 164; Roger Young and John Loxley, *Zambia: An Assessment of Zambia's Structural Adjustment Experience* (Ottawa, Ontario: The North-South Institute, 1990), 8; and "Copperbelt Rioting," *Africa Research Bulletin-Political Series*, June 15, 1987, 8518.

85. Ronald T. Libby, *The Politics of Economic Power in Southern Africa* (Princeton, N.J.: Princeton University Press, 1987), 230.

86. Phyllis Johnson and David Martin, *Apartheid Terrorism: The Destabilization Report* (Bloomington: Indiana University Press, 1989), 77–79.

87. Economic Commission for Africa, *South African Destabilization: The Economic Cost of Frontline Resistance to Apartheid* (New York: United Nations, 1989), 32–33.

88. Good, "Debt and the One-Party State," 307; and Carolyn Baylies and Morris Szeftel, "The Rise to Political Prominence of the Zambian Business Class," in *The Dynamics of the One-Party State in Zambia*, ed. Cherry Gertzel (Manchester, England: Manchester University Press, 1984), 58–60.

89. "Opposition Leader Arrested," *Africa Research Bulletin-Political Series*, July 15, 1987, 8547; and "Pretoria Coup Bid Claim," *Africa Research Bulletin-Political Series*, May 15, 1987, 8482.

90. U.S. Department of State, *Country Reports on Human Rights Practices for 1988*, 413–414.

91. Anglin, "Zambia in Southern Africa," 480.

92. "Zambia-South Africa, Let Us Talk About It," *Africa* (June 1982):18.

93. Deon Geldenhuys, *The Diplomacy of Isolation: South African Foreign Policy* (New York: St. Martin's Press, 1984), 213.
94. "Zambia-South Africa," 17.
95. "Kaunda Denies Aid Reason for Talks with the Republic of South Africa," *FBIS-AFR*, October 19, 1984, U5.
96. "De Klerk, Pik Botha Interview," *FBIS-AFR*, August 29, 1989, 38.
97. Colin Legum, ed., *Africa Contemporary Record* (New York: Africana Publishing Company, 1988), B876.
98. "Zambia Re-routing Will Hit Tazara," *South Scan* 5, no. 33 (September 7, 1990):249.
99. Colin Legum, "The Southern African Crisis 1986–1987," in *Africa Contemporary Record*, ed. Colin Legum (New York: Africana Publishing Company, 1988), p. A43.
100. "Minister Declares RSA Trade Ties Continue," *The Star* (Johannesburg), February 27, 1988, 8.
101. "Kaunda Warns Against Purchase of RSA Goods," *FBIS-AFR*, October 6, 1987, 17.
102. United Nations Industrial Development Organization, *Industrial Cooperation Through the Southern African Development Coordination Conference* (New York: United Nations, 1985), 85.
103. Joseph Hanlon, *Beggar Your Neighbor: Apartheid Power in Southern Africa* (Bloomington: Indiana University Press, 1986), 251.
104. "Oil Prices Increase Throughout Region," *South Scan* 5, no. 33 (September 7, 1990): 249; and "Government Requests Oil From South Africa," *FBIS-AFR*, May 6, 1985, U7.
105. Department of Foreign Affairs, *Mini Atlas of Southern Africa* (Pretoria: Department of Foreign Affairs, 1990), 15.
106. "Musokotwane: No Plans to Nationalize RSA Firms," *FBIS-AFR*, January 29, 1987, D8.
107. "Zambia Denies Reports of SA Trade Mission," *FBIS-AFR*, September 15, 1990, 15; and "South African Commerce Delegation Arrives," *FBIS-AFR*, November 16, 1988, 39.
108. Ben Arnold, "Southern Africa's Elder Statesman," *Africa Report* 35, no. 1 (March-April 1990):36.
109. "ANC Urges Members to Behave," *BBC World Service*, May 8, 1989, reprinted in *FBIS-AFR*, May 9, 1989, 23; and "Police Detain ANC Member on Murder Charge," *FBIS-AFR*, May 17, 1989, 12.
110. "Kaunda Reiterates Importance of de Klerk Talks," *FBIS-AFR*, August 21, 1989, 15–16; and "Kaunda Shows Growing Impatience with ANC," *FBIS-AFR*, August 21, 1989, 14.
111. Kenneth Good, "Zambia and the Liberation of South Africa," *The Journal of Modern African Studies* 25, no. 3 (1987):523.
112. James R. Scarritt, "The Effects of South Africa on Zambian Politics: Overt and Systematic Destabilization," in *South Africa in Southern Africa:*

Domestic Change and International Conflict, eds. Edmond J. Keller and Louis A. Picard (Boulder, Colo.: Lynne Rienner, 1989), 184–185.

CHAPTER 3: ASIA

1. Lucian Pye, *Asian Power and Politics: The Cultural Dimensions of Authority* (Cambridge, Mass.: Harvard University Press, 1985), 20.

2. Harish Kapur, "India's Foreign Policy Under Rajiv Gandhi," *The Round Table*, no. 304 (October 1987):477.

3. Marshall M. Bouton, "Foreign Relations: Elusive Regional Security," in *India Briefing, 1987*, ed. Marshall M. Bouton (Boulder, Colo.: Westview Press, 1987), 160.

4. William T. Tow, *Subregional Security Cooperation in the Third World* (Boulder, Colo.: Lynne Rienner, 1990), 8.

5. D. Anthony Low, "Development's Contexts: Asia, Africa," *Daedalus* 118, no. 1 (Winter 1989):18–23.

6. Catherine Gwin and Lawrence A. Veit, "The Indian Miracle," *Foreign Policy*, no. 58 (Spring 1985):81.

7. Francine R. Frankel, "India's Democracy in Transition," *World Policy Journal* 7, no. 3 (Summer 1990):53.

8. Swaminathan S. Aiyar, "Wooing Foreign Investors," *The Times of India*, July 18, 1990, 6.

9. World Bank, *India: Recent Developments and Medium-Term Issues* (Washington, D.C.: World Bank, 1989), XXII.

10. "India's External Debt Mounting," *The Hindu* (International Edition), July 21, 1990, 12; "Gulf Crisis Imposes $26 Billion Extra Oil Bill on Third World," *The Times of India*, September 20, 1990, 11.

11. Padma Srinivasan, "Ethnicity in the Politics of Africa and India," *The Indian Journal of Political Science* 47, no. 4 (1986):522.

12. Phillips Talbot, *India in the 1980s* (New York: Foreign Policy Association, 1983), 13.

13. Richard Sisson, "India in 1989: A Year of Elections," *Asian Survey* 30, no. 2 (February 1990):117; and James Clad, "Towards a Hindu Raj," *Far Eastern Economic Review*, September 20, 1990, 28.

14. Smriti Vohra, "Caste a Reality of Society," *The Times of India*, October 5, 1990, 4.

15. Pye, *Asian Power and Politics*, 134.

16. Jack Donnelly, *Universal Human Rights in Theory and Practice* (Ithaca, N.Y.: Cornell University Press, 1989), 128–131; and I. P. Desai, et al., *Caste, Caste Conflict and Reservations* (New Delhi: Ajanta Publications, 1985), 3.

17. P. A. Kluck, "Social Systems," in *India: A Country Study*, ed. Richard F. Nyrop (Washington, D.C.: U.S. Government Printing Office, 1985), 224.

18. Donnelly, *Universal Human Rights*, 135.

19. Suma Chitnis, "Positive Discrimination in India with Reference to Education," in *From Independence to Statehood: Managing Ethnic Conflict in Five*

African and Asian States, eds. Robert B. Goldmann and A. Jeyaratnam Wilson (London: Francis Pinter, 1984), 33.

20. Christopher Thomas, "Brahmins Tighten Grip on Top Jobs," *The Times* (London), January 25, 1991, 11.

21. Barbara Crossette, "Hiring Plan Angers India's Students," *The New York Times*, August 22, 1990, A4; and Sheila Tefft, "Caste Dispute Deepens India's Political Crisis," *The Christian Science Monitor*, December 28, 1990, 8.

22. "Mandela Hails Mandal Report," *The Times of India*, October 16, 1990, 18; and "Mandela Statement Flayed," *The Times of India*, October 16, 1990, 3.

23. Amnesty International, *Amnesty International Report 1989* (London: Amnesty International, 1989), 175.

24. Christopher Thomas, "Singh Links Drive to Assist Lowly Castes with Plight of Child Slaves," *The Times* (London), September 20, 1990, 11; and Sheila Rule, "British Group Finds Slavery is Flourishing," *The New York Times*, July 5, 1990, A49.

25. Joy Brain, "Indentured and Free Indians in the Economy of Colonial Natal," in *Enterprise and Exploitation in a Victorian Colony*, eds. Bill Guest and John M. Sellers (Pietermaritzburg: University of Natal Press, 1985), 202.

26. Anirdha Gupta, "India and Africa South of the Sahara," in *India's Foreign Policy*, ed. Bimal Prasad (New Delhi: Vikas Publishing House, 1979), 264.

27. T. G. Ramamurthi, *Fight Against Apartheid* (New Delhi: ABC Publishing House, 1979), 264.

28. Heribert Adam, "Ethnic Politics and Crisis Management: Comparing South Africa and Israel," *Journal of Asian and African Studies* 28, nos. 1–2 (1983):12.

29. "Official Statement on Killing of Innocent Africans in Soweto, June 19, 1976," in *India in Asia and Africa: Documents, 1976–1978*, ed. J. A. Naik (Atlantic Highlands, N.J.: Humanities Press, 1978), 506; and "South Africa," in *India in Asia and Africa: Documents, 1979*, ed. J. A. Naik (Atlantic Highlands, N.J.: Humanities Press, 1982), 121.

30. Ministry of Information and Broadcasting, *India: A Reference Manual* (New Delhi: Government of India, 1983), 471.

31. United Nations, "First Embassy of SWAPO Inaugurated," *Namibia Bulletin*, no. 6 (1986):23.

32. "One Man, One Vote, Only Way: Mandela," *The Times of India*, October 17, 1990, 1.

33. "India Endorses Mandela's Stand," *The Times of India*, October 16, 1990, 1; and "Rousing Welcome for Mandela," *The Times of India*, October 16, 1990, 10.

34. Hari Sharan Chhabra, "India and Africa: A Decade of Relations," in *Africa Contemporary Record*, ed. Colin Legum (New York: Africana Publishing Company, 1985), A243.

35. "Gandhi to Visit Four African States," *FBIS-South Asia*, May 6, 1986, E1; and "Vice President on Aid to Frontline African States," *FBIS-South Asia*, September 30, 1986, E1.

36. Andrew Meldrum, "On the Frontline," *Africa Report* 31, no. 4 (July-August 1986):14.

37. Rajiv Gandhi, "The Movement of Nonaligned Countries," *Africa Quarterly* 23, nos. 3–4 (1987):2.

38. International Labor Office, *Special Report of the Director-General on the Application of the Declaration Concerning Apartheid* (Geneva: ILO, 1988), 159.

39. Colin Legum, ed., *Africa Contemporary Record* (New York: Africana Publishing Company, 1988), B374.

40. Sunil Saraf and Fiammetta Rocco, "India and Africa: Economic Ties Lag Behind Political Links," *Africa Economic Digest*, August 31, 1985, 36; and "Sanctions on South Africa: Double-Edged," *The Economist*, August 16, 1986, 42.

41. Gita Piramal, "Rough Times for Indian Diamonds," *The Times of India*, June 21, 1990, 9.

42. "Ministries Differ on Gold Import Scheme," *The Times of India*, July 25, 1990, 9; and Sanjoy Hazarika, "India's Clandestine Market in Gold," *The New York Times*, January 18, 1988, D6.

43. Vijay Gupta, "India and Africa," *Africa Quarterly* 17, no. 4 (April 1978):111.

44. Signe Landgren, *Embargo Disimplemented: South Africa's Military Industry* (New York: Oxford University Press, 1989), 87.

45. "Commonwealth Games Boycott," *Africa Research Bulletin-Political Series*, August 15, 1986, 8171.

46. Deon Geldenhuys, *Isolated States: A Comparative Analysis* (New York: Cambridge University Press, 1990), 93; Efraim Inbar, *Outcast Countries in the World Community* (Denver, Colo.: University of Denver Press, 1985), 55; Robert E. Harkavy, "The Pariah State Syndrome," *Orbis* 21, no. 3 (Fall 1977):624–627; and Richard K. Betts, "Paranoids, Pygmies, Pariahs and Nonproliferation," *Foreign Policy*, no. 26 (Spring 1977):157–167.

47. Chang Liang-jen, ed., *Republic of China Yearbook 1989* (Taipei, Taiwan: Kwang Hwa Publishing Company, 1989), 227.

48. Thomas J. Bellows, "Taiwan's Foreign Policy in the 1970s: A Case Study of Adaptation and Viability," *Asian Survey* 16, no. 7 (July 1976):607.

49. Marc J. Cohen, *Taiwan at the Crossroads* (Washington, D.C.: Asia Resource Center, 1988), 226; and Sheryl WuDunn, "Taiwan's Mainland Efforts Widen," *The New York Times*, April 14, 1990, A19.

50. "Taiwan Trade Takes up Third of China Deficit," *Financial Times*, February 28, 1990, 6; and Elizabeth Cheng, "Thaw in China-Taiwan Relations Boasts Business Links," *Far Eastern Economic Review*, December 10, 1987, 90.

51. M. Shadid Alam, *Government and Markets in Economic Development Strategies: Lessons from Korea, Taiwan, and Japan* (New York: Praeger, 1989), 19.

52. Chalmers Johnson, "Political Institutions and Economic Performance: The Government-Business Relationship in Japan, South Korea and Taiwan," in

the Political Economy of the New Asian Industrialism, ed. Frederic C. Deyo (Ithaca, N.Y.: Cornell University Press, 1987), 152.

53. Johnson, "Political Institutions," 145; and John F. Copper, *Taiwan: A Nation-State or Province?* (Boulder, Colo.: Westview Press, 1990), 79.

54. Hung-mao Tien, "Social Change and Political Development in Taiwan," in *Taiwan in a Time of Transition*, eds. Harvey Feldman, et al. (New York: Paragon House, 1988), 8.

55. Tun-Jen Cheng, "Democratizing the Quasi-Leninist Regime in Taiwan," *World Politics* 41, no. 4 (July 1989), 474.

56. Cheng, "Democratizing the Quasi-Leninist Regime," 474.

57. Copper, *Taiwan*, 36.

58. Akira Kusuhara, *Apartheid and East Asia* (New York: UN Special Committee Against Apartheid, 1990), 5.

59. George T. Yu, "The Tanzania-Zambia Railway: A Case Study in Chinese Economic Aid to Africa," in *Soviet and Chinese Aid to African Nations*, eds. Warren Weinstein and Thomas H. Henrikson (New York: Praeger, 1980), 118.

60. Wei Liang-Tsai, *Peking Versus Taipei in Africa 1960–1978* (Taipei, Taiwan: The Asia and World Institute, 1982), 115.

61. Deon Geldenhuys, *The Diplomacy of Isolation: South African Foreign Policy Making* (New York: St. Martin's Press, 1984), 115.

62. Caryle Murphy, "South Africa, Taiwan Strengthen Ties," *The Washington Post*, October 25, 1980, A15.

63. Department of Foreign Affairs, *South Africa 1989–1990: Official Yearbook of the Republic of South Africa* (Pretoria: Government Printer, 1990), 202.

64. "Taiwan's Minister Chang Arrives in Johannesburg," *FBIS-AFR*, November 24, 1989, 13; and "Taiwan Parliamentary Official Begins Visit," *FBIS-AFR*, January 25, 1990, 5.

65. John Blakley, "South Africa Looks East," *The New York Times* November 22, 1987, D2; and UN Special Committee Against Apartheid, *The East Asian Region and International Action Against Apartheid* (New York: UN Special Committee Against Apartheid, 1990), 4.

66. U.S. Department of State, *Report to the Congress on Industrialized Democracies' Relations with and Measures Against South Africa* (Washington, D.C.: U.S. Department of State, 1987), 24; and "East Asia Has Sizeable Economic Ties with Pretoria," *Far Eastern Economic Review*, August 7, 1986, 16.

67. Commonwealth Committee of Foreign Ministers on Southern Africa, *South Africa: The Sanctions Report* (London: Penguin Books, 1989), 214–235.

68. Colin Legum, ed., *Africa Contemporary Record* (New York: Africana Publishing Company, 1980), B867; and Keith Ovenden and Tony Cole, *Apartheid and International Finance* (New York: Penguin Books, 1989), 137.

69. Madden Cole, "Mineral-Related Trade with Taiwan to Increase," *The Citizen*, October 12, 1988, 24. Reprinted in *FBIS-AFR*, December 8, 1988, 23.

70. Paul Conlon, *South African Coal Report* (New York: UN Center Against Apartheid, 1988), 10; Ovenden and Cole, *Apartheid and International Finance*,

169; and "Taiwan's Gold Imports Surge," *The New York Times*, April 13, 1988, D14.

71. Brent Melville, "Steel Company Wins Contract in PRC," *Business Day*, June 2, 1989, 16. Cited in *FBIS-AFR*, July 5, 1989, 14; and Robert Gentle, "PRC Purchases Ten Shipments," *Business Day*, June 21, 1989, 3. Reprinted in *FBIS-AFR*, July 3, 1989, 14–15.

72. C. M. Rogerson, "Decentralization and the Location of Third World Multinationals in South Africa," in *Regional Restructuring Under Apartheid*, eds. Richard Tomlinson and Mark Addleson (Johannesburg: Ravan Press, 1987), 294–304.

73. Steve Askin, "The Business of Sanctions Busting," *Africa Report* 34, no. 4 (January-February 1989), 19.

74. Eddie Koch, "Decentralization: A Prop for Inefficiency," *The Weekly Mail*, September 30–October 6, 1988, 13.

75. "Taiwanese Investments in Homelands Explained," *FBIS-AFR*, November 30, 1988, 10; John Pickles and Jeff Woods, "Taiwanese Investment in South Africa," *African Affairs* 88, no. 353 (October 1989):514; Jonathan Friedland, "South Africa Woos Asia," *Far Eastern Economic Review*, September 15, 1988, 83; and C. M. Rogerson, "Third World Multinationals and South Africa's Decentralization Program," *The South African Geographical Society* 68, no. 2 (September 1986):137.

76. Heloise Henning, "Taiwanese Create 40,000 Jobs in Country," *Business Day*, April 20, 1989, 1. Reprinted in *FBIS-AFR*, June 2, 1989, 35.

77. Robert G. Sutter, *Taiwan: Entering the 21st Century* (Lanham, Md.: University Press of America, 1988), 38; Landgren, *Embargo Disimplemented*, 224; and Andrew Tanzer, "The Saudi Connection," *Far Eastern Economic Review*, July 9, 1982, 28.

78. Betts, "Paranoids, Pygmies, Pariahs . . . ," 167; and Harkavy, "The Pariah State Syndrome," 641.

79. Amos Perlmutter, et al., *Two Minutes Over Baghdad* (London: Valentine, Mitchell and Company, 1982), 50.

80. Ronald W. Walters, *South Africa and the Bomb* (Lexington, Mass.: Lexington Books, 1987), 139.

81. Leonard S. Spector and Jacqueline R. Smith, *Nuclear Ambitions: The Spread of Nuclear Weapons 1989–1990* (Boulder, Colo.: Westview Press, 1990), 60.

82. "Tribute Paid to Taiwan's Chiang Ching-Kuo," *FBIS-AFR*, January 15, 1988, 14; and John Pickles and Jeff Woods, "Reorienting South Africa's International Links," *Capital and Class*, no. 35 (Summer 1988):51.

CHAPTER 4: LATIN AMERICA

1. "Anti-Apartheid Conference Ends in Caracas," *FBIS-LAT*, September 20, 1983, L1.

2. Edward Schumacher, "Argentina and Democracy," *Foreign Affairs* 62, no. 5 (Summer 1984):1070.

3. Pamela Constable and Arturo Valenzuela, "Chile's Return to Democracy," *Foreign Affairs* 68, no. 5 (Winter 1989/90):172; and Martin Edwin Andersen, "The Military Obstacle to Latin Democracy," *Foreign Policy*, no. 73 (Winter 1988/89):94–113.

4. Pedro-Pablo Kuczynski, "Latin American Debt," *Foreign Affairs* 61, no. 2 (Winter 1982/83):354.

5. Kuczynski, "Latin American Debt," 347.

6. Deon Geldenhuys, *The Diplomacy of Isolation: South African Foreign Policy Making* (New York: St. Martin's Press, 1984), 135.

7. "South African Navy Chief Arrives," *FBIS-LAT*, June 1, 1983, H1; and "Congressmen Depart for South African Visit," *FBIS-LAT*, June 1, 1983, H1.

8. Paul Sohr, "Reagan Alliance Woos South Africa," *South*, October 1981, 23.

9. U.S. Department of State, *Report to Congress on Industrialized Democracies' Relations with and Measures Against South Africa* (Washington, D.C.: U. S. Department of State, 1987), 3.

10. Edward Kannyo, "The Latin Balancing Act," *Africa Report* 27, no. 4 (July-August 1982):52–53.

11. David Kaplan, "The Industrialization of South African Capital: South African Direct Investment in the Contemporary Period," *African Affairs* 82 (October 1983):479.

12. United Nations, *International Trade Statistics Yearbook* (New York: The United Nations, 1985), 837; Paul Horowitz and Holly Sklar, "South Atlantic Triangle," *NACLA: Report on the Americas* 16, no. 3 (May-June 1982), 23; and Commonwealth Committee of Foreign Ministers on Southern Africa, *South Africa: The Sanctions Report* (London: Penguin Books, 1989), 214.

13. Roy Arthur Glasgow, "African Relations with Latin America and the Caribbean," in *Latin America and the Caribbean Contemporary Record*, ed. Jack Hopkins (New York: Holmes and Meier, 1985), 186.

14. "Nwachukwu Discusses Chile-RSA Ties at the UN," *FBIS-AFR*, October 3, 1988, 25; and Colin Legum, ed., *Africa Contemporary Record* (New York: Africana Publishing Company, 1981), B782.

15. "South Africa Wants to Transfer Military Technology," *FBIS-LAT*, March 8, 1984, E5.

16. "South African Armed Forces Chief Visits," *FBIS-LAT*, August 9, 1984, E2.

17. William Perry, *Contemporary Brazilian Foreign Policy: The International Strategy of an Emerging Power* (Beverly Hills, Calif.: Sage Publications, 1976), 67.

18. Georg Sorensen, "Brazil," in *Newly Industrializing Countries and the Political Economy of South-South Relations*, eds. Jerker Carlsson and Timothy M. Shaw (London: Macmillan Press, 1988), 106; and Ronald M. Schneider,

Brazil: Foreign Policy of a Future World Power (Boulder, Colo.: Westview Press, 1976), 58.

19. Bela Balassa, "Incentive Policies in Brazil," *World Development*, November-December 1979, 1023.

20. William G. Tyler, *Advanced Developing Countries as Export Competitors in Third World Markets: The Brazilian Experience* (Washington, D.C.: Center for Strategic and International Studies, Georgetown University, 1980), 19.

21. Juan de Onis, "Brazil on the Tightrope Toward Democracy," *Foreign Affairs* 68, no. 4 (Fall 1989):139.

22. James Brooke, "Bad Times, Bold Plans for Brazil," *The New York Times*, January 7, 1990, F4.

23. "Brazil Hits Oil Offshore," *The New York Times*, May 13, 1991, C4; and James Brooke, "Brazil's Remote Amazon Oil Effort," *The New York Times*, November 16, 1990, C1.

24. Thomas E. Skidmore, *The Politics of Military Rule in Brazil, 1964–1985* (New York: Oxford University Press, 1988), 284.

25. Skidmore, *The Politics of Military Rule*, 289.

26. Hermann Giliomee, "The Magic Moment? South America Between Past and Future," in *The American People and South Africa*, eds. Alfred O. Hero, Jr., and John Barratt (Lexington, Mass.: D.C. Heath and Company, 1981), 193.

27. Jose Augusto Lindgren Alves, "Implementation of the Program of Action for the Second Decade to Combat Racism and Social Discrimination" (New York: United Nations, 1986), 4.

28. Carlos A. Hasenbalg, *Race Relations in Modern Brazil* (Albuquerque: The University of New Mexico Press, 1981), 12; Thomas G. Sanders, "Racial Discrimination and Black Consciousness in Brazil," *American Universities Field Staff Reports*, no. 42 (1981):2–3; and Anani Dzidzienyo, "Brazil," in *International Handbook on Race and Race Relations*, ed. Jay A. Sigler (New York: Greenwood Press, 1987), 23.

29. Glasgow, "African Relations," 187.

30. Riordan Roett, "Brazil: Staying the Course," *The Wilson Quarterly* 7, no. 3 (Summer 1983):58.

31. Amnesty International, *Amnesty International Report 1989* (London: Amnesty International, 1989), 109.

32. "Foreign Minister on Policy Toward South Africa," *FBIS-LAT*, April 3, 1984, D1.

33. Jãnio Quadros, "Brazil's New Foreign Policy," *Foreign Affairs* 40, no. 1 (October 1961):24.

34. Quadros, "Brazil's New Foreign Policy," 27.

35. Wayne A. Selcher, *The Afro-Asian Dimension of Brazilian Foreign Policy* (Gainesville: University of Florida, 1974), 29; and Thomas G. Sanders, "Brazil's Foreign Policy in Africa," *American Universities Field Staff Reports*, no. 43 (1981):1.

36. Roy Glasgow, *Pragmatism and Idealism in Brazil's Foreign Policy in Southern Africa* (Pasadena: California Institute of Technology, 1974), 15.

37. David Fig, "The Political Economy of South African Penetration of Brazil: The Case of the Anglo-American Corporation," in *Newly Industrializing Countries*, 212.

38. "Malmierca, Sodre Discuss Various Issues," *FBIS-LAT*, January 21, 1988, 32.

39. James Brooke, "Dateline Brazil: Southern Superpower," *Foreign Policy*, no. 44 (Fall 1981):177; and Colin Legum, ed., *Africa Contemporary Record* (New York: Africana Publishing Company, 1981), B594.

40. "Brazil to Head UN Commission on Cuban Pullout," *FBIS-AFR*, December 19, 1988, 10.

41. Maria Y. Leite Linhares, "Brazilian Foreign Policy and Africa," *The World Today* 18, no. 12 (December 1962):539.

42. Fig, "The Political Economy of South African Penetration of Brazil," 211.

43. "Trade with Brazil Increasing Despite Sanctions," *FBIS-AFR*, July 27, 1988, 10; Horowitz and Sklar, "South Atlantic Triangle," 23; United Nations, *International Trade Statistics Yearbook* (1985), 837; and The Commonwealth Committee of Foreign Ministers on Southern Africa, *South Africa: The Sanctions Report*, 214.

44. "Trade with Brazil Increasing Despite Sanctions," 10; Horowitz and Sklar, "South Atlantic Triangle," 23; UN, *International Trade Statistics Yearbook* (1985), 837.

45. "Brasília to Deemphasize Trade with South Africa," *FBIS-LAT*, March 27, 1979, D2.

46. Kannyo, "The Latin Balancing Act," 54.

47. "Brazilian Gold Miners Seek Technical Aid," *The Star* (Johannesburg), November 21, 1988, 5.

48. "Brazilian Gold Miners Seek Technical Aid," 5

49. Anani Dzidzienyo and Michael Turner, "African-Brazilian Relations: A Reconsideration," in *Brazil in the International System: The Rise of a Middle Power*, ed. Wayne Selcher (Boulder, Colo.: Westview Press, 1981), 203.

50. Peter Howard Wetehein, "Brazil and Africa," *African Business*, October 1983, 59.

51. "Brazil," *South*, July 1985, 52.

52. Dzidzienyo and Turner, "African-Brazilian Relations," 206–207.

53. "Minister Cites Brazilian Arms Purchase," *FBIS-AFR*, March 14, 1989, 20.

54. Glasgow, "African Relations with Latin America," 188.

55. Marc Levinson, "What to do About Brazil Inc." *Across the Board*, March 1985, 42; and Michael Crabbe, "Brazil: Oil Self-sufficiency Within Reach," *Petroleum Economist*, February 1986, 48.

56. "Brazil: Trade and Investment Survey," *The Journal of Commerce and Commercial*, June 29, 1983, A8.

57. Andrew Hurrell, "The Politics of South Atlantic Security," *International Affairs* 59, no. 2 (Spring 1983):180.
58. Edward T. Rowe, *Strengthening the UN: A Study of the Evolution of Member State Commitments* (Beverly Hills, Calif.: Sage Publications, 1974), 57.
59. Glasgow, *Pragmatism and Idealism in Brazilian Foreign Policy*, 10.
60. Selcher, *The Afro-Asian Dimension*, 191.
61. "South African Solidarity Committee Established," *FBIS-LAT*, August 21, 1985, D5.
62. Selcher, *The Afro-Asian Dimension*, 193.
63. "Spokesman on Arms Sales to Iran, South Africa," *FBIS-LAT*, November 30, 1983, D3.
64. United Nations, *Special Report of the Special Committee Against Apartheid on the Implementation of the Arms Embargo Against South Africa*, Official Records of the General Assembly, 40th Session, Supp. no. 22A (October 14, 1985), 6; Roberto De Abreu Sodre, *Address on the Critical Economic Situation in Africa* (New York: Brazilian UN Mission, 1986), 15; UN Center Against Apartheid, *News Digest*, September-October, 1985, 6; and "Sarney Decrees Ban on Trade with South Africa," *FBIS-LAT*, August 12, 1985, D1.

CHAPTER 5: THE MIDDLE EAST

1. Frederick Cooper, *Plantation Slavery on the East Coast of Africa* (New Haven, Conn.: Yale University Press, 1977), 12; and Ali A. Mazrui, "Eurafrica, Eurasia, and African-Arab Relations," in *Independence in a World of Unequals: African-Arab-OECD Economic Cooperation for Development*, ed. Dunstan M. Wai (Boulder, Colo.: Westview Press, 1982), 26.
2. Arye Oded, *Africa and the Middle East Conflict* (Boulder, Colo.: Lynne Rienner, 1987), 83.
3. UNESCO, *Historical and Socio-Cultural Relations Between Black Africa and the Arab World from 1935 to the Present* (Paris: UNESCO, 1984), 49; and Victor T. Le Vine and Timothy W. Luke, *The Arab-African Connection: Political and Economic Realities* (Boulder, Colo.: Westview Press, 1979), 4.
4. R. D. McLaurin, Don Peretz, and Lewis W. Snider, *Middle East Foreign Policy* (New York: Praeger, 1982), 39.
5. James D. Rudolph, "Government and Politics," in *Saudi Arabia: A Country Study*, ed. Richard F. Nyrop (Washington, D.C.: U.S. Government Printing Office, 1985), 234–243; and Bahgat Korany, "Defending the Faith: The Foreign Policy of Saudi Arabia," in *The Foreign Policies of Arab States*, eds. Bahgat Korany and Ali E. Hillal Dessouki (Boulder, Colo.: Westview Press, 1984), 256–257.
6. Muhammad Muslih and Augustus Richard Norton, "The Need for Arab Democracy," *Foreign Policy*, no. 83 (Summer 1991):5.
7. Youssef M. Ibrahim, "An Affluent Kuwait Joins an Arab Trend Toward Democracy," *The New York Times*, March 11, 1990, A1.

8. Farid Esack, "Three Islamic Strands in the South African Struggle for Justice," *Third World Quarterly* 10, no. 2 (April 1988):497.

9. Rajen Harshe, "France, Francophone African States, and South Africa," *Alternatives* 9, no. 1 (Summer 1983):54.

10. United Nations, *Report of the Intergovernmental Group to Monitor the Supply and Shipping of Petroleum Products to South Africa* (New York: UN General Assembly, 1987), 13.

11. Olayiwola Abegunrin, "The Arabs and the Southern African Problem," *International Affairs* 60, no. 1 (Winter 1983/84):99.

12. Richard J. Payne, *The Nonsuperpowers and South Africa: Implications for U.S. Policy* (Bloomington: Indiana University Press, 1990), 127.

13. Payne, *The Nonsuperpowers*, 127; Naomi Chazan, "The Fallacies of Pragmatism: Israeli Foreign Policy Toward Africa," *African Affairs* 82 (April 1983), 172; and Jane Hunter, *Israeli Foreign Policy: South Africa and Central America* (Boston: South End Press, 1987), 25.

14. Payne, *The Nonsuperpowers*, 128.

15. Gideon Shimoni, *Jews and Zionism: The South African Experience* (Cape Town: Oxford University Press, 1980), 353; and Payne, *The Nonsuperpowers*, 129.

16. Menachem Shalver, "Officials Upset by South Africa Change," *The Jerusalem Post*, January 30, 1988, 4.

17. Deon Geldenhuys, *The Diplomacy of Isolation: South African Experience* (New York: St. Martin's Press, 1984), 117; and Arye Oded, *Africa and the Middle East Conflict* (Boulder, Colo.: Lynne Rienner, 1987), 150.

18. "South African National Council Group Meets Ghali," *FBIS-AFR*, December 18, 1979, D11.

19. "Direct Contact with South Africa Denied," *FBIS-NES*, June 28, 1988, 21.

20. F. R. Metrowich, *South Africa's New Frontiers* (Sandton, South Africa: Valiant Publishers, 1977), 129.

21. Colin Legum, "The Middle East Dimension," in *International Politics in Southern Africa*, eds. Gwendolen M. Carter and Patrick O'Meara (Bloomington: Indiana University Press, 1982), 116.

22. Geoffrey Allen, "Government Keeping Back Door Diplomat in South Africa," *Sunday Times* (Johannesburg), May 11, 1980, 13.

23. Colin Legum, "The Southern African Crisis 1986–87," in *Africa Contemporary Record*, ed. Colin Legum (New York: Africana Publishing Company, 1988), A71.

24. "Arab Summit Conference," *Africa Research Bulletin-Political Series*, November-December 1973, 2937.

25. Olusola Ojo, "Oil Sanctions and South Africa," in *Southern Africa in the 1980s*, eds. Olajide Aluko and Timothy Shaw (London: Allen and Unwin, 1985), 239.

26. Arthur Jay Klinghoffer, *Oiling the Wheels of Apartheid: Exposing South Africa's Secret Oil Trade* (Boulder, Colo.: Lynne Rienner, 1989), 37.

27. Paul Conlon, "International Oil Trade and South Africa's Energy Requirements," *Notes and Documents* (New York: UN Center Against Apartheid, 1989), 10.

28. Tareq Y. Ismael, *International Relations of the Contemporary Middle East* (Syracuse, N.Y.: Syracuse University Press, 1986), 257.

29. Shipping Research Bureau, *Fuel for Apartheid: Oil Supplies to South Africa* (Amsterdam: Shipping Research Bureau, 1990), 96; and "Paper Says Egypt Has Sold Oil to Israel and South Africa," *FBIS-ME*, March 23, 1979, C1.

30. UN, *Report of the Intergovernmental Group*, 57: Robert Whitehill, "The Sanctions That Never Were: Arab and Iranian Oil Sales to South Africa," *Middle East Review* 19, no. 1 (Fall 1986): 39; and Bernard Rivers and Martin Bailey, "How Oil Seeps into South Africa," *Business and Society Review*, no. 39 (Fall 1981): 58.

31. U.S. Congress, *Possible Violation or Circumvention of the Clark Amendment*, Hearing Before the Subcommittee on Africa of the Committee on Foreign Affairs, HR 100th Cong., 1st Sess., July 1, 1987 (Washington, D.C.: U.S. Government Printing Office, 1987), 26.

32. UN, *Report of the Intergovernmental Group*, 42.

33. UN, *Report of the Intergovernmental Group*, 23.

34. Colin Legum, ed., *Africa Contemporary Record* (New York: Africana Publishing Co., 1980), B866.

35. Oded, *Africa and the Middle East Conflict*, 152.

36. Metrowich, *South Africa's New Frontiers*, 130.

37. U.S. Congress, *Possible Violations or Circumvention of the Clark Amendment*, 2.

38. Abegunrin, "The Arabs and the Southern African Problem," 100.

39. Colin Legum, ed., *Africa Contemporary Record* (New York: Africana Publishing Co., 1975), B472.

40. Yehuda Litani, "London Sources Claim Jordan Sends Arms to RSA," *Jerusalem Post*, March 29, 1987, 1.

41. Kemal Kirisci, *The PLO and World Politics* (New York: St. Martin's Press, 1986), 73.

42. Legum, "The Middle East Dimension," 119.

43. Council of Ministers of the OAU, "Resolution on the Palestinian Issue," in *Africa Contemporary Record*, ed. Colin Legum (New York: Africana Publishing Co., 1979), C14.

44. Alan George, "PLO Makes its Presence Felt in Africa," *The Middle East*, July 1987, 19.

45. Yasir Arafat, "Speech at the OAU Meeting in Kampala, July 29, 1975," cited by Mohammed E. Selim, "The Foreign Policy of the Palestine Liberation Organization," in *The Foreign Policies of Arab States*, 214.

46. Richard J. Payne, *Opportunities and Dangers of Soviet-Cuban Expansion: Toward a Pragmatic U.S. Policy* (Albany: State University of New York Press, 1988), 14–18.

47. Galia Golan, "The Soviet Union and the Palestine Liberation Organization," in *The Soviet Union and the Middle East in the 1980s: Opportunities, Constraints, and Dilemmas*, eds. Mark V. Kauppi and R. Craig Nation (Lexington, Mass.: Lexington Books, 1983), 191.

48. Arye Oded, *Africa, the PLO, and Israel* (Jerusalem: The Leonard Davis Institute, 1990), 24–25.

49. "ANC, SWAPO Send Condolences to Arafat," *FBIS-AFR*, September 28, 1982, U3; and United Nations, "International Seminar on World Action for Immediate Independence of Namibia," *Namibia Bulletin*, no. 6 (1986):11.

50. "PLO's Arafat Arrives, Holds Talks with Kaunda," *FBIS-AFR*, April 29, 1987, U13.

51. "Intelligence Sources See Libyan Aid to ANC," *FBIS-AFR*, December 16, 1985, U4; and "P. W. Botha Links Libya to Expanding Unrest," *FBIS-AFR*, April 17, 1986, U3–U4.

52. Alan Riding, "Mandela Moves to Reassure Visiting Group of U.S. Jews," *The New York Times*, June 11, 1990, A6.

CHAPTER 6: POST-APARTHEID CHALLENGES

1. F. W. de Klerk, *Manifesto for the New South Africa* (Cape Town: Republic of South Africa, February 1, 1991), 4.

2. "Zimbabwe," *Africa Report* 35, no. 4 (September-October 1990):7.

3. Paul Lewis, "UN Freedom Index Angers Third World," *The New York Times*, June 23, 1991, A6. See the United Nations, *Human Development Report* (New York: Oxford University Press, 1991).

4. Lewis, "UN Freedom Index," A6.

5. Larry Diamond, "Beyond Autocracy: Prospects for Democracy in Africa," in *Beyond Autocracy in Africa: Working Papers for the Inaugural Seminar of the Governance in Africa Program* (Atlanta, Ga.: The Carter Center, 1989), 25.

6. Christopher S. Wren, "Even in New South Africa Apartheid's Legacy Lives On," *The New York Times*, June 23, 1991, A1.

7. F. W. de Klerk, *Address at the Opening of the Third Session of the Ninth Parliament of the Republic of South Africa, February 1, 1991* (Pretoria: Government Printer, 1991), 10.

8. Stephen R. Lewis, *The Economics of Apartheid* (New York: Council on Foreign Relations, 1990), 147.

9. Kenneth B. Noble, "Nigeria Weighs Ending Curbs on Pretoria," *The New York Times*, April 14, 1991, A3; and "South Africa," *Africa Report* 36, no. 2 (March-April 1991), 12.

10. "De Klerk Seeks Stronger Ties to Africa," *The Christian Science Monitor*, June 10, 1991, 6.

11. "Update: South Africa," *Africa Report* 36, no. 3 (May-June 1991):12.

12. Jane Perlez, "As Apartheid Falls, So Do Obstacles to Trade," *The New York Times*, June 13, 1991, A5.

13. Roy Laishley, "Looking Ahead at South Africa," *Africa Recovery* 5, no. 1 (June 1991):5.

14. Joseph Hanlon, "Post-Apartheid South Africa and its Neighbors," *The Third World Quarterly* 9, no. 2 (April 1987):440

15. Alan B. Durning, *Apartheid's Environmental Toll* (Washington, D.C.: Worldwatch Institute, 1990), 38.

Selected Bibliography

Abegunrin, Olayiwola. "The Arabs and the Southern African Problem." *International Affairs* 60, no. 1 (Winter 1983–84): 97–105.

Adam, Heribert. "Ethnic Politics and Crisis Management: Comparing South Africa and Israel." *Journal of Asian and African Studies* 28, no. 1–2 (1983): 4–21.

Adams, Bob. "High Technology Can Also Be Appropriate." *African Business* (March 1985): 60–61.

Adebisi, Busari. "Nigeria's Relations with South Africa, 1960–1975." *Africa Quarterly* 16, no. 3 (January 1977): 67–89.

Agbaje, Adigun. "Freedom of the Press and Party Politics in Nigeria." *African Affairs* 89, no. 355 (April 1990): 205–226.

Akinola, Anthony A. "A Critique of Nigeria's Proposed Two-Party System." *The Journal of Modern African Studies* 27, no. 1 (March 1989): 109–124.

Akinyemi, A. Bolaji. "Africa-Challenges and Responses: A Foreign Policy Perspective." *Daedalus* 111, no. 2 (Spring 1982): 243–254.

Al-Karie, Ahmed Youssef. "Mubarak's Africa Policy." *Africa Report* 27, no. 2 (March–April 1982): 27–30.

Alam, M. Shadid. *Governments and Markets in Economic Development Strategies: Lessons from Korea, Taiwan, and Japan.* New York: Praeger, 1989.

Allen, Caroline. "The Politics of Apathy." *Africa Report* 33, no. 3 (May–June 1988): 40–42.

Aluko, Olajide, and Timothy M. Shaw, eds. *Southern Africa in the 1980s.* London: Allen and Unwin, 1985.

Alves, Lindgren Augusto Jose. *Implementation of the Program of Action for the Second Decade to Combat Racism and Social Discrimination, April 30, 1986*. New York: United Nations, 1986.
Amnesty International. *Amnesty International Report 1989*. London: Amnesty International Publications, 1989.
"ANC Aid Pledge." *Africa Research Bulletin-Political Series*, January 15, 1987: 8327.
Andersen, Martin Edwin. "The Military Obstacle to Latin Democracy." *Foreign Policy*, no. 73 (Winter 1988–89): 94–113.
Anglin, Douglas G. "Zambia in Southern African Detente." *International Journal* 30, no. 3 (Summer 1975): 471–503.
Anglin, Douglas G., and Timothy M. Shaw. *Zambia's Foreign Policy: Studies in Diplomacy and Dependence*. Boulder, Colo.: Westview Press, 1979.
Arnold, Ben. "Southern Africa's Elder Statesman." *Africa Report* 35, no. 1 (March–April 1990): 36.
Askin, Steve. "The Business of Sanctions Busting." *Africa Report* 34, no. 4 (January-February 1989): 18–20.
Balassa, Bela. "Incentive Policies in Brazil." *World Development* (November-December 1979): 1023.
Barber, James. *Is There a South African Nation?* Braamfontein: The South Africa Institute of International Affairs, 1987.
Basu, Anup Ranjan. "India-Africa Relations." *Africa Quarterly* 20, nos. 1–2 (1981): 98–103.
Baum, Julian. "Taipei Hit by Saudi Decision to Recognize Peking." *Far Eastern Economic Review*, August 2, 1990: 49.
Bellows, Thomas J. "Taiwan's Foreign Policy in the 1970s: A Case Study of Adaptation and Viability." *Asian Survey* 16, no. 7 (July 1976): 593–610.
Betts, Richard K. "Paranoids, Pygmies, Pariahs and Nonproliferation." *Foreign Policy*, no. 26 (Spring 1977): 157–167.
Bhana, Surendra. "Indian Trade and Trader in Colonial Natal." In *Enterprise and Exploitation in a Victorian Colony*, edited by Bill Guest and John M. Sellers, 234–263. Pietermaritzburg: University of Natal Press, 1985.
Bissell, Richard E. *Apartheid and International Organizations*. Boulder, Colo.: Westview Press, 1977.
Bouton, Marshall M. "Foreign Relations: Elusive Regional Security." In *India Briefing, 1987*, edited by Marshall M. Bouton, 159–184. Boulder, Colo.: Westview Press, 1987.
Brain, Joy. "Indentured and Free Indians in the Economy of Colonial Natal." In *Enterprise and Exploitation in a Victorian Colony*, edited by Bill Guest and John M. Sellers, 198–233. Pietermaritzburg: University of Natal Press, 1985.
"Brazil: Trade and Investment Survey." *The Journal of Commerce and Commercial*, June 29, 1983: A8.
Brent, R. Stephen. "Aiding Africa." *Foreign Policy*, no. 80 (Fall 1990): 121–140.

Burdette, Marcia M. *Zambia: Between Two Worlds.* Boulder, Colo.: Westview Press, 1988.
Butts, Kent Hughes, and Paul R. Thomas. *The Geopolitics of Southern Africa: South Africa as a Regional Superpower.* Boulder, Colo.: Westview Press, 1986.
Chan, Stephen. "Zambia's Foreign Policy-Elitism and Power." *The Round Table*, no. 302 (April 1987): 223–233.
_____. *Exporting Apartheid: Foreign Policies in Southern Africa.* New York: St. Martin's Press, 1990.
Chazan, Naomi. "Ethnicity in Economic Crisis: Development Strategies and Patterns of Ethnicity in Africa." In *Ethnicity, Politics, and Development*, edited by Dennis L. Thompson and Dov Ronen, 137–158. Boulder, Colo.: Lynne Rienner, 1986.
Chazan, Naomi, Robert Mortimer, John Ravenhill, and Donald Rothchild. *Politics and Society in Contemporary Africa.* Boulder, Colo.: Lynne Rienner, 1988.
Cheng, Elizabeth. "Thaw in China and Taiwan Relations Boosts Business Links." *Far Eastern Economic Review*, December 10, 1987: 90.
Cheng, Tun-Jen. "Democratizing the Quasi-Leninist Regime in Taiwan." *World Politics* 41, no. 4 (July 1989): 471–499.
Chhabar, Hari Sharan. "India's Africa Policy." *India Quarterly* 41, no. 1 (1985): 68–73.
_____. "India and Africa: A Decade of Relations." In *Africa Contemporary Record*, edited by Colin Legum, A243–A248. New York: Africana Publishing Company, 1985.
"Civilian Rule Postponed to 1992." *Africa Research Bulletin-Political Series*, August 5, 1987: 8567.
Clad, James. "Towards a Hindu Raj." *Far Eastern Economic Review*, September 20, 1990: 27–28.
Cohen, Marc J. *Taiwan at the Crossroads.* Washington, D.C.: Asia Resource Center, 1988.
Commonwealth Committee of Foreign Ministers on Southern Africa. *South Africa: The Sanctions Report.* London: Penguin Books, 1989.
"Commonwealth Games Boycott." *Africa Research Bulletin-Political Series*, August 15, 1986: 8171.
Commonwealth Statement on Apartheid in Sport: The Gleneagles Agreement. London: Foreign and Commonwealth Office, June 15, 1977.
Conlon, Paul. *South African Coal Report.* New York: U.N. Center Against Apartheid, 1988.
_____. "International Oil Trade and South Africa's Energy Requirements." *Notes and Documents.* New York: U.N. Center Against Apartheid, April 1989.
Cooper, Frederick. *Plantation Slavery on the East Coast of Africa.* New Haven: Yale University Press, 1977.

Cooper, John F. *Taiwan: Nation-State or Province?* Boulder, Colo.: Westview Press, 1990.
Council of Ministers of the OAU. *Resolution on the Palestinian Question.* CM/Res. 1061 (XLIV), July 1986.
"Debt Drives Brazil into the Arms of the Third World." *Business Week,* April 2, 1984: 48.
Decalo, Samuel. *Psychoses of Power: African Personal Dictatorships.* Boulder, Colo.: Westview Press, 1989.
de Klerk, F. W. *Address to the Opening of the Third Session of the Ninth Parliament of the Republic of South Africa.* Pretoria: Government Printer, 1991.
Delors, Jacques. "Europe's Ambitions." *Foreign Policy,* no. 80 (Fall 1990): 14–27.
Department of Foreign Affairs. *Mini Atlas of Southern Africa.* Pretoria: Department of Foreign Affairs, 1990.
Department of Foreign Affairs. *South Africa 1989–1990: Official Yearbook of the Republic of South Africa.* Pretoria: Government Printer, 1990.
Department of State. *Country Reports on Human Rights Practices for 1988.* Reports Submitted to the Committee on Foreign Relations, U.S. Senate and Committee on Foreign Affairs, U.S. House of Representatives. Washington, D.C.: U.S. Government Printing Office, February 1989.
Department of State. *Report to the Congress on Industrialized Democracies' Relations with and Measures Against South Africa.* Washington, D.C.: U.S. Department of State, 1987.
Desai, I. P., et al. *Caste, Caste Conflict, and Reservations.* New Delhi: Ajanta Publications, 1985.
Diamond, Larry. *Class, Ethnicity, and Democracy in Nigeria.* Syracuse, N.Y.: Syracuse University Press, 1988.
Donnelly, Jack. *Universal Human Rights in Theory and Practice.* Ithaca, N.Y.: Cornell University Press, 1989.
Dryeyer, June Teufel. "Taiwan in 1989: Democratization and Economic Growth." *Asian Survey* 30, no. 1 (January 1990): 52–58.
Durning, Alan B. *Apartheid's Environmental Toll.* Washington, D.C.: Worldwatch Institute, 1990.
Dzidzienyo, Anani, and Michael Turner. "African-Brazilian Relations: A Reconsideration." In *Brazil in the International System: The Rise of a Middle Power,* edited by Wayne A. Selcher, 203. Boulder, Colo.: Westview Press, 1981.
"East Asia Has Sizeable Economic Ties with Pretoria." *Far Eastern Economic Review,* August 7, 1986: 14–16.
Economic Commission for Africa. *South African Destabilization: The Economic Cost of Frontline Resistance to Apartheid.* New York: United Nations, 1989.
Egedo, Ihebom. "Nigeria and Apartheid." *The Round Table,* no. 301 (January 1987): 33–39.

Eke, Kenoye Kelvin. *Nigeria's Foreign Policy Under Two Military Governments, 1966–1979*. Lewiston, N.Y.: The Edwin Mellen Press, 1990.

El-Khawas, Mohamed. "The Third World Stance on Apartheid: The U.N. Record." *The Journal of Modern African Studies* 9, no. 3 (October 1971): 443–452.

Ergas, Zaki, ed. *The African State in Transition*. New York: St. Martin's Press, 1987.

Esack, Farid. "Three Islamic Strands in the South Africa Struggle for Justice." *Third World Quarterly* 10, no. 2 (April 1988): 473–498.

Fatton, Robert. "Liberal Democracy in Africa." *Political Science Quarterly* 105, no. 3 (1990): 455–473.

Feldman, Harvey, Michael Y. M. Kau, and Illpyong J. Kim. *Taiwan in a Time of Transition*. New York: Paragon House, 1988.

Forrest, Tom. "Brazil and Africa: Geopolitics, Trade, and Technology in the South Atlantic." *African Affairs* 81, (January 1982): 3–20.

Frankel, Francine R. "India's Democracy in Transition." *World Policy Journal* 7, no. 3 (Summer 1990): 521–556.

Frankel, Fracine R., and M.S.A. Rao, eds. *Dominance and State Power in Modern India: Decline of a Social Order, Vol. 2*. Delhi: Oxford University Press, 1980.

Friedland, Jonathan. "South Africa Woos Asia." *Far Eastern Economic Review*, September 15, 1988: 83.

Gambari, Ibrahim A. *Theory and Reality in Foreign Policy Making: Nigeria After the Second Republic*. Atlantic Highlands, N.J.: Humanities Press International, 1989.

Gandhi, Rajiv. "The Movement of Nonaligned Countries." *Africa Quarterly* 23, nos. 3–4 (1987): 1–9.

Ganguly, Shivaji. "India's Foreign Policy Initiatives." *India Quarterly* 41, nos. 3–4 (1985): 390–400.

Geldenhuys, Deon. *The Diplomacy of Isolation: South African Foreign Policy Making*. New York: St. Martin's Press, 1984.

———. *Isolated States: A Comparative Analysis*. New York: Cambridge University Press, 1990.

Gertzel, Cherry, ed. *The Dynamics of the One-Party State in Zambia*. Manchester, England: Manchester University Press, 1984.

Giliomee, Hermann. "The Magic Moment? South America Between Past and Future." In *The American People and South Africa*, edited by Alfred O. Hero, Jr., and John Barratt, 177–197. Lexington, Mass.: D. C. Heath and Company, 1981.

Glasgow, Roy. *Pragmatism and Idealism in Brazil's Foreign Policy in Southern Africa*. Pasadena: California Institute of Technology, 1974.

Golan, Galia. "The Soviet Union and the Palestine Liberation Organization." In *The Soviet Union and the Middle East in the 1980s: Opportunities, Constraints, and Dilemmas*, edited by Mark V. Kauppi and R. Craig Nation, 189–210. Lexington, Mass.: Lexington Books, 1983.

Goldmann, Robert B. and A. Jeyaratnam Wilson, eds. *From Independence to Statehood: Managing Ethnic Conflict in Five African and Asian States.* London: Francis Pinter, 1984.

Good, Kenneth. "Zambia and the Liberation of South Africa." *The Journal of Modern African Studies* 25, no. 3 (1987): 505–540.

———. "Debt and the One-Party State in Zambia." *The Journal of Modern African Studies* 27, no. 2 (1989): 297–313.

Gupta, Anirudha. "India and Africa South of Sahara." In *India's Foreign Policy: Studies in Continuity and Change*, edited by Bimao Prasad, 261–276. New Delhi: Vikas Publishing House, 1979.

Gupta, Vijay. "India and Africa." *Africa Quarterly* 18, no. 1 (July 1977): 77–85.

———. "India and Africa." *Africa Quarterly* 17, no. 4 (April 1978): 110–123.

Gwin, Catherine, and Lawrence A. Veit. "The Indian Miracle." *Foreign Policy*, no. 58 (Spring 1985): 79–98.

Hanlon, Joseph. *Beggar Your Neighbor: Apartheid Power in Southern Africa.* Bloomington: Indiana University Press, 1986.

———. "Post-Apartheid South Africa and its Neighbors." *Third World Quarterly* 9, no. 2 (April 1987): 437–449.

Hardgrave, Robert L., and Stanley A. Kochanek. *India: Government and Politics in a Developing Nation.* New York: Harcourt Brace Jovanovich, 1986.

Harkavy, Robert E. "The Pariah State Syndrome." *Orbis* 21, no. 3 (Fall 1977): 623–650.

Harsche, Rajen. "France, Francophone African States, and South Africa." *Alternatives* 9, no. 1 (Summer 1983): 51–72.

Hasenbalg, Carlos A. *Race Relations in Modern Brazil.* Albuquerque: The University of New Mexico Press, 1981.

Hawkins, Tony. "Africa May Come Second." *Financial Times Survey*, March 19, 1990: 4.

Hearing, Roger. "When Copper was King." *Africa Report* 33, no. 5 (September-October 1988): 38–40.

Hendersen, Robert. "Nigeria: Future Nuclear Power?" *Orbis: Journal of World Affairs* 25, no. 2 (Summer 1981): 409–423.

Holman, Michael. "Nigeria: A Question of Debt Relief." *Financial Times Survey,* March 19, 1990: 1.

Horowitz, Donald L. *A Democratic South Africa? Constitutional Engineering in a Divided Society.* Berkeley: University of California Press, 1991.

Huntington, Samuel P. "Will More Countries Become Democratic?" *Political Science Quarterly* 99, no. 2 (Summer 1984): 193–218.

Hurrell, Andrew. "The Politics of South Atlantic Security." *International Affairs* 59 (Spring 1983): 179–193.

Ihonvbere, Julius O. "Resource Availability and Foreign Policy Change in Nigeria: The Impact of Oil." *India Quarterly* 39, no. 2 (1983): 111–136.

Inbar, Efraim. *Outcast Countries in the World Community.* Denver, Colo.: University of Denver Press, 1985.

International Labor Office. *Special Report of the Director-General on the Application of the Declaration Concerning the Policy of Apartheid in South Africa.* Geneva: ILO, 1988.

Ismael, Tareq Y. *International Relations of the Contemporary Middle East.* Syracuse, N.Y.: Syracuse University Press, 1986.

Jackson, Robert H., and Carl G. Rosberg. "The Marginality of African States." In *African Independence: The First Twenty-Five Years*, edited by Gwendolen M. Carter and Patrick O'Meara, 45–70. Bloomington: Indiana University Press, 1985.

Johnson, Chalmers. "Political Institutions and Economic Performance: The Government-Business Relationship in Japan, South Korea, and Taiwan." In *The Political Economy of the New Asian Industrialism*, edited by Frederic C. Deyo, 136–164. Ithaca, N.Y.: Cornell University Press, 1987.

Johnson, Phyllis, and David Martin. *Apartheid Terrorism: The Destabilization Report.* Bloomington: Indiana University Press, 1989.

Joseph, Richard A. "Class, State, and Prebendal Politics in Nigeria." *Journal of Commonwealth and Comparative Politics* 21, no. 3 (1983): 21–38.

Kannyo, Edward. "The Latin Balancing Act." *Africa Report* (July-August 1982): 52–53.

Kaplan, David. "The Internationalization of South African Capital: South African Direct Investment in the Contemporary Period." *African Affairs* 82 (October 1983): 465–494.

Kapur, Ashok. "Indian Foreign Policy: Perspectives and Present Predicaments." *The Round Table*, no. 295 (July 1985): 230–239.

Kapurk, Harish. "India's Foreign Policy Under Rajiv Gandhi." *The Round Table*, no. 304 (October 1987): 469–480.

Kirisci, Kemal. *The PLO and World Politics.* New York: St. Martin's Press, 1986.

Klinghoffer, Arthur Jay. *Oiling the Wheels of Apartheid: Exposing South Africa's Secret Oil Trade.* Boulder, Colo.: Lynne Rienner, 1989.

Kuczynski, Pedro-Pablo. "Latin American Debt." *Foreign Affairs* 61, no. 2 (Winter 1982–83): 344–364.

Kurata, Phil. "The Outcasts Forge New Bonds." *Far Eastern Economic Review*, November 7, 1980: 40–41.

Kusuhara, Akira. *Apartheid and East Asia.* New York: UN Special Committee Against Apartheid, 1990.

Laishley, Roy. "Gulf Crisis Threatens Further Setbacks to African Economies." *Africa Recovery* 4, no. 2 (July-September 1990): 1.

———. "Looking Ahead at South Africa." *Africa Recovery* 5, no. 1 (June 1991): 5.

Lall, Rajiv. "Indian Overseas Investment and Exports of Technology and Manufactures." In *South-South Trade: Trends, Issues, and Obstacles to Its Growth*, edited by Vivianne Ventura-Dias, 291–308. New York: Praeger, 1989.

Landgren, Signe. *Embargo Disimplemented: South Africa's Military Industry.* New York: Oxford University Press, 1989.

Legum, Colin, ed. *Africa Contemporary Record.* New York: Africana Publishing Company, 1975.

———. *Africa Contemporary Record.* New York: Africana Publishing Company, 1978.

———. *Africa Contemporary Record.* New York: Africana Publishing Company, 1981.

———. "The Middle East Dimension." In *International Politics in Southern Africa*, edited by Gwendolen M. Carter and Patrick O'Meara, 115–121. Bloomington: Indiana University Press, 1982.

———. *Africa Contemporary Record.* New York: Africana Publishing Company, 1983.

———. *Africa Contemporary Record.* New York: Africana Publishing Company, 1984.

———. "Democracy in Africa: Hopes and Trends." In *Democracy and Pluralism in Africa*, edited by Dov Ronen, 175–188. Boulder, Colo.: Lynne Rienner, 1986.

———. *Africa Contemporary Record.* New York: Africana Publishing Company, 1987.

———. "The Southern African Crisis 1986–87." In *Africa Contemporary Record*, edited by Colin Legum, A3–A79. New York: Africana Publishing Company, 1988.

———. "The Southern African Crisis 1987–88." In *Africa Contemporary Record*, edited by Colin Legum, A3–A23. New York: Africana Publishing Company, 1989.

———. "The Coming of Africa's Second Independence." *The Washington Quarterly* 13, no. 1 (Winter 1990): 129–140.

Le Vine, Victor T., and Timothy W. Luke. *The Arab-African Connection: Political and Economic Realities.* Boulder, Colo.: Westview Press, 1979.

Levinson, Marc. "What to do About Brazil Inc." *Across The Board*, March 22, 1985: 42.

Lewis, Stephen R. *The Economics of Apartheid.* New York: Council on Foreign Relations, 1990.

Liang-jen, Chang, ed. *Republic of China Yearbook, 1989.* Taipei, Taiwan: Kwang Hwa Publishing Company, 1989.

Liang-Tsai, Wei. *Peking Versus Taipei in Africa 1960–1978.* Taipei, Taiwan: The Asia and World Institute, 1982.

Libby, Ronald T. *The Politics of Economic Power in Southern Africa.* Princeton, N.J.: Princeton University Press, 1987.

Lone, Salim. "UN Counts Cost to Frontline of South Africa Destabilization." *Africa Recovery* 3, no. 3 (December 1989): 6.

———. "Donors Demand Political Reforms." *Africa Recovery* 4, no. 2 (July-September 1990): 3.

_____. "Challenging Conditionality." *Africa Report* 35, no. 4 (September-October 1990): 31–32.
Longer, V. *The Defense and Foreign Policies of India*. New Delhi: Sterling Publishers Private Ltd., 1988.
Low, D. Anthony. "Development's Contexts: Asia, Africa." *Daedalus* 118, no. 1 (Winter 1989): 17–30.
Manifesto for the New South Africa. Cape Town: Republic of South Africa, February 1, 1991.
Manley, Michael. "Southern Needs." *Foreign Policy*, no. 80 (Fall 1990): 40–51.
Mathew, M. J. "Indo-Africa Trade 1970–1982." *Foreign Trade Review* 18, no. 3 (October-December 1983): 327–344.
Mazrui, Ali A. "Eurafrica, Eurasia, and African-Arab Relations. In *Interdependence in a World of Unequals: African-Arab-OECD Economic Cooperation*, edited by Dunstan M. Wai, 26. Boulder, Colo.: Westview Press, 1982.
McLaurin, R. D., Don Peretz, and Lewis W. Snider. *Middle East Foreign Policy*. New York: Praeger, 1982.
Meldrum, Andrew. "On the Frontline." *Africa Report* 31, no. 4 (July-August 1986): 14–16.
Metrowich, F. R. *South Africa's New Frontiers*. Sandton, South Africa: Valiant Publishers, 1977.
Meyers, Benjamin D. "African Voting in the United Nations General Assembly." *The Journal of Modern African Studies* 4, no. 2 (October 1966): 213–228.
Ministry of Information and Broadcasting. *India: A Reference Manual*. New Delhi: Government of India, 1983.
Moberly, Patrick. "The World and South Africa: A New Perspective." *The World Today* 46, no. 4 (April 1990): 62–66.
Modi, B. K. "Indo-African Cooperation." *New African*, (February 1983): 63–65.
Moore, Jonathan. "Taiwan Will Do Away with Middlemen in Eastern Bloc Trade." *Far Eastern Economic Review*, April 14, 1988: 56–57.
_____. "Social Unease the Price of Development." *Far Eastern Economic Review,* September 15, 1988: 52–53.
Morna, Colleen Lowe. "The Pariah's New Pals." *Africa Report* 36, no. 3 (May-June 1991): 28–30.
Mugomba, Agrippah T. *The Foreign Policy of Despair: Africa and the Sale of Arms to South Africa*. Nairobi: East African Literature Bureau, 1977.
Mugyenyi, Meddi. "Development First, Democracy Second." In *Democratic Theory and Practice in Africa*, edited by Walter O. Oyugi, et al., 178–190. London: James Currey, 1988.
Mukela, John. "The IMF Fallout: Zambia." *Africa Report* 32, no. 1 (1987): 65–67.

Munoz, Heraldo, and Joseph Tulchin, eds. *Latin America in World Politics*. Boulder, Colo.: Westview Press, 1984.
Muslish, Muhammad, and Augustus Richard Norton. "The Need for Arab Democracy." *Foreign Policy*, no. 83 (Summer 1991): 3– 19.
Nadelman, Ethan A. "Israel and Black Africa: A Rapprochement?" *The Journal of Modern African Studies* 19, no. 2 (June 1981): 183–219.
Naik, J. A., ed. *India in Asia and Africa: Documents: 1976–1978*. Atlantic Highland, N.J.: Humanities Press,1981.
———. *India in Asia and Africa: Documents: 1979*. Atlantic Highland, N.J.: Humanities Press, 1982.
"Nigeria: Hope and Apathy as Vote Nears." *Africa News* 33, no. 6 (April 1990): 8–9.
Novicki, Margaret A. "Interview with Kenneth Kaunda, President of Zambia." *Africa Report* 28, no. 3 (May-June 1983): 4–8.
Nyrop, Richard F., ed. *India: A Country Study*. Washington, D.C.: U.S. Government Printing Office, 1985.
Oded, Arye. *Africa and the Middle East Conflict*. Boulder, Colo.: Lynne Rienner, 1987.
———. *Africa, the PLO, and Israel*. Jerusalem: The Leonard Davis Institute, 1990.
Ojo, Olatunde J. C. B., D. K. Orwa, and C. M. B. Utete. *African International Relations*. New York: Longman, 1985.
Onis, Juan de. "Brazil on the Tightrope Toward Democracy." *Foreign Affairs* 68, no. 4 (Fall 1989): 127–143.
"Opposition Leader Arrested." *Africa Research Bulletin-Political Series*, July 15, 1987: 8547.
Ovenden, Keith, and Tony Cole. *Apartheid and International Finance*. New York: Penguin Books, 1989.
Pachai, P. *The International Aspects of the South African Indian Question*. Cape Town: C. Struik Ltd., 1971.
Payne, Richard J. *The Nonsuperpowers and South Africa*. Bloomington: Indiana University Press, 1990.
———. *The West European Allies, the Third World, and U.S. Foreign Policy*. New York: Praeger, 1991.
Perlmutter, Amos, Michael Handel, and Uri Bar-Joseph. *Two Minutes Over Baghdad*. London: Valentine, Mitchell and Company, Ltd., 1982.
Permanent Mission of Israel to the United Nations, *Arab Oil Trade with South Africa Exposed*. New York: Permanent Mission of Israel to the UN, 1986.
Perry, William. *Contemporary Brazilian Foreign Policy: The International Strategy of an Emerging Power*. Beverly Hills, Calif.: Sage Publications, 1976.
Pickles, John, and Jeff Woods. "Reorienting South Africa's International Links." *Capital and Class*, no. 35 (Summer 1988): 49–55.

―――――. "Taiwanese Investment in South Africa." *African Affairs* 88, no. 353 (October 1989): 507–528.
Pinto, Brian. "Nigeria During and After the Oil Boom: A Policy Comparison with Indonesia." *The World Bank Economic Review* 1, no. 3 (1987): 419–445.
"Pretoria Coup Bid Claim." *Africa Research Bulletin-Political Series*, May 15, 1989.
Pye, Lucian. *Asian Power and Politics: The Cultural Dimensions of Authority*. Cambridge: Harvard University Press, 1985.
Quadros, Jânio. "Brazil's New Foreign Policy." *Foreign Affairs* 40 (October 1961): 24–27.
Ramamurthi, T. G. *Fight Against Apartheid*. New Delhi: ABC Publishing House, 1984.
Ravenhill, John. "Reversing Africa's Economic Decline." *World Policy Journal* 7, no. 4 (Fall 1990): 703–732.
Ray, Vanita. "India-Africa Relations." *Africa Quarterly* 18, nos. 2–3 (January 1979): 75–96.
Rivers, Bernard, and Martin Bailey. "How Oil Seeps into South Africa." *Business and Society Review*, no. 39 (Fall 1981): 53–59.
Roett, Riordan. "Brazil: Staying the Course." *The Wilson Quarterly* 7, no. 3 (Summer 1983): 46–61.
Rogerson, C. M. "Third World Multinationals and South Africa's Decentralization Program." *The South African Geographical Society* 68, no. 2 (September 1986): 132–143.
―――――. "Decentralization and the Location of Third World Multinationals in South Africa." In *Regional Restructing Under Apartheid*, edited by Richard Tomlinson and Mark Addleson, 294–308. Johannesburg: Ravan Press, 1987.
Rothchild, Donald. "State and Ethnicity in Africa: A Policy Perspective." In *Ethnic Preference and Public Policy in Developing States*, edited by Neil Nevitte and Charles H. Kennedy, 15–61. Boulder, Colo.: Lynne Rienner, 1986.
Rothstein, Robert L. *The Weak in the World of the Strong*. New York: Columbia University Press, 1977.
Rowe, Edward T. *Strengthening the UN: A Study of the Evolution of Member State Commitments*. Berkeley, Calif.: Sage Publications, 1974.
Rudolph, James D. "Government and Politics." In *Saudi Arabia: A Country Study*, edited by Richard F. Nyrop, 203–250. Washington, D.C.: U.S. Government Printing Office, 1985.
"Sanctions on South Africa: Double-Edged." *The Economist*, August 16, 1986: 42–44.
Sandbrook, Richard. "Taming the African Leviathan." *World Policy Journal* 7, no. 4 (Fall 1990): 673–702.
Sanders, Thomas G. "Brazil's Foreign Policy in Africa." *American Universities Field Staff Reports*, no. 43 (1981): 1–5.

---. "Racial Discrimination and Black Consciousness in Brazil." *American Universities Field Staff Reports*, no. 42 (1981): 2–3.
Saraf, Sunil, and Fiammetta Rocco. "India and Africa: Economic Ties Lag Behind Political Links." *Africa Economic Digest*, August 31, 1985: 34–40.
Scarritt, James R. "The Effects of South Africa on Zambian Politics: Overt and Systematic Destablization." In *South Africa in Southern Africa: Domestic Change and International Conflict*, edited by Edmond J. Keller and Louis A. Picard, 179–195. Boulder, Colo.: Lynne Rienner, 1989.
Schneider, Ronald M. *Brazil: Foreign Policy of a Future World Power*. Boulder, Colo.: Westview Press, 1976.
Schumacher, Edward. "Argentina and Democracy." *Foreign Affairs* 62, no. 5 (Summer 1984): 1070–1095.
Selcher, Wayne A. *The Afro-Asian Dimension of Brazilian Foreign Policy, 1956–72*. Gainesville: University Presses of Florida, 1974.
Selim, Mohamed E. "The Foreign Policy of the Palestine Liberation Organization." In *The Foreign Policies of Arab States*, edited by Bahgat Korany and Ali E. Hillal Dessouki, 197–240. Boulder, Colo.: Westview Press, 1984.
Sesay, Amadu, Olusola Ojo, and Orobola Fasehun. *The OAU After Twenty Years*. Boulder, Colo.: Westview Press, 1984.
Shagari, Alhaji Shehu. *Africa Report* 27, no. 1 (January-February 1982): 20–22.
Shipping Research Bureau. *Fuel for Apartheid: Oil Supplies to South Africa*. Amsterdam: Shipping Research Bureau, 1990.
Sigler, Jay A., ed. *International Handbook on Race and Race Relations*. New York: Greenwood Press, 1987.
Sisson, Richard. "India in 1989: A Year of Elections." *Asian Survey* 30, no. 2 (February 1990): 111–125.
Skidmore, Thomas E. *The Politics of Military Rule in Brazil, 1964–85*. New York: Oxford University Press, 1988.
Sodre, De Abreu Roberto. *Address to the Special Session of the General Assembly on the Critical Economic Situation in Africa*. New York: Brazilian UN Mission, 1986.
Sohr, Raul. "Reagan Alliance Woos South Africa." *South*, October 1981: 23.
Sorensen, George. "Brazil." In *Newly Industrializing Countries and the Political Economy of South-South Relations*, edited by Jerker Carlsson and Timothy M. Shaw, 101–120. London: Macmillan Press, 1988.
"South Africa." *Africa Report* 36, no. 2 (March-April 1991): 12.
"South Africa and Hungary: When Foes Turn to Friends." *Africa Report* 35, no. 1 (March-April 1990): 10.
South African Reserve Bank. *Annual Economic Report 1990*. Pretoria: South African Reserve Bank, 1990.

Spector, Leonard S., and Jacqueline R. Smith. *Nuclear Ambitions: The Spread of Nuclear Weapons 1989–1990*. Boulder, Colo.: Westview Press, 1990.
Spring, Martin. "Letter from Johannesburg." *Far Eastern Review,* November 14, 1975: 62.
Srinivasa, Padma. "Ethnicity in the Politics of Africa and India." *The Indian Journal of Political Science* 47, no. 4 (1986): 509–531.
Stremlau, John J., ed. *The Foreign Policy Priorities of Third World States*. Boulder, Colo.: Westview Press, 1982.
Stultz, Newell M. "The Apartheid Issue at the General Assembly: Stalemate or Gathering Storm?" *African Affairs* 86, no. 342 (January 1987): 25–46.
Sutter, Robert G. *Taiwan: Entering the 21st Century*. Lanham: University Press of America, 1988.
Talbot, Phillips. *India in the 1980s*. New York: Foreign Policy Association, 1983.
Tanzer, Andrew. "The Saudi Connection." *Far Eastern Economic Review*, July 9, 1982: 28–29.
Tasker, Rodney. "Trade Overcomes Diplomatic Isolation." *Far Eastern Economic Review*, May 22, 1981: 36–45.
Tharoor, Shashi. *Reasons of State: Political Development and India's Foreign Policy Under Indira Gandhi*. New Delhi: Vikas Publishing House, 1982.
Thompson, Jato. "Can This Farm Plan Stay the Course?" *African Business,* April 1990: 39–41.
_____. "Shuttle Diplomacy Brings Home the Bacon." *African Business,* April 1990: 39.
Touval, Saadia. *The Peace Brokers: Mediators in the Arab-Israeli Conflict, 1948–79*. Princeton, N.J.: Princeton University Press, 1982.
Tow, William T. *Subregional Security Cooperation in the Third World*. Boulder, Colo.: Lynne Rienner, 1990.
Tyler, William G. *Advanced Developing Countries as Export Competitors in Third World Market: The Brazilian Experience*. Washington, D.C.: Center for Strategic and International Studies, Georgetown University, 1980.
UNESCO. *Historical and Socio-Cultural Relations Between Black Africa and the Arab World from 1935 to the Present*. Paris: UNESCO, 1984.
United Nations. *Special Report of the Special Committee Against Apartheid on Implementation of the Arms Embargo Against South Africa*. Official Records of the General Assembly, 40th Session, Supplement no. 22A, October 14, 1985.
United Nations. "International Seminar on World Action for Immediate Independence of Namibia." *Namibia Bulletin*, no. 6 (1986): 2–19.
United Nations. *Apartheid Policies of the Government of South Africa: Concerted International Action for the Elimination of Apartheid*. New York: UN General Assembly, 1987.

United Nations. *Report of the Intergovernmental Group to Monitor the Supply and Shipping of Petroleum Products to South Africa.* New York: UN General Assembly, 1987.
United Nations Center Against Apartheid. *Declaration on the Question of South Africa by the Ad-Hoc Committee on Southern Africa of the Organization of African Unity.* New York: United Nations, 1989.
United Nations Industrial Development Organization. *Industrial Cooperation Through the Southern African Development Coordination Conference.* New York: United Nations, 1985.
United Nations Special Committee Against Apartheid. *The East Asian Region and International Action Against Apartheid.* New York: UN Special Committee Against Apartheid, 1990.
"Update: South Africa." *Africa Report* 36, no. 3 (May-June 1991): 12.
"Update: Zambia." *Africa Report* 34, no. 1 (January-February 1989): 12.
U.S. Congress. House Committee on Foreign Affairs. Hearing on Possible Violation or Circumvention of the Clark Amendment. 100th Congress, 1st sess., July 1, 1987. Washington, D.C.: U.S. Government Printing Office, 1987.
Uwazurike, P. Chudi. "Confronting Potential Breakdown: The Nigerian Redemocratization Process in Critical Perspective." *The Journal of Modern African Studies* 28, no. 1 (March 1990): 55–78.
Vail, Leroy. "Introduction: Ethnicity in Southern African History." In *The Creation of Tribalism in Southern Africa,* edited by Leroy Vail, 1–19. Berkeley: University of California Press, 1989.
Walters, Ronald W. *South Africa and the Bomb.* Lexington, Mass.: Lexington Books, 1987.
Welch, Jr., Claude E. "Human Rights as a Problem in Contemporary Africa." In *Human Rights and Development in Africa,* edited by Claude E. Welch, Jr., and Ronald I. Meltzer, 11–32. Albany: State University of New York Press, 1984.
Weteheim, Peter Howard. "Brazil and Africa." *African Business,* October 1983: 59.
Whitaker, Jennifer Seymour. *How Can Africa Survive?* New York: Council on Foreign Relations Press, 1988.
Whitehill, Robert. "The Sanctions that Never Were: Arab and Iranian Oil Sales to South Africa." *Middle East Review* 19, no. 1 (Fall 1986): 38–46.
Wiseman, John A. *Democracy in Black Africa: Survival and Revival.* New York: Paragon House Publishers, 1990.
World Bank. *India: Recent Developments and Medium Term Issues.* Washington, D.C.: The World Bank, 1989.
World Bank. *Sub-Saharan Africa: From Crisis to Sustainable Growth.* Washington, D.C.: The World Bank, 1989.
World Bank. *World Development Report 1990: Poverty.* New York: Oxford University Press, 1990.

Wulf, Jurgen. "Zambia Under the IMF Regime." *African Affairs* 87, no. 349 (October 1988): 579–594.

Young, Crawford. "Beyond Partrimonial Autocracy: The African Challenge." In *Beyond Autocracy in Africa: Working in Africa Program*, edited by The Carter Center, 21–23. Atlanta, Ga.: The Carter Center, 1989.

Young, Roger, and John Loxley. *Zambia: An Assessment of Zambia's Structural Adjustment Experience*. Ottawa: The North-South Institute, 1990.

Yu, George T. "The Tanzania-Zambia Railway: A Case Study in Chinese Economic Aid to Africa." In *Soviet and Chinese Aid to African Nations*, edited by Warren Weinstein and Thomas H. Henriksen, 117–144. New York: Praeger, 1980.

"Zambia-South Africa: Let Us Talk About It." *Africa*, no. 130 (June 1982): 17–18.

Zartman, William. "The African States as a Source of Change." In *South Africa into the 1980s*, edited by Richard E. Bissell and Chester A. Crocker, 107–132. Boulder, Colo.: Westview Press, 1979.

"Zimbabwe." *Africa Report* 35, no. 4 (September-October 1990): 7.

Index

Accra Conference of Independent African States (1958), 23
Adamishin, Anatoly, 8
Addis Ababa Summit, 24
Adebisi, Busari, 30
Aerlineas Argentinas, agreement with South African Airways, 102
Africa Fund, 76
African Americans, and democratic reforms in Africa, 16
African Liberation Committee, 25
African National Congress (ANC): collaboration with China, 86; compared to the PLO in Jordan, 60; impact of Kaunda's dialogue with de Klerk on, 60; India's support of, 75–76; Kenya's support of, 28; Libya's assistance to, 136; meeting in Dakar, 29; Nigerian assistance to, 42–43; perceived as threat to Zambia, 55–56; relations with Moscow, 8; suspension of armed struggle, 7; ties with PLO, 126; ties with South African Indian Congress, 74

Afro-Arab cooperation, Israel's influence on, 124
Akinyemi, Bolaji, 31, 42
Algeria, 128; reasons for anti-apartheid stance of, 130–131; war with France, 131
Alves, Lindgren, on racial harmony in Brazil, 108
Al-Sadat, Anwar: assassination of, 136; the Camp David Accords, 135; visit to Israel, 135
Anglo-American Corporation, investments in Brazil, 115–116
Angola: Brazil's assistance to, 118; involvement of Petrobras in, 117, 119; Portugal's control of, 111; relations with Brazil, 111; South Africa's support for UNITA, 40; trade with Brazil, 117, 119; withdrawal of Cuban troops from, 113
Anti-Apartheid Day, in Brazil, 122
Anti-Slavery Society for the Protection of Human Rights, 73
Apartheid: compared to Humanism, 46; divisive nature of, 74. *See*

also South Africa; *specific countries' policies toward*
Arab League, oil embargo, 27
Arab States: human rights violations in, 129; oil embargo against South Africa, 138; Operation Desert Storm, 127; sub-Saharan criticism of, 139. *See also* Middle East; *specific countries*
Arabs: African views of, 127; perceptions of Africans, 127; in Senegal, 127
Arafat, Yasir: comparisons between Israel and South Africa, 146; relations with Kaunda, 147; supported by Nelson Mandela, 147
Argentina: British influence in, 100; family links to South Africa, 100; import substitutution, 99; Nonaligned Movement, 100; North-South issues, 100; ties with the United States, 100; trade with South Africa, 101–102

Babangida, Ibrahim, 32
Balewa, Tafaw Abubaker, 31, 40
Bamieh, Sam T., Saudi Arabia's covert trade with South Africa, 140
Barbosa, Gibson, 117
Barclays Bank, 43–44
Bastani, M. A., 137
Begin, Menachem, 135
Belafonte, Harry, and Mandel's support of the PLO, 148
Bella, Ahmed Ben, and the National Liberation Front (Algeria), 131
Beltrao, Helio, 122
Bharatiya Janata Party (BJP), 70
Bharatiya Mazdoor Sangh, and sanctions against South Africa, 78
Biafran conflict, 38; white minority regimes and, 38
Bihar famine, 68
Boesak, Allan, 86

Bophuthatswana National Development Corporation, efforts to attract Taiwanese investments, 93
Botha, Pik, 8, 100, 103
Brahmins, influence of, 68, 72
Branco, Hamerto, 111
Brazil: commerical relations with South Africa, 113–115; compared to South Africa and the United States on race, 107–108; compared to Taiwan, South Korea, Japan, and Hong Kong, 104–105; connection between race and class in, 108; criticism of U.S. aid to UNITA, 113; debt problems, 99, 105, 106, 114; emphasis on African heritage, 110; emphasis on economic development, 104; energy policy of, 106–107; factors influencing policy toward South Africa, 103–123; foreign policy-making process in, 104–105; human rights abuses in, 108; import substitution, 99, 104, 105; incentives to exporters, 119; income distribution in, 107; influence of race on Brazil's foreign policy, 198; military rule in, 111; as a newly industrializing country, 105; opposition to a South Atlantic Treaty Organization, 119; opposition to UN resolutions against South Africa, 120–121; racial policies criticized, 108; reduced diplomatic ties with South Africa, 112; relations with Portugal, 111–112; relationship between the army and navy during military rule, 120; role in Cuban troop withdrawal from Angola, 113; support for African self-determination, 112; trade with Africa, 117–120; treatment of indigenous people, 109; view of

South Africa as competitor, 106; view on sanctions, 121, 122
Brazilian Committee on Solidarity with South Africa and Namibia, 121
Brent, R. Stephen, 22
Britain: Central African Federation, the, 48; Chinese laborers in South Africa, 95; colonial domination of India, 66; colonial rule in Nigeria, 43; democracy in India, 69; indentured Indians in Natal, 74; influence in Argentina, 100; leadership role in the Commonwealth, 80; Nigerian oil embargo, 44; Nigeria's sanctions against companies from, 43–44; position on sanctions against South Africa, 28; Tafawa Balewa's cooperation with, 40; termination of anti-apartheid sanctions, 61; trade with South Africa, 89; trade with Zambia, 58
British Foreign Office, on Jordan's arms sales to South Africa, 143
British Petroleum (BP), Nigerian sanctions against South Africa, 44
British South Africa Company, 48
Buhari, Muhammadu, 32
Bush, George, Operation Desert Storm, 129

Callaghy, Thomas, 20
Camp David Accords, 135
Canada, 2, 23, 27, 41, 48, 74, 77; economic sanctions against South Africa, 88
Castro, Fidel, 8
Central African Federation, 48
Chang, John H., 88
Chia Ho, false labeling operation, 92
Chile: Fourth International Air Fair, 103; military collaboration with South Africa, 103; participation in the South Africa Republican Festival, 103; South African policy, 100; South Africa's fishing industry, 101; trade with South Africa, 101–102
Chiluba, Frederick, 14, 52
Ching-Kuo, Chiang, 95
Chinkuli, Kingsley, 57
Chissano, Joaquim A., 14
Clark Amendment, 143
Coetzee, Johann, 95
Committee of Trade Unions Against Apartheid, 77–78
Commonwealth, 5, 6, 23, 27, 41, 44, 45; Gleneagles Declaration, the, 28; India, 80; Zambia's dependence on, 53, 61
Commonwealth Eminent Persons Group, 41
Concert of Medium Powers, 31
Congress Party, 70
Coordination Council for North American Affairs of Taiwan, 82
Cotia Comercio Exportacao, Brazil's trade with Nigeria, 118
Crocker, Chester, the Angolan-Namibia issue, 136
Cuban-Soviet alliance, 8

De Beers Central Selling Organization, 4, 8
De Beers of South Africa: agreement with Soviet Union, 8; and India's diamond industry, 78–79
Decentralization Board, 93
de Klerk, F. W.: African initiatives of, 29; attempts to enlist European support, 7; economic growth and constitutional reform link, 154; negotiations with Kaunda, 55–56, 60–61; 1992 referendum on reforms, 149; reforms in South Africa, 7, 75, 95; views in Manifesto for a New

South Africa, 149; visits to sub-Saharan Africa, 155
de Mello, Fernanado Collor: creation of homeland for Yanomamis, 109; efforts to deal with problems of "the lost decade," 106; energy self-sufficiency, 106–107
Democracy: developments in Africa, 20–21; impact of ethnic groups on, 13; in Latin America, 98; in Nigeria, 33–36; relationship between development and, 12–13; religion and, 12. *See also specific countries*
De Wet, Carel, private visit to Saudi Arabia, 141
Diamond, Larry, 151
Dome of the Rock, importance to Islam, 128
Drake Networking Systems, cooperation with Taiwanese, 93

East Asia, emphasis on economic growth, 88
Economic Intelligence Unit, 43
Ecuador, assistance from South Africa, 101
Edwards, A. M., South African technical cooperation with Taiwan, 90
Egypt: democratic reforms in, 130; foreign policy-making in, 128; influence of Arab-Israeli conflict on policy towards South Africa, 131–133; involvement with UNITA, 143; oil sales to South Africa, 140; relations with South Africa, 136
Elgin, Colin, 55

Fegueredo, João, visit to Africa, 117
Foreign policy: constraints on, 5; levels of change in, 6
Franco-African Summit, 17

Frontline States, xiv, 53, 67

Gandhi, Indira, 68
Gandhi, Mahatma: nonviolent campaign in South Africa, 66, 74; role in India's independence, 66
Gandhi, Rajiv, 76, 77, 78, 80
Garba, Joseph, 40
Garcia, Ricardo, 102
Geisel, Ernesto, improvement of ties with Africa, 117
Geldenhuys, Mike, 103
General Mining Company, activities in Brazil, 116
German unification, 9
Ghali, Boutros, and Egypt's opposition to apartheid, 136
Ghana, 21, 24, 25, 40, 117
Gleneagles Declaration, 28
Gold Control Act, 79
Gorbachev, Mikhail: new thinking, xii; support for negotiated settlement between ANC and Pretoria, 8
Gossens, Salvador Allende: Chile's 1973 coup, 98; nationalization of Chile's industries, 101
Goulart, João, Brazil's ties to Africa, III
Government of India Act, 69
Gowon, Yakubu, 31, 43
Group Areas Act, 74
Group of Seven, 17
Guerreiro, Saraiva, 109

Heath, Edward, 27
Hindustan Diamond Company: De Beers corporation, 78; Indian government ownership of, 78
Holocaust, 5; awareness of dangers of racial ideologies, 30; impact of Israel's self-perception, 126
Hong Kong: anti-apartheid groups in, 86; opposition to sanctions,

88; reintegration into China in 1997, 91; role in clandestine trade with South Africa, 89, 91
Honorary whites, 5
Horn, Gyuna, 8
Houphouet-Biogny, 25, 29; reluctance to support OAU's policy on South Africa, 29
Humanism, compared to U.S. moralism, 46–47
Hungary, links to South Africa, 8–9
Huntington, Samuel, 10

India: xiv, 24; assistance to liberation movements, 75–76; British influence on, 69; caste system compared to apartheid, 63–64; continuing significance of the caste system, 70–72; democracy in, 69–70; foreign investment and, 68–69; Gold Control Act, 79; Green Revolution in, 68; human rights violations in, 73; impact of the Gulf War on, 69; importance of diamond trade to, 79; introduction of apartheid issue to UN, 66; nonalignment in foreign policy, 67; position on sanctions, 77–80; as a regional superpower, 67; support for arms embargo against South Africa, 80; support of the ANC's armed struggle, 74
Informal Permanent Machinery, 23
Inter-American Development Bank, ties with South Africa's Reserve Bank, 114
International Monetary Fund (IMF), 15, 17–35; Zambia and, 49–50
Iran: aid to the OAU's Liberation Committee, 137; historical ties to South Africa, 130; military cooperation with South Africa, 142; oil sales to South Africa, 138; opposition to sanctions against South Africa, 137; policies toward South Africa, 137
Iran's Revolutionary Council: abhorrence of apartheid, 137; repudiation of Shah's foreign policies, 137
Iraq, arms trade with South Africa, 142
Ironsi, Johnson, 31
Islamic Development Bank, 130
Israel: compared to South Africa, 134–135; contributions to the OAU's Liberation Committee, 133; influence of Jewish fundamentalists, 145; military collaboration with South Africa and Taiwan, 93–95; South African Jewish donations to, 132; South African support of, 134; sub-Saharan attitudes toward, 132; support for sanctions against South Africa, 132
Itamaraty: impact of Third World nationalism on, 110, 117; influence on Brazil's foreign policy, 104; recognition of Anti-Apartheid Day, 122; reforms in South Africa, 121
Ivory Coast: de Klerk's visit to, 29; policy toward South Africa, 25

Jackson, Robert, 19
Jains, dominance of India's diamond industry, 79
Janata Dal Party, 70
Johnson, Chalmers, 84
Jordan, arms sales to South Africa, 143–144
Joseph, Richard, 15, 34

Kai-shek, Chiang, retreat with anticommunist supporters to Taiwan, 84

Kaunda, Kenneth, 2, 25, 35; assistance to the ANC, 51; democratic reforms 52; emphasis on negotiations with South Africa, 47, 54, 55, 56; emphasis on South African threat, 61–62; influence on Zambia's foreign policy, 46–48; negotiations with John Vorster, 54; problems with the IMF, 49–50; support for strong anti-apartheid sanctions, 56–57
Kenya: anti-apartheid actions, 28–29; demonstrations for democracy in, 14; support for the ANC, 28; U.S. policy towards, 16. *See also* Sub-Saharan Africa
Khomeini, Ayatollah, and South Africa, 137, 138, 141
Klopper, Donald, 116
Kotzember, H., visit to Brazil, 121
Kou-Tsai, Liu, visit to South Africa, 88
Kuria, Gibson Kamau, 16
Kuwait: Operation Desert Storm, 127; pressures for democratic reforms in, 130

Lagos Apartheid Conference, 39
Latin America: economic cooperation with South Africa, 101–102; lack of democracy in, 98; military relations with South Africa, 103; pattern of industrialization and foreign debt, 99; reasons for low levels of interaction with South Africa, 97; role of military in, 98. *See also specific countries*
Latin American Regional Conference for Action Against Apartheid (1983), 97
Le Grange, Louis, 88
Libya, 129; assistance to ANC, 136; factors shaping South African policies of, 129

Ling, Du, 88

Macedo, Edmundo, 122
Major, John, and the link between aid and "good government," 17
Malawi: Central African Federation, the, 48; diplomatic links with South Africa, 28
Mandal Commission, 70, 72, 73
Mandela, Nelson, 7, 73; support for PLO, 147; visit to India, 76
Manley, Michael, 9
Marais, Piet, and Chile's Fourth International Air Fair, 103
Massachusetts Institute of Technology (M.I.T.), and Taiwan's nuclear weapons program, 94
Mauritanians: race relations, 127; in Senegal, 127
Mauritius: Gandhi's visit to, 78; relations with India, 78; trade with South Africa, 78; view on sanctions, 78
Meir, Golda, and the 1973 war, 145
Middle East: convergence of interests with sub-Saharan Africa, 125, 135; enslavement of black Africans, 126–127; factors shaping South African policies of, 126; foreign policy-making in, 128; human rights violations in, 129; military links with South Africa, 142
Mitterrand, François, and aid to Africa, 17
Moi, Daniel arap, opposition to competitive party politics, 14–15
Mozambican National Resistance Movement (Renamo), 14, 62; Saudi assistance to, 143
Mozambique: movement toward multiparty politics, 14; Mozambican National Resistance Movement (Renamo), 14, 62;

Portugal's policies in, 111; target of South Africa's military attacks, 61
Mubarak, Hosni: and democratic reforms, 130; policies towards South Africa, 136
Mugabe, Robert, 2; State of Emergency in Zimbabwe, 52; suppression of political dissent, 14
Mugomba, Agrippah, 26
Mugyenyi, Meddi, 12
Muller, Hildgard, visit to Brazil, 121
Mushala, Adamson, 61

Namibia, Brazilian Committe on Solidarity with, 121. *See also* South West African People's Organization (SWAPO)
Nasser, Gamal: influence on Egypt's foreign policy, 128; support for anti-apartheid struggle, 131
National Chinese Association of Commerce and Industry, 90
National Committee Against Apartheid, 39
National Conference of Bishops, and Brazil's human rights record, 108–109
National Union for the Total Independence of Angola (UNITA), 40, 112, 113, 143
Nehru, Jawaharlal, 66
New Zealand, sporting contacts with South Africa, 45
Nigeria: agricultural reforms in, 36; aid to the Frontline states, 42; anti-apartheid groups in, 39; anti-apartheid stance, 1; anti-apartheid strategies, 38–45; and British Petroleum, 44; Chile's ties with South Africa, 102; compared to Zambia, 45–46; criticism of Brazil's racial policies, 108; demonstrations against economic programs, 35; discrimination and human rights abuses in, 36–37; economic decline of, 21; 34; economic relations with Brazil, 117–119; establishment of an Economic Intelligence Unit, 43; ethnic and religious rivalries in, 31–33; factors shaping foreign policies of, 30–32; influence on the UN Anti-Apartheid Committee, 40; National Electoral Commission of, 33; nationalization of Barclays Bank, 43, 44; outflow of foreign investment from, 35; participation in the Eminent Persons Group, 41; political and economic reforms in, 33–36; as a regional superpower, 42, 43; response to South Africa's agreement with Equatorial Guinea, 42; Robbery and Firearms Tribunals in, 37; South Africa's role in civil war, 38; sports boycott, 45; support for liberation groups, 42–43
Nigerian Enterprises Promotion decree, 35
Nkrumah, Kwame, 24
Nonaligned Movement, 1, 26, 27; and Argentina, 100; India's leadership in, 67
Nujoma, Sam, 75
Nwachukwa, Ike, 35, 39; position on Chile's ties with South Africa, 120
Nyerere, Julius, 55
Nzo, Alfred, 9

Obasanjo, Olusegun, 40, 43
Operation Desert Storm, 15–16, 127
Organization of African Unity (OAU), 5, 23; Addis Ababa summit, 24; arms embargo, 26; assis-

tance from OPEC, 26–27; attempts to influence British poicy, 28; beginning of direct contact with Pretoria, 29; on democracy in South Africa, 24; strategy for ending apartheid, 24–26
Organization of Islamic Conference, 32
Organization of Petroleum Exporting Countries (OPEC), 26; impact on Brazil's foreign policy, 111

Pahlavi, Muhammad Reza Shah: ties to South Africa, 137; view of economic sanctions, 137
Palestine Liberation Organization: collaboration with ANC and SWAPO, 126, 145, 146; compared to ANC in Zambia, 60; Israel's view of, 126; Kaunda's support of, 147; and Nigeria, 147; Soviet assistance, 146; ties with sub-Saharan Africa, 144–148; UN observer status, 145
Palestine National Conference, and cooperation between Palestinians and African Liberation Movements, 146
Pan-Africanist Congress (PAC), 42
Paraguay, 99; economic aid from South Africa, 99–100
Pariah states, 4, 64, 65, 81; Chile's status as, 100; military collaboration among, 93–95; preoccupation with security, 64–65. *See also* Israel; Taiwan; South Africa; South Korea
Patrimonial administrative state, 20
People's Republic of China (PRC), 64, 65, 82, 83, 86; competition with Soviet Union, 86; diplomatic relations with Saudi Arabia, 87; and Hong Kong, 91; leadership in Nonaligned Movement, 86; ties with South Africa, 86–87, 91
Peron, Juan Domingo, 98
Personal rule: consequences of, 21; objectives of, 21
Petrobrãs, 106, 117, 118, 119
Polisario, 143
Political Bureau, 32; functions and recommendations of, 32–33
Popular Movement for the Liberation of Angola (MPLA), 112
Portugal, policies in Angola and Mozambique, 111
Preservation of Public Security Act, 52–53
Program of Fiscal Benefits for Exports, 119
Putter, Andres Petrus, 100
Pye, Lucian, 67

Qaddafi, Mu'ammar: Nonaligned Movement, 129; self-perception of Nasser's heir, 129
Qatar, and oil sales to South Africa, 140–141
Quadros, Jânio: and Brazil's foreign policy 110–111; and Portuguese control of Angola and Mozambique, 111; relations with Africa, 110

Rabin, Yitzhak, 145
Reagan, Ronald: Brazil's support for the independence of, 121; and constructive engagement, 41; India's policy toward, 75–76; linkage of independence with Cuban troops in Angola, 41; support for a South Atlantic Treaty Organization, 119; and U.S. debt, 99
Rhoodie, Eschel, the South African Department of Information, 87

Rio Treaty, 120
Robbery and Firearms Tribunals, 37
Rosberg, Carl, 19
Rothchild, Donald, 13

Safari, and trade with South Africa, 89
Sarney, José: implementation of anti-apartheid sanctions, 122; reduced Brazilian diplomatic ties with South Africa, 112
Saudi Arabia: diplomatic relations with China, 87; foreign policy-making in, 128; as guardian of holy places, 129; links to Taiwan, 87, 93; oil sales to South Africa, 140–141; purchases of South African gold, 141; in southern Africa, 140, 143
Scheduled Castes (untouchables), 70; and job reservations, 72
Seko, Mobutu, resistance to democratic reform, 14
Senegal, treatment of Mauritanians in, 127
Shagari, Alhaji, 32, 41; criticism of Ronald Reagan's constructive engagement policy, 41
Shah, Reza, and South Africa, 130
Shapi, Alex, and restrictions on the ANC, 60
Sharpeville Massacre, 6, 24, 99
Shatila and Sabra refugee camps, massacres in, 146–147
Shipping Research Bureau, 140
Signal and Control Corporation: link to U.S. Central Intelligence Agency, 142; U.S. arms supplies to South Africa and Iraq, 142
Singh, V. P., 72, 73, 76
Six Day War, impact on Israel's relations with sub-Saharan Africa, 125

Smith, Ian, 38; and sanctions against Rhodesia, 50
"Soft state," 20
South Africa: agreement with Equatorial Guinea, 42; AIDS problem in, 154; arms sales to Iraq, 142; assistance to Ecuador, 101; as Brazil's competitor, 106; Brazil's criticism of aid to UNITA, 113; collaboration with Israel, 134; Commonwealth and, 23; compared to Brazil on race, 107–108; cooperation with France in Algeria, 131; cultural links with Taiwan, 95; decentralization program in homelands, 92–93; economic aid to Paraguay, 99–100; economic and political ties with Eastern Europe, 8–9; economic and technical cooperation with Taiwan, 90; economic cooperation with Latin American, 101–102; efforts to reduce isolation, 29; emphasis on common interests with Taiwan, 88; factors affecting Third World relations with, 3; family links to Argentina, 100; Group Areas Act, 74; impact of economic sanctions on, 7; influences on Nigeria's policy towards, 37–41; interest in a South Atlantic Treaty Organization, 119; investments in Brazil, 115–116; involvement in Angola, 40; military cooperation with Taiwan, 93–95; military relations with Latin America, 103; Nigeria's policies towards, 37–45; oil trade with Middle East, 140–141; opposition to PRC's admission to UN, 87; post-apartheid challenges for, 154–158; reasons for low levels of interaction with Latin America, 97–98; regional destabilization program,

51; relations with Zambia, 53–62; role in Nigeria's civil war, 38; and SADCC after apartheid, 157; sanctions against neighboring countries, 56–57; settlement of Indians in Natal, 73–74; Sharpeville Massacre, 6; source of uranium for Taiwan, 94; Taiwan's investments in, 91–94; Taiwan's policy toward, 87–95; ties with China, 86; trade with Brazil, 113–115. *See also* Apartheid

South African Communist Party, 7

South African Department of Information: covert campaign to enlist PRC's support, 87; efforts to improve relations with Middle East, 136; Eschel Rhoodie and, 87

South African Foreign Trade Organization, and commerce with Taiwan, 90

South Africa's Republican Festival, Chile's participation in, 103

South African Reserve Bank, 7

South African Weapons Corporation (Armscor), 103

South African Youth Revolutionary Council (SAYRCO), 42–43

South Asian Association for Regional Cooperation (SAARC), 67

South Asian Coalition on Children in Servitude, and child labor in India, 73

South Atlantic Treaty Organization (SATO): Brazil's naval officer's support of, 120; Brazil's opposition to, 119–120; and the Cuban-Soviet threat, 120; favored by the Reagan Administration and South Africa, 119

Southern African Development Coordination Conference (SADCC), xiv, 47; India's assistance to, 76

South Korea: and apartheid, 63; as a capitalist developmental state, 84; democratic reforms, 9; 12; economic development in, 105; impact of Gulf War on, 16; national security policy of, 95; opposition to sanctions, 88; pariah status of, 4, 64, 81; trade with South Africa, 89

South West African Peoples Organization (SWAPO), 28; India's support for, 75. *See also* Namibia

Soviet Union: alliance with Cuba in Angola, 8; on clandestine trade between China and South Africa, 91; competition with China, 86; diplomatic contacts with South Africa, 8; involvement in Angola, 87; relations with Taiwan, 86; support for the ANC, 8, 86–87; trade with Brazil, 104, 105

Soweto riots, impact on Indian's South African policy, 75

State Security (Detention of Persons) Decree (1984), 37

Steinmuller-Lavis, exports to China, 91

Stroessner, Alfredo, relations with South Africa, 99–100

Subramaniam, K., 70

Sub-Saharan Africa: anti-apartheid activities in the UN, 26; anti-colonial movements in, 20; attempts to influence Britain on South Africa, 28; Brazil's identification with, 110–112; compared to South Africa and India, 10; convergence of interests with Middle East, 125; domestic influences on relations with South Africa, 19–23; economic deterioration in, 21–22; government involvement in the private sector of, 22; human rights and

democratic reforms in, 9–17; impact of Gulf War on, 16; implications of the end of the Cold War for, 17; personalization of power in, 20–21; poor governance, 21; positive attitudes toward Israel, 132; as "soft states," 20; struggle for "second independence," 10; ties with the PLO, 144–148. *See also individual countries*
Sun, Yun-suan, on Taiwan-South Africa alliance, 88
Superwave Systems, involvement in South Africa, 93
Sutton, John, 100
Suzman, Helen, 55
Swaziland, venue for false labeling, 92

Taiwan: xiii, 4, 5; anti-apartheid groups in, 86; cultural links with South Africa, 95; development strategy, 84; dominance of mainland Chinese, 84; economic and technical cooperation with South Africa, 90; economic development and democratic reforms, 85; Gulf crisis and Taiwan's vulnerability, 91; impact of great power rivalries on alliance with Pretoria, 86; imports from South Africa, 90–91; investments in the homelands, 91–94; links with Eastern Europe, 86; military collaboration with South Africa, 93–95; nuclear weapons program, 94–95; pariah status, 64, 65, 81; perception of communist threat, 86; policy of flexible diplomacy, 82; policy toward South Africa, 87–95; preoccupation with security, 64–65; purchases of South African uranium, 94; relations with People's Republic of China, 82–83; relations with South Africa, 86–95; role in South Africa's decentralization program, 92; role of trade in foreign policy, 82; trade with South Africa, 89–91; treatment of aboriginal groups, 85
Taiwan-South Africa Chamber of Commerce, and economic and technical cooperation, 90
Tambo, Oliver, 75
Tanzania, 25, 56, 57
Tazara railway, 56
Thatcher, Margaret, 44–45, 61
Third World: constraints on foreign policies of, 5; European pressures for reforms in, 9; factors influencing policies toward South Africa, 1–5; as an ideological concept, xiii; influence on foreign policies of, 5; and moral parochialism, 2; and nonalignment, xii; support for sanctions, 7

Ugarte, Pinochet Augusto: and Chile's South African Policy, 100; economic policies of, 101–102
UN Anti-Apartheid Committee, 40
UN Human Rights Seminar on Apartheid, organized by Brazil, 121
UN Security Council, 26, 27
UN Special Committee on the Policies of Apartheid, appeals to Brazil to cancel flights to South Africa, 122
United Arab Emirates: and the oil embargo against South Africa, 140; purchases of South African gold, 141
United Bank for Africa, 118

United National Independence Party (UNIP), 50, 51
United States: Brazil's criticism of aid to UNITA, 113; Brazil's debt, 106; Clark Amendment, the, 143; compared to Brazil on race, 107–108; Department of State and Taiwan's nuclear program, 94; economic sanctions against South Africa, 88; military cooperation among Taiwan, South Africa, and Israel, 93–95; Nigeria's criticism of, 41; P. W. Botha's views of, 88; restrictions on Taiwan's exports, 92; ties with Argentina, 100; trade with South Africa, 89
Universal Declaration of Human Rights, 6
Uruguay, 99; trade with South Africa, 102

Van Zyl, Alex, 116
Viljoen, Constand, and Pretoria's military links with Chile, 103
Volkswagen do Brazil, and Nigeria, 118
Vorster, John: African diplomatic efforts, 54; support for upgrading relations with Brazil, 121; visit to Israel, 145; visits to Uruguay and Paraguay, 199

Welch, Claude, 11
World Bank, 15; and African economic decline, 22
Worldwide Shipping Group, and petroleum shipments to South Africa, 89

Yanomamis, 107
Yom Kippur War, 27

Zaire, 14, 16; economic and political ties to South Africa, 29
Zambia: agreement with the IMF, 49–50; compared to Nigeria, 45–46; complexity of policy toward South Africa, 2; complexity of South African policies, 46; contradictions in sanctions policy, 56–58; economic decline of, 21, 48–51; economic links with South Africa, 56–60; influence of Kaunda on foreign policy of, 46–48; Preservation of Public Security Act, 52–53; South African military attacks on, 61–62; South Africa's destabilization program, 51. *See also* Sub-Saharan Africa
Zanzibar, 127

About the Author

RICHARD J. PAYNE is Professor of Political Science at Illinois State University. Among his earlier publications are *The Nonsuperpowers and South Africa* (1990) and *The West European Allies, The Third World, and U.S. Foreign Policy* (Greenwood and Praeger, 1991).